WHITE WOMEN'S CHRIST AND
BLACK WOMEN'S JESUS

American Academy of Religion Academy Series

edited by
Susan Thistlethwaite

Number 64
WHITE WOMEN'S CHRIST AND
BLACK WOMEN'S JESUS
Feminist Christology and Womanist Response

by
Jacquelyn Grant

Jacquelyn Grant

WHITE WOMEN'S CHRIST AND BLACK WOMEN'S JESUS
Feminist Christology and Womanist Response

Scholars Press
Atlanta, Georgia

WHITE WOMEN'S CHRIST AND BLACK WOMEN'S JESUS
Feminist Christology and Womanist Response
by
Jacquelyn Grant

Library of Congress Cataloging in Publication Data

Grant, Jacquelyn.
    White women's Christ and Black women's Jesus : feminist
christology and womanist response / Jacquelyn Grant.
        p.   cm. -- (American Academy of Religion academy series : no.
    64)
    Bibliography: p.
    ISBN 1-55540-302-6 -- ISBN 1-55540-303-4 (pbk.)
        1. Jesus Christ--History of doctrines--20th century. 2. Feminist
    theology--History--20th century. 3. Black theology--History--20th
century. 4. Liberation theology--History--20th century. 5. Jesus
Christ--Person and offices. I. Title. II. Series
BT198.G67 1989
232'088042--dc19   88-33323
                                                                         CIP

Printed in the United States of America
on acid-free paper

In memory of my grandmother,
Mrs. Eliza Ward,
Who in the stillness of a coma,
When she heard the name Jesus,
moved.

To my parents,
The Rev. Joseph J.
and
Mrs. Lillie Mae Grant

TABLE OF CONTENTS

PREFACE

Feminist theology is a recent discipline in theology which is an articulation of the significance of the gospel as read in the context of women's experience. It is an attempt to take seriously women's experience as the primary source and context for understanding the nature of God and God's Word to humanity. In considering the nature of God, feminist theologians have uncovered a direct relationship between exclusive male imagery of God and the structural oppression of women. For this reason, Christology is especially problematic for feminists. Because Jesus was undebatably male and because the Christian church claims him as the unique God-bearer, feminist christology has as the critical task the explaining of the significance of this male Godbearer for women, and the constructive task of creating adequate christological models for women today.

This subject was of particular interest to me given my own religious upbringing. As grandchildren of religious grandparents (maternal and paternal), as children of an African Methodist Episcopal minister, my siblings and I were quite accustomed to the name Jesus. The love and kindness, the giving and sacrifices, and the community service and political interest we witnessed in our parents were in the name of Jesus.

The theology of somebodiness which they lived out without pretension, conveyed to their children that inspite of the world's denial of you, Jesus (God) affirms you. So you must go on. . . . Hence, the personal commitment I made to Jesus as a youngster was not one that restricted me as a Black person or as a female, but affirmed me and projected me into areas where, I later learned, "I was not supposed to go" by virtue of my race and gender.

When introduced to christological issues from a feminist perspective, I understood the problem. Though I was not conscious of limitations of a male saviour during my upbringing, in my adulthood I was able to see the issues in my life–my studies and my ministry. For in my adulthood, not only did I recognize the sexual politics in theology in a patriarchal society, but also the racial politics in theology in a racist society.

I decided to research this project for two reasons: 1) because of the challenge which Christology presented for women, I wanted to explore the feminist responses to the christological question; and 2) because in Black women's religious experiences we see both an oppressive and liberating Christology at work. The oppressive (White) Christology was used to keep Blacks (and women) in their place. The liberating Christology emerged in that Black women (and people) did not always accept the oppressive interpretations handed down to them; instead, they articulated their own liberative christologies. I was interested in comparing some of the responses of Black women to those articulated by contemporary White feminist thinkers. Given the differences between Black women and White women's history, culture and experiences, my operating hunch was that a corollary difference in their interpretation of Jesus Christ is expectant.

Data out of the experience of Black women provides the basis for beginning the construction of a womanist theology and Christology that emerges from the tri-dimensional reality of Black women which is characterized by the convergence of racism, sexism, and classism.

ACKNOWLEDGEMENTS

I am appreciative for the support and services of many persons who assisted in the completion of this work. To James Cone, I am eternally indebted for his continuous guidance and support throughout my graduate studies. For her long-suffering assistance with the first draft and helpful conversations I am indebted to Beverly Harrison.

I am grateful to Christopher Morse for his helpful conversations, and to Tom Driver and William Kennedy for serving on my committee. I thank James Washington and Gayraud Wilmore for helping me to talk out some problematic issues. For reading the work in its entirety and offering critical comments and dialogues, I am grateful to Elizabeth Lunz and Mary Anne Bellinger.

For reading the work in part, I thank Noel Erskine and Willie Coleman; and for his seemingly endless critical questions and evaluation, I am indebted to R. Clifton Potter.

I was able to complete my first draft because John Diamond reduced my work-load by teaching one of my classes himself; to him I am grateful. Special thanks to Jocelyn W. Jackson, Pauline Davis, Alvin T. Riley, Nicolene Durham, Blondella James, Dell O. Grant, Marla Coulter, Polly Smith and Joseph Troutman (of the Woodruff Library of the Atlanta University Center).

For financial assistance, I thank the Fund for Theological Education for supporting me through fellowships. I also thank Major Jones formerly of Gammon Theological Seminary of the Interdenominational Theological Center for providing a study grant which assisted in my revision process.

Finally, I am eternally grateful to my sister, Dorothy M. Grant for typing the work in its entirety.

INTRODUCTION

Christology represents the central doctrine in most of Christian theology. Throughout the history of Christian theology, European and American white men have formulated christologies in the continual response to Jesus' question, "Who do you say that I am?"[1] Recently this question has been addressed by Black and other Third World theologians who have argued that theology and Christology are not unrelated to social, political and economic realities of human existence. Essentially, the argument of these theologians is three-fold: (1) Human condition results from the conscious (or unconscious) ethical decisions of human beings; (2) The divine reality is on the side of the oppressed poor, the outcast, the wretched, the downtrodden; and (3) Therefore the gospel reveals that the primary intention of God in the incarnation is one of liberation.[2] These liberation theologians attempted to construct theological perspectives which emerge out of the particular experiences of oppressed peoples. In so doing they have sought to contextualize theology. That is to say "(People) must be reached in their *lebenswelt* if faith is to be a live option. Theology as developed in Europe and America is limited when it approaches the majority of human beings."[3] When theology and Christology are contextualized, the oppressed become actual participants in the process rather than mere recipients of theological and christological dogma which have claims of universality. This participation in the theological process places oppressed peoples in a position to discuss the meaning of the gospel for the oppressed.

In analyzing the nature of God and Jesus Christ vis-a-vis the variety of human conditions, these theologians have argued that there is a relationship between Western articulated theologies and christologies and Western supremacist ideology which tends to perpetuate the oppression of the oppressed. Specifically, one who does not challenge the concept of a God and Christ who allow the evils of a socially unjust society is merely a tool of White supremacist ideology.[4]

Consistent with this trend, some Christian Feminists have identified women's experience as the proper context for discovering the significance of Jesus for women. For much of Christian theology, Jesus has been the Christ–the unique God bearer whose task it is to save the world. However, given the significance of being male throughout patriarchal history, many women are asking if a male can be a savior of women.[5] This concern is lodged among a variety of other questions: Why is Jesus used as a "weapon" against (the "progress" or "advancement" of) women in the church? What is the relationship between the maleness of Jesus and the salvation of women? How did Jesus challenge the established order–particularly in reference to women–or did he accept what was said about women by status quo oriented people? In what way(s) can Jesus be considered the savior of women?

These questions reflect the changing ways in which women are rearticulating their experience of Jesus and wrestling with Christology. They are the result of women claiming the right to raise questions out of their own experiences–that is contextualizing Christology. Therefore, they have challenged preconceived notions and more established interpretations about the place of women and the ways in which Jesus or Christology sanctioned that place. Some women theologians are beginning to re-evaluate Christology, appealing to women's experience as the primary context in which this is done.

I shall explore feminist responses to the above questions. By tracing the development of feminist Christology, I will make these responses evident. Also evidenced will be the limitations of feminist Christology when the primary source and context–women's experiences–is challenged by Black women's experience. I shall argue that racism/sexism/ classism, as a conglomerate representation of oppression, is the most adequate point of departure for doing the kind of wholistic theology and Christology which, as we shall see, feminist theologians advocate. Black women representing an embodiment of this triply oppressive reality possess the potential for an wholistic analysis that can provide for the development of wholistic theological and christological construction which are wholly rather than partially liberating.

METHODOLOGY AND ORGANIZATION OF THE STUDY

As a methodological procedure, I am employing the concept of contextualization. In so doing, I am recognizing the locus of feminist theology in the context of women's experiences and struggles in the church and society. Likewise, since Christology must be understood as a part of an overall system of Christian teaching, the feminist perspectives in Christology must be located in the larger feminist theological perspective.

The feminist theologies which I examine regard human experience in general and women's experience in particular as primary sources for doing theology. Not only that, but women's experience represents the context out of which feminist theologies emerge. Chapter I provides this context by focusing upon selected aspects of women's experience. After establishing the context, we are able to propose reasons that the subject Christology is simultaneously critical and problematic for women. This is done in Chapter II.

Christian feminists tend to agree upon the following: (1) Even when experience has been considered a source for theology it has actually invoked an abstract experience or it has spoken of it as if human experience equaled a "phantom" universal male experience;[6] (2) The use of the Bible in much of the White, male-articulated theologies has reinforced the oppression of women; and (3) Appeals to tradition in mainstream male articulated theologies often have been nothing more than a way of reinforcing male patriarchal history. Women, it is agreed, need liberation from all of these oppressive uses of sources and must develop alternative sources and/or interpretations of sources.

Although there are these and other common experiences and analyses which inform the development of a feminist theological perspective, feminist theology is hardly a monolithic movement. Three broad perspectives will be identified: (1) the Biblical Feminist Perspective; (2) the Liberation Feminist Perspective; and (3) the Rejectionist Feminist Perspective.

Biblical feminists are those who see Scripture as the primary source of theology. As such, the Bible provides a central authority which cannot be evaded. These persons are not biblical literalists and, in fact, do approach the Bible with a critical, exegetical eye. Those whom I will discuss in the evangelical camp are sometimes referred to as "evangelical liberals" who maintain scriptural revelation as normative. In Chapter III, I analyze the work of three women–Virginia Mollenkott (who represents one of the major evangelical biblical feminist thinkers), Nancy Hardesty and Letha Scanzoni. In this context, I also discuss the works of a "self-proclaimed" feminist, Paul Jewett, who has influenced Biblical feminists, and another, Leonard Swidler, whose work has provided supportive research for Biblical feminism.

In Chapter IV, I will examine the second position I have designated as "liberation feminists." Women who represent this position embrace the methodology developed in liberation theology, but their primary interest is the liberation of women in particular, within the broader struggle to liberate all humanity. Even though general human liberation is the conceptualized goal, women's liberation is the starting point. Two divisions within Christian liberation feminism are evident–those who view Scripture as central authority and define their position primarily, though not exclusively, in relation to it; and those who view Scripture as simply one, but not an overriding, source for doing theology. On the one hand Letty Russell represents the former position, seeking to remain biblically sound by continually testing her assertions against Scripture. On the other hand, Rosemary Ruether gives more primacy to women's experience as a source for critical reassessment of Christian tradition. Because these women see the liberation of women as intertwined with other liberation struggles, they have addressed the interrelationship and the interstructuring of various forms of oppressions. Although a central one, gender subjugation is not the only structure of oppression which a human liberation theology must address.

Whereas liberationists see the women's struggle as a focus within all other struggles, some radical feminist proponents insist that woman's struggle toward liberation must be disengaged from a presumed "general" human liberation. Other struggles, at best, turn out to be para-patriarchal movements whose primary goals still leave male domination intact. Women in this group view both scripture and tradition as irredeemably oppressive. Therefore, both are rejected as sources for the reflections of serious religious feminist thinkers. It is for this reason, that I have characterized this position in White feminism as "Rejectionist." This perspective is examined in Chapter V, utilizing Mary Daly as its primary proponent.

As is to be expected, one finds a correlation between the larger theological views of these feminists and their respective christologies. The greater the emphasis upon human experience, the less the emphasis upon the Bible and tradition. In their emergent christologies, the greater the emphasis upon women's experiences, the less the emphasis upon and importance of Jesus as divine. This relationship is clear in Chapter VI as I engage these various feminists in dialogue upon certain christological themes and analyze their christological offerings.

Although the White feminist christologies assessed here offer a radical critique of historical and contemporary male-articulated christologies, I shall argue that their critique is inadequate because they do not transcend their own criticisms of other christologies. The seriousness of the charge White feminists make regarding inappropriate male universalism is undercut by the limited perspective which presumes the universality of women's experience. White feminism does not emerge out of the particularity of the majority of women's experience.[7] Here I shall focus on the realities of the experiences of Black women as the evaluative criterion for testing the limitations of the feminist perspective in theology and Christology, because Black women are a significant minority group of women in the United States and because they have claimed that Jesus Christ has played a dominant role in their lives.

The analytical principle for determining the adequacy or inadequacy of White feminist Christology is twofold: (1) Because a single issue analysis has proven inadequate to eliminate oppression, a multi-issue analysis must be constructed. The race/sex/class analysis must be embraced as a representative corporate analysis for the destruction of oppressive structures; and (2) because Jesus located the Christ with the outcast, the least, Christology must emerge out of the condition of the least. The representative corporate analysis of race/sex/class is one such situation of the least. Indeed, Black women's tradition is where these three contradictions intersect.

The Black women focused upon in this project were selected because of their contributions to feminist discussions, by negative implications, or by positive affirmation, in the Black Church and community during the nineteenth and twentieth centuries. The same contextualization method is employed in Black women's resources. Two significant historical phenomona best describe the context of Black women in America: 1) Black women during slavery and 2) Black women in domestic service. By examining these two entities in Black women's existence, we are able to see the interworkings of racism, sexism, and classism in their lives.

Although Black women were not "systematic" theologians one can find in their work (speeches, biographies, writings, and so forth), theological fragments which give us some glimpses into their theological perspectives and christological beliefs. Chapter VII contains an examination of some of these resources and a discussion of how Black women's experiences challenge White feminist analysis, as well as ways in which Black women themselves are challenged.

NOTES

[1] Mark 8:27.

[2] See James Cone, *A Black Theology of Liberation* (New York: Lip-pincott, 1970); J. Deotis Roberts, *Liberation and Reconciliation* (Phil-adelphia: Westminster Press, 1971); Gustavo Gutierrez, *A Theology of Liberation* (New York: Orbis, 1973); Jose Miguez Bonino, *Doing Theology in a Revolutionary Situation* (Philadelphia: Fortress Press, 1975); Rosemary Ruether, *Liberation Theology* (New York: Paulist Press, 1972). Also see the documents of the Ecumenical Association of Third World Theologians: Kofi Appiah-Kubi and Sergio Torres, eds., *African Theology en Route* (Maryknoll, New York: Orbis Books, 1979); Virginia Fabella, ed., *Asia's Struggle for Full Humanity* (Maryknoll, N.Y.: Orbis Books, 1980); Virginia Fabella and Sergio Torres, eds., *Irruption of the Third World: Challenge to Theology* (Maryknoll, New York: Orbis Books, 1983); Sergio Torres and John Eagleson, eds., *The Challenge of Basic Christian Communities* (Maryknoll, N.Y.: Orbis Books, 1981).

[3] J. Deotis Roberts, "Contextual Theology: Liberation and Indigenization," *Black Theology Today: Liberation and Contextualization* (New York: The Edwin Mellen Press, 1983), p. 106. For Black liberation theologians, the primary experience of op-pression is the Black experience. For Feminist theologians it is women's experience and for Latin Americans it is the experience of the poor Latin American. Contextualization means making one's own experiences the framework for doing theology. The context determines the questions asked of the theologians, as well as the form of the answers given. Liberation theologians reject the imposition of the oppressor's questions upon the oppressed peoples. See also Shoki Coe "Contextualizing Theology," in *Mission Trends No. 3: Third World Theologies*, ed. Gerald H. Anderson and Thomas Stransky (New York: Paulist Press, 1976), pp. 19-24.

[4] See Vincent Harding, "Black Theology and the American Christ," in *Black Theology: A Documentary History, 1966-1979*, eds. Gayraud Wilmore and James Cone (New York: Orbis Books, 1979), pp. 35-42.

[5] See Chapter IV for the discussion of Ruether's raising of the questions in this form.

[6] According to Rita Gross, this is experience interpreted androcentrically: the male experience becomes synonomous with human experience. ". . . in androcentric thinking, the male norm and the human norm are collapsed and become identical." See "Androcentrism and Androgyny in the Methodology of History of Religion," in *Beyond Androcentrism: New Essays on Women and Religion,* ed. Rita Gross (Missoula, Montana: Scholars Press, 1977), p. 9. Paul Tillich speaks of experience as "the 'medium' through which the sources 'speak' to us." See *Systematic Theology,* Vol. I (Chicago: The University of Chicago, 1956), Chapter I.

[7] It is significant to note that Black and other ethnic women of color comprise a vast majority of the female population of the world.

I

WOMEN'S EXPERIENCE AS THE CONTEXT AND A SOURCE FOR DOING FEMINIST THEOLOGY AND CHRISTOLOGY

What is women's experience? Women's experience is a complex of events, feelings and struggles which are shared by women in various circumstances of life. It would be possible to examine several dimensions of women's experience—the historical, political, psychological, social, religious and theological. Other studies have been done on various aspects of women's experience.[1] This study presumes an interrelationship of the dimensions of women's experience, and will draw from a combination of these dimensions particularly the historical and political aspects of women's experience. Since feminist theology is related to the church, my primary focus is the church though the larger societal question regarding women will be discussed in order to provide a more adequate context for the development of feminist theology. As I shall argue in Chapter II, the (contemporary) ordination and leadership of women issue is one concrete way in which the christological problem manifests itself. It is sufficient to say at this point that the struggle of women in the church is not only one of the political process of ordination or leadership, but it involves, as we shall see, theological issues, such as, are women human and can women represent Christ? Therefore much of what is described in this chapter addresses these theological questions via religio-political struggles of women in the church. What is described represent the context in which women began to forge new questions, such as the christological one: In light of the struggle of women today, what is the meaning of Jesus Christ?

A. *Women's Experience and Men's Experience:*
the Particular Challenges the Universal

What does it mean to do Christology out of the context of women's experience? Many traditional male articulated theological and christological arguments defined the task of theology and Christology in universal terms. Barth's minimizing of human experience, and his projection of The Word of God alone as the starting point of theology, is a prime example of this universal approach to theologizing. Feminist theologians, as liberation theologians, utilize the particular experience of women to determine the questions asked regarding the significance of Jesus. Liberation theologians including Christian feminists, charge that the experience out of which Christian theology has emerged is not universal experience but the experience of the dominant culture. It is a kind of shaking of this foundation of theology that is called for by proponents of the theology of liberation. Recognizing inherent problems in the universalist approach to the doing of theology, liberationists therefore, propose that theology must emerge out of particular experiences of the oppressed people of God.

James Cone, in *God of the Oppressed*, addresses this issue in terms of the way in which we image God:

> Because Christian theology is human speech about God, it is always related to historical situations, and thus all of its assertions are culturally limited. . . . Although God, the subject of theology, is eternal, theology itself is, like those who articulate it, limited by history and time. . . . [Our image of God] is a finite image, limited by the temporality and particularity of our existence. Theology is not universal language; it is interested language and thus is always a reflection of the goals and aspirations of a particular people in a definite social setting.[2]

Likewise Christology, in liberation theology, is grounded in the particular experience of the oppressed. This is not to say that liberation Christology is not concerned with universal principles, or "the whole" or universal picture that Gordon Kaufman talks about.[3] Jon Sobrino articulates the possible meaning of the universal while remaining faithful to his concern for the oppressed:

> If Christ is the foundation of all, then any study of Christ must undertake to explain first what that 'all' signifies. In short, it must offer some understanding of the world, the person, history, sin, liberation, and so forth; or at the very least, it must spell out at the start how it focuses on that 'all'. Of course Christological study will in turn explain, retouch, or perhaps even radically alter our way of focusing on the 'all'.[4]

Two crucial differences appear in Sobrino's idea of the "all" which are not in Kaufman's idea of the "whole." One is the inclusion of "liberation", and the other is the idea that perhaps the whole will be radically altered when liberation of the oppressed is considered as an integral part of the whole.

Black Theology, through the work of James Cone, more explicitly exemplifies use of the particular/universal approach to Christology: "The Jesus of the black experience is the Jesus of Scripture. The dialectic relationship of the black experience and Scripture is the point of departure of Black Theology's Christology."[5] The particular black experience is the starting point but not the stopping point.

For women, nothing short of a shaking of the male universal foundation of theology is required to construct an adequate feminist Christology. Since experience is the context in which christological interpretation takes place, before women begin to reflect on Jesus Christ, they must claim the power to name themselves and their experience so that their christological reflections would be authentically theirs. Historically, the woman's experience has been consumed by "generic" (male) experiences and camouflaged by generic (male) language regarding that universal (male) experience. One of the first women to address this issue is Valerie Saiving Goldstein, she says:

> . . . I am no longer as certain as I once was that, when theologians speak of "man," they are using the word in its generic sense. It is, after all, a well-known fact that theology has been written almost exclusively by men. This alone should put us on guard, especially since contemporary theologians constantly remind us that one of man's strongest temptations is to identify his own limited perspective with universal truth.[6]

Lifting up the Christian notion of sin and love,[7] Goldstein suggests that the identification of these notions with self-assertion and selflessness respectively, functions differently in masculine experience and feminine experience. She explains further:

> Contemporary theological doctrines of love have, I believe, been constructed primarily upon the basis of masculine experience and thus view the human condition from the male standpoint. Consequently, these doctrines do not provide an adequate interpretation of the situation of women—nor, for that matter, of men, especially of certain fundamental changes now taking place in our own society[8]

Because of their feminine character, love for women takes the character of nurturing, supporting and servicing their families. Consequently if women believe "the theologians, she will try to strangle those impulses in herself. She will believe that, having chosen marriage and children and thus being face to face with the needs of her family for love, refreshment, and forgiveness, she has no right to ask anything for herself but must submit without qualification to the strictly feminine role."[9]

Goldstein then argues that when experience in theology is scrutinized, we will discover that because it has been synonymous with masculine experience, it is inadequate to deal with the situation of women. Feminist theology, as a theology of liberation, is concerned about exposing this false universalism and reinterpreting the experiences of women. In so doing, it is following the lead of liberation theology.

Sheila Collins indicates how the experience of women is important in doing theology by making experience an active integral part of the process. Collins' approach to theology stems from her basic differentiation between theology and theologizing. Theology is a "systematized body of knowledge about God", whereas theologizing is "that dialectical process of action/reflection which generates ever new questions."[10] This distinction opens the discipline for the participation of many people, theologizing out of their own experiences, for "theologies arise out of a cultural context."[11] This fact, however, is often ignored. Instead we are presented with theologies which have become "legislated." These legislated theologies have as their basis patriarchalism.[12]

Theology, in Collins' original formulation, must begin "exorcising this Patriarchal Demon." This process begins by affirming our own experience in "doing" theology. In the light of that experience women must break with the patriarchalism of "his-story" and affirm "her-story" which has been ignored in traditional Judeo-Christian theology. In order for this to be done, history must be reread and rewritten with the feminist perspective in mind, thereby centralizing the experience of women.

White women have begun to take an active role in naming themselves and their experiences. Taking place under the umbrella of the women's liberation movement, they have moved in the sphere of the larger society as well as in the church. The development of this movement is critical for understanding and putting into perspective the development of feminist theology and Christology. It is important to note even at this point that White feminists have attempted to identify the particular experience out of which feminist theory emerges. The acts of naming and identifying extend beyond present women's reality into past history. Below I will examine the past and present realities and struggles of women. Later, I shall examine the question of whether particularity as identified by feminists is sufficiently particular, or whether White women succeeded or failed in creating an inclusive woman's experience by incorporating the experiences of Black women and other Third World women.

1. Nineteenth Century Background for the Development of Feminist Christology

Feminist theology is a unique development of the contemporary feminist movement. It is unique because, whereas feminism is not new, the theology of feminism is new and distinct from any past developments in the feminist movement. Feminists in nineteenth century America, in a rather sporadic way, addressed the issue under the larger umbrella of religion.[13] Some women were able to see the relationship between religion and the oppression of women. Others merely employed feminist imagery to make religion more relevant to them (women).[14]

During the nineteenth century, the church with remarkable success resisted the impact of the women's movement. The resistance took the form of teachings on the virtues of womanhood lauding the feminine qualities of women as godly and Godgiven. Nancy Cott described the indoctrination which women received regarding their role in the church and family. Women populated the church by a majority as early as the mid-seventeenth century. They were kept in line however by the constant teaching that they were special having "female values." Being seduced by the minister's teachings that they were "of conscientious and prudent character, especially suited to religion," women became well indoctrinated in what was expected of them.[15]

Cott characterized early nineteenth century religion's treatment of women in this way:

> No other public institutions spoke to women and cultivated their loyalty so assiduously as the churches did. Quickened by religious anxiety and self-interest, the clergy gave their formulations of women's roles unusual force. They pinned on women's domestic occupation and influence their own best hopes. Their portrayal of women's roles grew in persuasive power because it overlapped with republican commonplaces about the need for virtuous citizens for a successful republic. It gained intensity because it intersected with new interest in early childhood learning. Ministers declared repeatedly that women's pious influence was not only appropriate to them but crucial for society.[16]

Inspite of their ecclesiastical/religious oppression, however, women from time to time did challenge the church at the point of its role in perpetuating such oppression. The speeches of Sarah and Angelina Grimke, directed to Christian women and advocating the equality of the sexes, elicited angry reactions from the clergy of the church. One church body responded to the work of the Grimke sisters with a proclamation that God condones the "protected" and "dependent" state of women. The General Association of the Church wrote the following:

> The power of woman is her dependence, flowing from the consciousness of that weakness which God has given her for her protection, and which keeps her in those departments of life that form the character of individuals and of the nation.[17]

In spite of these kinds of "divinely-inspired" attacks, women began to claim and articulate revelations to the contrary.

Sarah Grimke affirmed that the appropriate duties and influence of women are revealed in the New Testament. In her words, "No one can desire more earnestly than I do that women may move exactly in the sphere which her creator has assigned her; and I believe her having been displaced from that sphere has introduced confusion into the world."[18] Grimke felt that the New Testament in its untarnished form can be used as a guide for women. Having been contaminated by the interpretations and translations of men, the Bible and commentaries there upon have been distorted especially with regards to women.

Grimke's position was obviously reformist. She was joined by many others who attempted to reform Christian and biblical dogma. By 1885 at the Annual Convention of the National Woman Suffrage Association a rather reformist resolution was proposed by what could be called the Christian apology contingent. They wrote:

"WHEREAS, The dogmas incorporated in religious creeds derived from Judaism, teaching that woman was an after-thought in the creation, her sex a misfortune, marriage a condition of subordination, and maternity a curse, are contrary to the law of God (as revealed in nature), and to the precepts of Christ, and,"WHEREAS, These dogmas are an insidious poison, sapping the vitality of our civilization, blighting woman, and, through her, paralyzing humanity; therefore be it "Resolved, That we call on the Christian ministry, as leaders of thought, to teach and enforce the fundamental idea of creation, that man was made in the image of God, male and female, and given equal rights over the earth, but none over each other. And, furthermore, we ask their recognition of the scriptural declaration that, in the Christian religion, there is neither male nor female, bond nor free, but all are one in Christ Jesus."[19]

Though passage of this resolution is not indicated,[20] its mere proposal reflected the growing belief that essentially, the problem regarding women is not with Christianity or the Bible, but with distortion of them.

Elizabeth Cady Stanton repudiated this view. Without apology, she attributed the entire situation of women to the use of the Old and New Testaments, and responded by editing and writing a commentary upon the Bible which she entitled *The Woman's Bible.* All bodies—religious, social and political she argued—undergird and sustain the inferiority of women: "The canon and civil law; church and state; priests and legislators all political parties and religious denominations have alike taught that woman was made after man, of man, and for man, an inferior being, subject to man."[21]

Stanton's position on religion was considered extreme for her time and was not widely shared. Women were afraid to join forces with her. This "reluctance" contributed to the strength of the Church's stifling of the progress of the movement. Consequently, the issue in the church was not actively or consistently addressed. Radical and reform feminists alike saw little possibility of change within the church. Thus, "while the moral crusaders shied away from a fundamental examination of the church . . ., the radicals simply assumed that religion was dead. . . ."[22]

2. *The Contemporary Secular Woman's Liberation Movement*

A significant aspect of contemporary feminism recaptures the spirit of nineteenth century feminists such as Elizabeth Cady Stanton, in identifying religion as the root of the oppression of women. This aspect of contemporary feminism consists of religious feminists who are engaging in systematic analysis of religion as the root of the oppression of women. Many feminists who have chosen to function within the realm of religion (and even some who have moved outside of religion) have made the important connection between legal, political, economic and social statuses of women and the image of women presented in religion. They have been able to relate the state of powerlessness of women in the society to the belief that woman was responsible for the relative power-lessness of man through the eating of the forbidden apple (The Fall). More specifically, they have been able to see the perceived connections made between the exclusion of women from leadership and the exclusion of women from the rank of disciples of Jesus (New Testament). Feminist Christology emerged in a context of radical struggles in the process toward the liberation of women from social and political and ecclesiastical oppression. Women began to analyze the various institutions which historically had oppressed them. A look at how women viewed the issues in the wider secular society and the church and particularly in theology will indicate how feminist theology and then Christology emerged from women's experience. It will also indicate how they both function as an oppressive tool used against women.

a. *Women's Liberation—A Societal Movement*

The second wave of the women's liberation movement began during the early 1960s. The publication of *The Feminine Mystique* (1963)[23] by Betty Friedan represented the commencement of what Sheila Rothman has termed the era of the "Woman as person."[24] Friedan's thoughts represented the early part of this era. She advances the notion that American women—particularly middle-class women—suffer from a feminine mystique which forces them into feminine conformity. That is, they suffer from an identity crisis because of the general belief that their identity is merged into the identity of others (husband and children) as wife and mother and, of course, housewife. The feminine mystique forces women to achieve, in fact to live, vicariously through men (husbands) and children. Friedan suggests that women can find fulfillment as wives and mothers only by fulfilling their own potentials as separate persons.[25] To do this, she proposes that women must adopt a new life plan which will reject the feminine mystique. In this connection, she says that:

> Ironically, the only kind of work which permits
> an able woman to realize her abilities fully, to
> achieve identify in society in a life plan that can
> encompass marriage and motherhood, is the kind
> that was forbidden by the feminine mystique; the
> lifelong commitment to an art or science, to
> politics or profession.[26]

It is only when women are able to reject totally the feminine
mystique that they can make the necessary "serious professional commitment" to any of these areas. Friedan, therefore,
suggests that women can achieve their own identities, goals
and aspirations as persons without giving up marriage and
family life. It is only as women achieve their potentials as
full human beings that they will be able to put into perspective marriage and family life. Friedan states:

> As boys at Harvard or Yale or Columbia or
> Chicago go on from the liberal arts core to study
> architecture, medicine, law, and science, girls
> must be encouraged to go on, to make a life plan. It
> has been shown that girls with this kind of a
> commitment are less eager to rush into early mar-
> riage, less panicky about finding a man, more
> responsible for their sexual behavior. Most of
> them marry of course, but on a much more mature
> basis. Their marriages then are not an escape but
> a commitment shared by two people that becomes
> part of their commitment to themselves and soci-
> ety. If, in fact, girls are educated to make such
> commitments, the question of sex and when they
> marry will lose its overwhelming importance. It
> is the fact that women have no identity of their
> own that makes sex, love, marriage, and children
> seem the only and essential facts of women's
> life.[27]

It was Friedan's book, along with various other events in the 1960s, which led to the development of the National Organization of Women (NOW) in 1966. Another event leading to the development of NOW was the struggle of women for the inclusion and implementation of the sex clause in Title VII of the Civil Rights Act of 1964.[28] Additionally, the Equal Employment Opportunity Commission's (EEOC) inability or refusal to enforce the provision of the Civil Rights Act aided in producing the atmosphere for the emergence of the first civil rights movement for women—NOW.[29] The chief objective of NOW was that women be allowed to reach their "full human potential." Friedan expressed this aim as she wrote the first sentence of the statement of purpose of NOW. NOW committed itself to "take action to bring women into full participation in the mainstream of American society now, exercising all the privileges and responsibilities thereof, in truly equal partnership with men."[30] The organization took on such concerns as "equal pay for equal work," economic independence for women, reform of family and societal structures.

Friedan admitted that "women also had to confront their sexual nature, not deny or ignore it as earlier feminists had done."[31] However, she argued that:

> Society had to be restructured so that women, who happened to be the people who give birth, could make a human, responsible choice whether or not—and when—to have children, and not be barred thereby from participating in society in their own right. This meant the right to birth control and safe abortion; the right to maternity leave and child care centers if women did not want to retreat completely from adult society during the childbearing years; and the equivalent of a GI bill for retraining if women chose to stay home with the children. For it seemed to me that most women would still choose to have children, though not so many if child rearing was no

longer their only road to status and economic support—a vicarious participation in life.[32]

The critical point of the argument is that women will be able to become professionals and yet be family persons— mothers and wives—at the same time. Although, one could argue that the goals of Friedan and her followers in NOW were modest compared to what was to happen later, they represented nonetheless a remarkable beginning of a movement which was to become momentous. Young radical women attempted to radicalize NOW. The mild call for equality had met with so much resistance that some young radical women began to preach "man-hating sex/class warfare."[33] Rothman wrote that the women's movement had shifted "from partnership to a war between the sexes."[34] "NOW had begun in 1966 as a Civil Rights Organization; by 1971, it was a women's liberation organization."[35] The agenda as well as the underlying assumptions had changed. Many women were no longer interested in partnership with men. Rather they were interested in liberation. To be full persons, women had to be liberated from the oppression and suppression of familial and societal structures. The issue for many was no longer spacing children but the right to have *no* children. Similarly, no longer was the issue mere abortion but "abortion on demand." In some expressions of the movement, "for the first time, it appeared that women's interests, family interests and societal interests were in conflict."[36]

A major part of the quest for liberation became expressed in the struggle for passage of the Equal Rights Amendment (ERA)—a struggle which was to last for several years, ending (temporarily) in defeat.[37]

b. *The Woman's Movement versus The Black Movement*

There is much in common between the contemporary women's movement and the Black movement just as there was in the abolition movement and the women's movement of the 19th century.[38] In both periods, the women's movement was influenced by the earlier Black movement. Rothman suggests two ways in which this was true of the contemporary movement. First, the language of the Black civil rights movement was conciliatory in its optimism and progressivism. Martin Luther King's dream was for "brotherhood." That is, he stressed searching for the togetherness of all peoples. In a similar vein, women spoke of "partnership", that is the togetherness of the sexes. Just as the civil rights movement gave way to the Black power movement, the women's rights movement gave way to the more radical women's liberation movement.

Second, in the civil rights movement serious challenges were made about the operating assumptions regarding "learning patterns of American children." Psychologists and educators began to challenge the notion that the presently structured IQ tests could adequately reflect the learning capabilities of Black children. It was argued that the IQ tests were culturally biased towards middle-class, White children. It was further argued that the results of the tests were socially (pre-) determined. In observing the performance differentials between Blacks and Whites, women began to look at the differentials between boys and girls and to assess the degree to which social expectation functioned in determining the results of the tests.[39] One could argue, then, that just as the tests were unfair for Blacks, they were likewise unfair for women and did not, in fact, could not, accurately test intelligence.[40] Women were not only influenced by the Black movement but some actively began their civil rights involvement in that context and then moved to the women's movement. An account of the evolution from one movement to the other is given in an autobiographical manner by Sara Evans in her book *Personal Politics: The Roots of Women's Liberation in the Civil Rights Movement and The New Left*.[41] Evans gives a history of her personal involvement and the involvement of other White women in the Black movement. She portrayed these women as being similar to the nineteenth-century White female abolitionist who saw the injustices of a racist society and was willing to volunteer her services for (and perhaps in some cases commit herself to) the Black struggle toward liberation. But there was sexism, expressed and unexpressed, in organizations such as the Student Non-Violent Coordinating Committee (SNCC), the Southern Student Organization Committee (SSOC), and Students for a Democratic Society (SDS). Fermenting under the surfaces of the activities of the women were the makings of a women's movement:

> Building on their new strengths, looking consciously to new models both black and white, southern white women in SNCC as early as 1960 sensed that the achievement of racial equality required fundamental changes in sex roles. To them the term "southern lady" was an obscene epithet.[42]

These women saw a relationship between racism and southern sexism. "Racism 'propped up notions about White women and repression'. . . ."[43] However, because of some of the sexism of the Black movement, they began to see themselves in a different light.

Evans says further of some of the southern women's involvement in the movement:

> It was from this network of southern women, whose involvement dated from the beginning of SNCC and who understood their commitment in the theological formulas of ultimate commitment, that the earliest feminist response emerged. These women had recognized from the very beginning of their involvement in the movement that they, like their male associates, were at war with their own culture. Unlike the Grimke sisters, they did not leave the south; but like them, as they confronted the racial

oppression of southern culture, they would be forced to challenge the most subtle assumptions behind their role as southern whites who were also women. The sexual distinction was fraught with psychic and cultural torment. Unlike their male companions these young, driven, committed white women had also to challenge roles forced upon them by friends and enemies alike— assumptions about female behavior, goals, and responsibilities that were not only a part of the general culture, but naturally and painfully a part of themselves. Thus from within a movement led by southern blacks, young white women had of necessity to forge a new sense of themselves, to redefine the meaning of being a woman quite apart from the flawed image they had inherited. As a result they were being prepared (quite unbeknown to themselves) to play a significant role in articulating the intensifying dilemmas of a growing number of activist women.[44]

As a result, many women eventually left the Black movement and other new left movements and began to focus on self-affirmation which was denied them even in those leftist movements. They committed themselves to political-social strategies for full participation in the human race.

Unfortunately the close relationship between the Black movement and the Women's movement still did not prevent racism from emerging in the White women's liberation movement. Consequently, Black women, by and large, rather than exiting with White women, remained in the Black movement.

3. *The Contemporary Ecclesiastical Women's Liberation Movement*

As women in the larger society had begun to agitate and advocate liberation for women, women in the church began to do the same. The churches, it was discovered, were, just as the larger society, patriarchal institutions and therefore women began to challenge the traditional structures of the church.

Women within and across denominational lines have formulated organizations and caucuses, all designed to foster full participation of women in the life and ministry of the church. For the most part this was, and continues to be, a difficult struggle in the denominations. An examination of the contemporary movements in several predominately White denominations will serve to document this struggle.

a. *The Roman Catholic Tradition*

The Catholic Church has consistently maintained its rigid prohibitions against the leadership of women. The contemporary women's struggle in the Catholic Church has become centered on the development of the organization called Women's Ordination Conference.[45] It was in November of 1975 that the church—primarily women of the church—met in Detroit, Michigan, on the question of the ordination of women in the Roman Catholic Church. This meeting led to the establishment of the Women's Ordination Conference, which met in Chicago in 1976 to discuss "the ordination of women to a renewed priestly ministry."

Fuel was added to the fire in January of 1977 with the "Vatican Declaration" that women could not image Jesus in the priesthood. According to this declaration, only the male priest could image Christ, that is, only he can act *in persona Christi*, to achieve the desired result—that the faithful perceives in him the image of Christ, because he in fact represents Christ.

It is this ability to represent Christ that St. Paul considered as characteristic of his apostolic function (cf. 2 Cor. 5:20; Gal. 4:14). The supreme expression of this representation is found in the altogether special form it assumes in the celebration of the eucharist, which is the source and center of the church's unity, the sacrificial meal in which the people of God are associated in the sacrifice of Christ; the priest, who alone has the power to perform it, then acts not only through the effective power conferred on him by Christ, but *in persona Christi*, taking the role of Christ, to the point of being his very image, when he pronounces the words of consecration. . . .

The same natural resemblance is required for persons as for things: when Christ's role in the eucharist is to be expressed sacramentally, there would not be this "natural resemblance" which must exist between Christ and his minister if the role of Christ were not taken by a man: in such a case it would be difficult to see in the minister the image of Christ. For Christ himself was and remains a man.[46]

The central point of the declaration was that "[t]he Church, in fidelity to the example of the Lord, does not consider herself authorized to admit women to priestly ordination."[47]

This declaration put the issues into perspective for many women, increasing sensitivities as well as anger in many conscious Roman Catholics, because it seemed to close the door on the ordination question for women. This move led to the planning and implementation of the Baltimore conference in 1978 with its focus on "New Woman, New Church, New Priestly Ministry", to call the church to justice for women in the elimination of the sin of sexism from the church.[48] Roman Catholic women, however, have been unable to break down the thick oppressive wall built in their church.

b. *The Episcopal Tradition*

On December 15, 1973, at the Cathedral of St. John the Divine in New York, ten Deacons were presented for ordination, but only five were accepted for ordination. The five men were ordained, and the five women were not allowed ordination. The struggle was intensified as a result.

The culmination of the struggle of women in the Episcopal Church occurred on July 29, 1974, at the Church of the Advocate in Philadelphia, Pennsylvania, when eleven women were ordained by four bishops in violation of church law and tradition.[49] Prior to this "illegal" and controversial ordination service women had been allowed to enter the order of deacon (since 1970), but by no means could they be full-fledged elders in the Episcopal Church.

The story of the struggle in the Episcopal Church is told in the autobiographical work of Carter Heyward in *A Priest Forever*, as she discusses what might be called "the making of a priest."[50] As one of eleven women ordained at Philadelphia at the church of the Advocate in 1974, her personal journey is a testimony of the struggle in the Episcopal Church.

Prior to that service, the several ordinants had been in conversation with some of the bishops of the church. Heyward speaks often of her correspondence with her friend and bishop of New York, Paul Moore, especially after having been denied ordination by her own bishop in North Carolina. After several meetings among the women, petitions to various bishops by the women, and an occasional church petition to bishops, the women organized an ordination service to be performed by three bishops, two of whom were retired. The ordination did not lead to an enthusiastic acceptance of the women by the general church.

Instead, women were asked to refrain from performing any priestly duties until the matter had been resolved by the general church. In an emergency meeting of the bishops in August 15, 1974, the bishops resolved to reconsider the matter of the ordination of women but not without condemning the participants of the illegal service and calling upon them to wait for the general church connection decision. Because of the action, Heyward and others decided to terminate their agreement to refrain from priestly functions. Agitation continued, but in 1976 the General Assembly of the Episcopal Church granted women the right to full ordination.

c. *The United Methodist Tradition*

The recent struggles in the United Methodist Church were not centered on the ordination issue and consequently did not take the same activist form as in the Episcipal Church. Women in this church body received the right to ordination in 1956. But in spite of this fact, the structural nature of sexism in the church had meant that still women did not share *equally* in the program and policy making channels of the church. Around 1968, the Women's Division of the Board of Missions of the Methodist Church petitioned the Church for the creation of "a study of the extent to which women are involved at all structural levels in program and policy-making channels and agencies of the United Methodist Church."[51] The 1970 General Conference approved this study commission and consequently, its work commenced.

The Study Commission functioned with the following purpose:

1. To make a study of the extent to which women are involved in program and policy-making decisions at all levels of The United Methodist Church.
2. To review the language of The Book of Discipline in the light of the issue of the role of women in the denomination.
3. To develop an awareness of the issue of the involvement of women in the life of the denomination, the factors contributing to the present situation and the changes which are needed.

4. To formulate some recommendations to The
   United Methodist Church and its constituent
   parts to enable and facilitate the involvement
   of women in the life and work of the church.[52]

The findings of the Study were perhaps revealing for some and served merely as verification of previous empirical observations for others. It was documented that on the connectional level women were concentrated, in fact relegated, to traditional women's areas of work rather than the top *leadership* positions of the church. It reported:

> Women in executive positions in The United
> Methodist Church agency structures tended to be
> concentrated in the Board of Missions and the
> Board of Education. The Board of Missions cur-
> rently has the highest ranking women executives
> in the denomination on its staff. The participa-
> tion of women in the structures of the denomina-
> tion still reflects the traditional patterns to a
> large extent. Women were found in the member-
> ship and on the staffs of agencies which relate to
> missions and education, the "historic channels"
> for women's work. This was true of the member-
> ship of the annual conference agencies as well.
> The largest proportion of women were found on
> the annual conference agencies of missions, educa-
> tion, worship and ecumenical affairs. The
> business functions, either on the general or the an-
> nual conference level, were largely reserved for
> men. This was true of annual conference
> Commissions on World Service and Finance and
> the Program Councils and their national counter-
> parts. Activities having to do with some aspect
> of the professional ministry, boards of ministries,
> pension activities, education and recruitment of
> clergy, were almost exclusively the domain of
> men.[53]

On the local church organizations level, the same was documented:

> Women were found in those organizational activities which have been rather traditionally ascribed to them, namely education, missions and the Council on Ministries. Men predominated in the Administrative Board, the Committee on Finance, the Board of Trustees and the Pastor-Parish Relations Committee, all of which are crucial in determining policy and direction for the local congregation.[54]

Now, participation of women in the ministry represents a particular problem. For even though the rights to full ordination were granted in 1956, the right to full participation in the Clergy (the professional ministry) has not become actualized.

The study found the following:

> A number of research reports have indicated that women clergy face obstacles in their professional careers which are not placed before men. There is an underlying prejudice against having women as clergy, particularly in the parish ministry. Women are harder to place because many congregations do not want a woman as pastor. In relation to a recent research project, the bishops of the United Methodist Church were asked to comment on issues relating to the appointment of women. Twelve of the thirty-eight respondents indicated that problems arose because of the history of male domination in professional ministry. Twelve pointed to the special problems which related to the placement of married women clergy. The bishops also indicated that many congregations are unwilling to accept a

woman minister. Supporting evidence of this type of bias can be found in almost all studies of the professional ministry which have dealt with the topic of women clergy.[55]

The study made specific recommendations for the advancement of women's participation in the church. This included the establishment of a Commission on the Role and Status of Women in the United Methodist Church. The recommendations to and action of the 1972 General Conference ranged from reform in legislation to reform in language.

Agitation on various levels continued in the Church until in 1980, the first woman bishop, Margaret Matthews, was elected. In 1984 two other women, Leontyne Kelly (a Black woman) and Judith Craig were elected bishop. The struggle for the liberation and full participation continues in order to maintain successes and to make further advancements.

d. *The Presbyterian Tradition*

In *In But Still Out: Women in the Church*, Elizabeth Howell Verdesi gives a history of the struggles of women in the United Presbyterian Church in the U.S.A.[56] Women, she feels, gained formal ecclesiastical status in 1956 with the achievement of the right to ordination.[57] The other significant event relative to the status of women in the United Presbyterian Church in the U.S.A. was the election of Thelma Adair as the first woman moderator (Black) of the General Assembly in 1971. This event represented the culmination of the journey toward ecclesiastic equality.[58]

Towards the end of the 1960s women's issues began to receive special attention in the general church. In 1967, a special committee was formulated for a "study of the status and participation of women in society and in the judicatories and agencies of the Church."[59] The report of this committee, in 1969 resulted in the commissioning of a three-year study of the role and status of women in the church and society. After the study, the Task Force on Women reported nine working principles which basically affirmed the equality of women and the need for wholeness in responsible relationship between men and women in the church. Nineteen-seventy-three brought about the formation of the Council on Women and the Church (COWAC). COWAC's duties related specifically to women's advocacy.

Other activities in the United Presbyterian Church U.S.A. included special studies in fields of theological education and investigations into various kinds of supports (financial and others) available to women, as well as mandates for representative participation of women in various agencies and organizational bodies of the church. Representative participation was dealt with in the area of employment as well.

As a reflection of the need to deal with foundational causes of the situation of women, this church has addressed the matter of language. In 1975, in a report entitled "Language About God—Opening the Door" the church committed itself to a "study of cultural and theological implications of changing language about God."[60] This was one of the first ecclesiastical bodies to study seriously the issue of language as it relates to women's oppression. However, its report was never implemented.

With the 1983 merger into the Presbyterian Church (U.S.A.) of the United Presbyterians, U.S.A. and the Presbyterian Church, U.S., some fear that the relative conservatism of the southern body will endanger the gains made by women in the northern body.

These four representative traditions provide some insights into the struggles of White Christian women in the churches.[61] Likewise the same spirit of justice and freedom moved among women in other religious institutions such as the Seminary.

e. *Women's Liberation in the Seminary*

The resurgence of the feminist movement in the church and society brought about an increase in the enrollment of women in seminaries. Women found themselves as a minority in the man's world of the seminary, an often hostile environment. They were often not taken seriously, neither in the classroom context nor in their ministries. Susan Copenhauer Barrabee, in her "Education for Liberation: Women in the Seminary," discusses her experiences as a woman seminarian.[62] She observes that women suffer from distorted images in the seminary context. Either they are husband hunting or they are escaping life.

The institutional responses to women's presence in the seminaries were similar to individual responses. For the purpose of support building and collective lobbying, women began to form caucuses on seminary campuses across the country:

> Once committed to defining themselves as such, they quickly start to confront administrative, faculty, and student structures with the need to do some self-examining and changing around the woman question. They have met with every type of response, from mutual concern to ridicule. In the main they have run into a few nervous laughs and a brick wall of patronizing tolerence. Of course any of these responses is accompanied by indignant denial of discrimination against women, ("After all, some of our best friends are women") in recruitment procedures, financial aid, job placement, and so on, but until we see some real activity in these areas for women—activity which results in their showing up in our campuses and in our parishes in much larger numbers—signs of officially neutral intentions are small comfort.[63]

Faced with a real sense of powerlessness and self-negation, women in seminary saw the need to create a context wherein women not only participate in the process of consciousness raising but also claim the power of theologizing and redefining theology. Grailville became the symbol of women theologizing. Doing theology at Grailville began with a Church Women United Conference in 1972, out of which emerged a booklet entitled "Women and Theology."[64] Subsequent Grailville experiences became somewhat more structured into a seminary quarter. Seminary Quarter at Grailville became the quasi-institutional expression of women theologizing:

> Since 1974 Seminary Quarter at Grailville has offered a six-week program primarily for women in theological education. Participants lived together in the community of Grailville, shaping their own learning, asking questions often treated as peripheral in their seminary curriculum, and moving from a passive to an active learning stance.[65]

Within the traditional seminary walls, women began mobilization for action to increase the presence of women in seminary. This presence was not only a numerical presence, for women were steadily increasing in enrollment as students. But this presence which was being sought was in terms of women faculty as well as theological curriculum development. Women lobbied for the hiring of women and especially of those with the feminist perspective. What ranged from sporadic individual courses to full-fledged women's studies program began to emerge in the seminary context.

Perhaps one of the most substantive and significant programs was the "Research/Resource Associate in Women's Studies Program," established at Harvard Divinity School, Cambridge, Massachusetts. The program was established to encourage and support research of women; to provide course offerings in women's studies at Harvard Divinity School; and to create a presence of women at the faculty level. In 1980, this program was upgraded and became the "Women's Studies in Religion Program" with the following as its purpose:

Its purpose is to encourage and guide the development of women's studies in the various fields of religion. Such scholarship promises to transform the study of religion to more adequately reflect the study of human religious experience. Through the application of gender as a primary category of analysis, it explores women's distinctive religious experience and perspectives and examines male-centeredness and sexism in religious traditions.[66]

Other seminaries have responded to the demands of women in different ways. For example, at Union Theological Seminary in New York, while there was an increase in the numbers of courses in women's studies, the number of women faculty was increased from two (2) full time women to four (4) full-time women, from 1972-1981.[67] In addition to these full-time appointments, one or two other women received part time appointments.

On an interseminary level, around 1972, women organized an Annual Women's Inter-Seminary Conference which met, and continues to meet, on different seminary campuses across the country. These women organized to identify primary needs of women in the seminary context and to strategize ways and means of addressing those needs. Involved in consciousness-raising, intellectual growth in feminist studies, and the creation of support structures for women in seminary, the conference became a significant reality in the lives of women seminarians.

Most recently, twenty-one (21) women meeting in Cambridge, Massachusetts, in June of 1980, proposed what is presently known as "The Feminist Theological Institute, Inc." For the primary purpose of providing "a resource for feminist education, advocacy for women, and sister celebrations."[68] The institute professes to be for women who are "unapologetically both feminist and religious."[69] This resource and networking agency is interested in justice for all women. By employing a feminist theological critique, these

women seek to actualize their commitment "to working together for fundamental changes in social, economic, political
and religious systems," and "to furthering (women's)
survival, growth, self-imaging and creativity."[70]
    The concern for feminist theology is most concentrated in
the seminary context. It is here that feminist thought as a
theological discipline has received more serious, consistent
and passionate treatment. Women have begun to articulate
their experience theologically.
    One significant point to be noted from the above discus-
sion is that it is easy to observe the remarkable absence of
Black women in these developments. In the larger societal
context, when the White women left the Black movement,
Black women, by and large remained with what may be
called their "first allegiance." Even when some Black women
moved into the feminist circles they clearly illustrated their
primary concern as racism. Whereas, some White women began to fight both sexism and racism, the agenda which had
to be adopted by Black women centered not only around the
sexism of Black and White men but also the racism by White
men and women.[71] The reality of racism in the feminist
movement is testified to by the conspicious absence of large
numbers of Black women in the women's movement, and by
the establishment of such organizations as National Black
Feminist Organization (founded in 1973). The significance of
this organization is that it challenged the racist attitudes
and behaviours in the women's movement without
acquiescing to the sexism in the Black Movement and without
abandoning concern for the latter.
    In the Church and seminaries as women's groups arose,
Black women in covert ways—as with Theressa Hoover in
Church Women United[72]—and overt ways—as in the formal
and informal Black women's caucuses at seminaries across the
nation—challenged both the subtle and "not so subtle" racism
of White women as reflected in their organization and attitudes.[73] Many of the problems and frictions which existed
between White and Black women were evidenced on the
seminary campuses. As in the larger movement, the agenda of

Christian White women was suspect by Black women because of the inability and sometimes unwillingness of these White women to eliminate racism from their community. The theology which emerged then, did so primarily out of Christian White women's experiences with only token nuances given to Black women. The significance of this problematic will be addressed further in Chapter VII.

B. *Feminist Theology and Theologians: Emergent Perspectives*

The religio-political struggles in the churches and seminaries led to new discussions around some theological tables with the introduction of feminist questions. But like any other movement, feminism is not a monolithic movement. Likewise, feminist theory is not a monolith. Rather, there are diverse perspectives in feminism; some are more conservative than others, and as we shall see, some are more radical than others in their views.

Christian feminists in the churches and seminaries may be categorized according to various perspectives as well. The following discussion elevates some of the categories of feminism.

1. *Perspectives in Feminism*

As described by Marian Schneir, "feminism is one of the basic movements for human liberty."[74] The term and concept of feminism itself is relatively recent in usage. Contrary to William O'Neil's belief that feminism was commonly used in the nineteenth century, Rossi suggests that the term emerged in the 1890s in the writings of women and it meant then what it means today, "opinions and principles of the advocates of the extended recognition of the achievements and claims of women."[75] Feminism, however, not only concerns the recognition of achievements but advocacy as well. This advocacy means that the liberation of women is a precondition for the realization of the equality among human

beings which women seek. It is not just concerned with
women's rights but also about women's liberation and
liberation in all spheres of life—political, economic,
reproductive, sexual, educational, cultural and household.[76]
Given this description of contemporary feminism, one could
argue that any feminist commitment necessarily implies at
least political liberalism. Clear-cut demarcations cannot
always be made, however. Alison Jagger identifies four
political and ideological positions in feminism: liberal
feminism, marxist feminism, radical feminism and socialist
feminism.[77] All of these perspectives have certain common
insights about our present existence:

> One is that profound changes in traditional
> social structures such as the family will be
> needed before women are in an important sense
> equal. Another is that, whether as cause or as
> effect, the economic role and power of women will
> change. Finally, fundamental attitudes and per-
> sonal relationships must also be affected if the
> improvement is to be lasting.[78]

In other words, all of these perspectives share in challenging
the conservative views of the role of women in the society.
"The conservative view" as characterized by Alison Jaggar
is:

> . . . the view that the differential treatment of
> women, as a group, is not unjust. Conservatives
> admit, of course, that some individual women do
> suffer hardships, but they do not see this suffer-
> ing as part of the systematic social oppression of
> women. Instead, the clear roles are rationalized
> in one of two ways. Conservatives either claim
> that the female role is not inferior to that of the
> male, or they argue that women are inherently
> better adapted than men to the traditional fe-
> male sex role. The former claim advocates a kind

of sexual apartheid typically described by such phrases as "complementary but equal"; the latter postulates an inherent inequality between the sexes.[79]

This conservative view is seen in the "total woman" movement, and other anti-feminist movements. Marabel Morgan and Phyllis Schafley, respectively, represent these perspectives.[80] Liberation is believed to be degrading of women. Some, such as Ashley Montagu, go to the extent of arguing that woman in her "womanness—her natural womanness—is actually superior to man's nature.[81] All feminist theory can be seen as over-against these conservative views. However, a brief discussion of four perspectives will indicate the differences in feminist analysis.

Liberal feminism is actually "moderate" feminism. Feminists in this group believe that the laws should not only guarantee equality, but that they should "make discrimination illegal." Equality and freedom are recurring themes for liberal feminists. Consequently, they are primarily concerned with human and civil rights for women. Women are seeking the freedom to determine their own destiny and the right to participate in the church and society on an equal basis. There is no real critique of the existing social system as itself being the problem. For the most part, the systematic structures are not challenged: "The liberal does not believe that it is necessary to change the whole existing social structure in order to achieve women's liberation."[82]

Jean Elshtain says that "Liberal feminists in action, behave like other interest groups bent on 'maximizing (their) effectiveness'." The ultimate aim of such groups is integration of group members into the ongoing political structure—the public sphere—with its attendant schedule of benefits and rewards.[83] Liberal feminists are not exclusively concerned about women's liberation, but it is argued that the flip side of women's liberation is men's liberation. Men will be freed from the burdens of a "macho" society.

The second group of feminists falls under the category of classical *marxist feminism*. Unlike liberal feminism, marxist feminists locate the central problem of women in the capitalist mode of the control of production and its ensuing class stratification. Relying upon the work of Karl Marx and Friedrich Engels, these feminists take seriously the economic realities of existence which are primary contributors to the perpetuation of the oppression of women. They would not go to the extent of saying that the present system of capitalism is totally and exclusively responsible for the oppression of women, but they would argue that capitalism undergirds the oppression of women.

One can discuss the problem even at the basic unit of the family. Whereas in the larger society, [the rich constitutes the bourgeois and that poor constitutes the proletariat,] "within the family (the husband is the bourgeois and the wife represents the proletariat."[84] It is generally the wife who suffers from the burden of uncomparable domestic work. In this view, socialism is seen as the appropriate social/political system for the structuring out of society, because it eradicates, (or at least severely challenges the assumptions held in) class oppression.

The third group of feminists is from the category of *radical feminism*. These feminists locate the origin of women's oppression at the point of biology and/or the primacy of gender oppression over other structures. Because women are bearers and rearers of children and because of their biological weakness, they are dependent upon the stronger independent men. Whereas liberal and marxist feminists identify civil rights and economic rights respectively, as the primary points of contradiction in the church and society, the radical feminist reject both notions and instead

> . . . she reverses the emphasis of the classical Marxist in terms of class society: She believes that the battle against capitalism and against racism are both subsidiary to the more fundamental struggle against sexism.[85]

Thus the oppression of women is the primary contradiction, and all other forms of oppression emerges from it. Sexism is based on the biological differences between men and women. It is at the point of these differences that the revolution is perceived necessary. Women must be relieved from the biological function which serves to oppress them:

> As the radical feminist sees them, those other prerequisites are: the full self-determination including economic independence of women (and children); the total integration of women (and children) into all aspects of the larger society; and the freedom of all women (and children) to do whatever they wish to do sexually.[86]

Radical feminists look to technology for liberation from biological and economic injustices. Some would even eliminate the need for women to be burdened with the bearing and rearing of children. Likewise, the notion of family would be radically changed. There would no longer be the need for sexual and role differentiation, but "humanity could finally resort to its natural 'polymorphosy perverse' sexuality."[87] Radical feminists unapologetically identify the male as the problem. It is this male being which has, with remarkable success, distorted the female and the male being. He has dominated over and oppressed the female. He is "corrupt to the core." Obsessed with power, his intention is to control for the sake of his own interest. Men according to this view are the enemy who must be dethroned. They are woman blood sucking vampires that must be destroyed.[88]

Elshtain has characterized radical feminists succinctly in the following way:

> The radical feminist portrait of man represents, in some ways, an inversion of misogynist views of women. Even as woman has been portrayed historically as an evil temptress or a format of idealized goodness rather than as a complex

flesh-and-blood creature who is both noble and
ignoble, radical feminists sketch a vision of the
male that is unrelenting and unforgiving in its
harshness. The view of male and female natures,
respectively, forms the core of radical feminist
thought. It is important to note that the radical
feminist position on male and female natures is
frequently couched on the level of ontology, that
is male and female being (or Being, as some prefer
to put it) is given a priori. Men and women, for
some leading radical feminists, are born "that
way." The problem historically has been that
the male, an aggressive and evil being, has dominated, oppressed, exploited, and victimized the
female as being of a very different sort.[89]

The fourth group of women is *socialist feminists* which is
related to the second category, marxist feminists. Actually
socialist feminism takes the best of both marxist feminism
and radical feminism and develops a model which is
socialist in structure but which moves beyond mere socialism
in order to address the existence of sexism even in a socialist
context. "The socialist feminist reestablishes the classical
marxist connection between class society and sexism but denies
the contention that sexism is the less fundamental."[90] In
addressing sexism in this context, the barriers which keep
women out of "public production" must be broken.
Consequently, both classism and sexism must be eliminated
from our society.[91]

2. Christian Conservatism on the Woman's Question

The aforementioned perspectives in feminism all challenge the oppressive realities resulting from conservative
perspectives on women. Likewise, feminist theology challenges the conservative Christian perspectives on women.
This conservative view is basically anti-feminist in nature as
is reflected in the work of Susan Foh. In her work, *Woman*

and The Word of God, this author argues that feminists are in error on the woman's question in the Christian community.[92] While advancing the notion of "ontological equality" (that is, both men and women are in the image of God and are saved through faith in Christ), she argues that the Bible also teaches "that women are to submit themselves to their husbands and not to hold positions of ruling or teaching in the church (economic or functional subordination)."[93] Interestingly, Foh removes the discussion from the question of whether or not men are superior and women inferior. Women are not inferior but they are subordinate. Subordination does not imply inequality, for there is ontological equality. In fact, Foh goes further to argue that the concept of equality, particularly as employed by feminists, is unbiblical. In her view, feminists use the word to mean "role-interchangeability"; in addition, it serves as the basis for the "demand for rights."[94] When it comes to defining Christian relationships between men and women, one cannot demand rights. For the Bible "does not frequently speak of rights (other than the 'right' to God's presence through Christ), not even the right of life, liberty and the pursuit of happiness."[95] Feminists' notions of equality are derived, not from the Bible but from contemporary cultural environment. Because of this genesis, it is impossible for them to arrive at correct ways in which women should be governed. We can only know the status of women by way of God's word. The question is neither superiority versus inferiority nor equality. But the issue is what has God said via the Bible? God has, in fact, according to Foh, said that women, though ontologically equal, are to be submissive or subordinate to men.[96]

This theologically conservative view on women represents that to which religious feminism responds. Feminists, however, respond to the reality of women's oppression and the conservative view in different ways.

3. *Perspectives in Feminist Theology*

If the conservative view of the man-woman relationship is that men and women are equal in their inequality and women's subordination is a natural part of that relationship, then any interpretation which rejects one or both of their claims falls to the left of the conservative perspective.

The question then is, given the nuances of different meanings of feminism itself, how can we adequately categorize perspectives of feminist Christian theology? Jaggar's categories are helpful in understanding the different trends in secular feminism, but do not fully portray differences in religious feminism. Defining the feminist challenge of religion as not only a "change in the understanding of the core symbolism of Western religion but also for a change in the core symbolism itself," Carol Christ sees that two groups of feminists have emerged—the reformists and the revolutionaries. For Christ, any continuing allegiance to woman's religious tradition is reformist. The reformists "claim allegiance to an 'essential core' of Christian truth, expressed in such statements as 'in Christ there is neither Jew nor Greek, slave nor free, male nor female'." (Galatians 3:28)[97] The revolutionaries have moved beyond this essential core which they argue, is inherently patriarchal. In short, they feel that the reformists' approach is fruitless because "Christianity is not reformable."[98] An examination of a wider body of Christian and post Christian feminist literature, however, suggests that three divisions should be made. I have found Elizabeth Fiorenza's characterization of Christian Feminist theology helpful. She identifies three strands or approaches to theology. One approach employs the notion of complementarity of the sexes. There are some gifts which are unique to the feminine person and would enhance the quality of leadership in the church. The feminine, then, complements the masculine and is equally important.[99]

The second approach is called "a critical theology of liberation" because it acknowledges and critically analyzes the oppressive sexist structures of the Christian church and tradition while at the same time rediscovers the liberating tradition and elements of Christian faith and community."[100] Fiorenzo places herself into this category.

The third approach views Christianity as essentially patriarchal and therefore unable to be an adequate religious expression for the conscious woman.[101] Those women believe that Christianity is irredeemably oppressive of women. They, therefore, have moved into a realm beyond Christianity into the post-Christian era.

With some modifications the feminist theologians discussed in this work are characterized by one of these three approaches. However, before speaking of the differences which characterize these theologians, I will discuss the common goals of the theologians representing these three approaches.

C. General Goals of Feminist Theology and Christology

There are several goals of feminist theology and Christology which characterize the perspective in general.[102] First, feminist theology seeks to develop a wholistic theology. Feminist theology rejects the traditional forms of oppressive and one-sided, male dominated theologies which arise out of patriarchal religion(s).[103] Women have begun to see that their continuous oppression in the church and society has its basis in these patriarchal religion(s). Historically, these theologies have emerged out of the experiences of only one-half of the human race, making the theologies representative thereof. Feminist theology seeks to bring about a more realistic and wholistic picture of the universe by developing a more wholistic theology.

Second, in seeking to be a wholistic theology, feminist theology mandates the eradication of the dualisms in existence which are inherent in patriarchy. A patriarchy, as will be discussed in Chapter II, is characterized by male-domination and female submission and subordination. In such a society, men are considered strong, intelligent, rational and aggressive; women are considered weak, irrational, and docile.

Feminists propose that the passive, weak traits are no more the sole possession of women. Women and men to varying degrees and independently of sex, have both passive and active traits, strong and weak personality characteristics.[104]

A third function of feminist theology is to conceptualize new and positive images of women. Throughout history, including the history of theology, women have been protrayed in negative ways. They have been sources of evil (snakes), authors of trickery (witches), and stimulants (therefore causes) for the sexual perversions of men (temptresses and prostitutes).[105] These negative images must be changed to reflect reality.

Finally, feminist theology must evaluate male articulated doctrines. Doctrines developed under a system of patriarchy merely perpetuate patriarchal structures. As the system is challenged, so are the doctrines. For example, let us consider the doctrine of God. God is known primarily as Father, Lord, King, and Master. All of these names are masculine ones. We are given to believe that the masculinity of God is neither accidental nor incidental. In Collins' words, "God's maleness . . . was not derivative but was in the very nature of things, just as his other qualities of infiniteness, omnipresence and omnipotence were."[106] God was viewed as a "male Lord of hosts . . . a God who was as different from man as man was from woman. . . ."[107] Feminist theology seeks to "exorcize" this patriarchal view of God to open the way for replacing it with a wholistic view of God. God is not *He*, therefore. God can no longer be uniquely imaged in masculine form. Some feminist have begun to image God as being as much feminine as masculine. Some others have chosen to image God as female. Many have made their flight to various goddess spirituality movements.[108]

For feminists, the central dilemma of the Christian doctrinal discussion is located at the point of Christology, which is why it is the central concern of this project. In challenging this doctrine, feminists have commenced the development of feminist Christology, which, in line with the larger discipline of feminist theology, specifically articulates the meaning of the gospel of Jesus Christ for us today and promotes the liberation of women from oppressive structures which have negated their humanity.

It is to the christological point that I now turn in order to examine in greater detail the developments of feminist christological views. Most of the feminist theologians in this study fall under the category which Carol Christ calls reformist, that is, they accept an "essential core" as Christian truth. For my purposes here, I have divided this group into two. The one group is Biblical feminists and the other is Liberationist feminists. The rationale for this discussion will become clear in the next two chapters. These two categories represent a sharpening of Fiorenzo's division as well.

Mary Daly represents a major exception to these two categories. She represents the extreme position which I shall call Rejectionist, because she rejects any level of Christian "truth" as authority; additionally she specifically rejects the notion that Christology is important for women's understanding of themselves and their function in the church and society.

D. *Summary*

Feminist Christology challenges the theological community to take a new look at women's experience in relation to theology and Christology. When taken as a legitimate source for doing theology, women's experience gives theology a radically different twist. To be sure, even in the white world, women's experience is not a monolith. Consequently, the particular background and context of different women result in varying perspectives in the feminist camp. Regardless of the differences, however, they share certain commonalities which keep them identified as feminist. After sharply focusing the christological problem in Chapter II, in Chapters III,

IV and, V I will examine the three feminist theological perspectives and their emergent christological correlates.

NOTES

[1] Cf. Judith Plaskow, *Sex, Sin and Grace: Women's Experience and the Theologies of Reinhold Niebuhr and Paul Tillich* (Washington, D.C.: University Press of America, Inc., 1980); Anne Wilson Schaef, *Women's Reality: An Emerging Female System in the White Male Society* (Minneapolis, Minnesota; Winston Press, Inc., 1981); Penelope Washbourn, *Becoming Woman: The Quest for Wholeness in Female Experience* (New York: Harper and Row Publishers, 1977); and Ann Belford Ulanov, *Receiving Women: Studies in the Psychology and Theology of the Feminine* (Philadelphia: The Westminster Press, 1981).

[2] James Cone, *God of the Oppressed* (New York: Seabury Press, 1975), p. 39.

[3] Gordon Kaufman, *An Essay in Theological Method* (Missions, Mountain: Scholar Press, 1975). Kaufman attempts to deal with the problem of universals in theology. He argues that the parts must give way to the whole. ". . . [T]heology does not confine itself to this or that segment or fragment of experience attempting to set it forth clearly and distinctly, but rather addresses itself to the whole within which all experience falls. In painting his or her picture of the whole, the theological artist must draw on wide ranges and types of experience, showing how each is grasped in the integrating vision and what each means, for the "whole" is nothing, an empty abstraction, apart from the parts that make it up. Moreover, the picture which results dare not be highly idiosyncratic or "subjective"; it must be recognizably of our world, our life, our experience." (pp. 30-31) God and Christ function as relativizers. That is, "the concept of God (and Christ) relativizes the concept of world—thus destroying its absoluteness and finality—by holding that the world is in fact dependent upon and grounded upon something beyond itself" (p. 43). In the essay Kaufman argues that theological systems are fundamentally grounded "in the language and tradition which shape experience" (p. 7). The theologian draws upon different types of experiences, relating them all to the whole. The result is a reflection of our experience yet it is not "idiosyncratic" or "subjective." Many current the-

ologians are parochial, idiosyncratic and serve the interest of special groups.

What Kaufman fails to give sufficient attention to is the fact that both tradition and language were developed in a patriarchal context. Both reek of sexism and racism. Though, he recognizes that other cultures may experience different religious traditions and languages, he does not make the same allowance for "subcultures"—Blacks, women, the poor, etc.—within Western Christian history. It would appear to me that in order to do wholistic theology and Christology, we need, not God and Christ the relativizer, but God and Christ the liberator. (It is possible to relativize and not liberate.) Thus God and Christ would liberate people from oppression perpetuated in tradition, language and various other expressions of it.

4 Jon Sobrino, *Christology at the Crossroads* (New York: Orbis Books, 1978), p. 18.

5 James Cone, *God of the Oppressed* (New York: Seabury Press, 1975), p. 113.

6 Valerie Saiving Goldstein, "The Human Situation of a Feminine View," *The Journal of Religion* 40 (April 1960):100.

7 Goldstein uses these notions as expressed in the works of Anders Nygren and Reinhold Niebuhr. (*Ibid.*, p. 100.)

8 *Ibid.*, p. 101.

9 *Ibid.*, p. 110.

10 Sheila Collins, *A Different Heaven and Earth* (Valley Forge, Pa.: Judson Press, 1974), p. 14.

11 *Ibid.*, p. 33. See also James Cone, *A Black Theology of Liberation.*

12 Patriarchalism will be defined later in this chapter. Also the theology which challenges this patriarchalism in mainline male articulated theologies—feminist theology—will be defined in greater detail later in the chapter.

13 For a documentary history of the women's movement see Alice Rossi, ed., *Feminist Papers: From Adam to de Beauvoir* (New York: Bantam Books, 1974); Mariam Schneir, ed., *Feminism: The Essential Historical Writings* (New York: Vintage Books, 1972); Aileen S. Kraditor, *Up From the Pedestal: Selected Writings in the History of American Feminism* (Chicago: Quadrangle Books, 1968); William O'Neill, *Everyone was Brave: The Rise and Fall of Feminism in America* (Chicago: Quadrangle

Books, 1969); *The Woman's Movement: Feminism in the United States and England* (New York: Barnes and Noble Inc., 1969);— The first half is a brief discussion of the history of women and the second half contains primary documents. Kraditor, *The Ideas of the Women Suffrage Movement* (New York: Columbia University Press, 1965); Eleanor Flexner, *Century of Struggle: The Woman's Rights Movement in the United States* (Cambridge, Mass.: The Belknap Press of Harvard University Press, 1975). For more general histories see Gerda Lerner, *The Woman in American History* (Reading, Massachusetts: Addison-Wesley Publishing Company, 1971). For specific religious histories see Alice Rossi "Introduction: Social Roots of the Women's Movement in America" in Rossi's *The Feminist Papers*, pp. 241-281. Donald Dayton, "The Evangelical Roots of Feminism" in *Discovering An Evangelical Heritage* (New York: Harper and Row Publishers, 1976), pp. 85-98. Lerner, *The Women in American History*, pp. 20-21 and 112-114; Kraditor, *Up From the Pedestal*, pp. 108-121. Hilah F. Thomas and Rosemary Skinner Keller, eds., *Women in New Worlds: Historical Perspective in the Wesleyan Tradition*, Vol. I (Nashville: Abingdon, 1981), see especially Part II, "The Spiritual Empowerment of Women" and Part IV, "The Status of Women in Institutional Church Life." Rosemary Skinner Keller, Louise L. Queen and Hilah Thomas, eds., *Women in New Worlds: Historical Perspective in the Wesleyan Tradition*, Vol. II (Nashville: Abingdon, 1982), see especially section 4, "Professions in the Church: Individual and Corporate Responsibility"; and Rosemary Ruether and Eleanor McLaughlin, eds., *Women of Spirit: Female Leadership in the Jewish and Christian Traditions* (New York: Simon & Schuster, 1979), see especially chapters 8, 11 and 13.

[14] For a brief discussion of nineteenth century women's efforts at employing female religious imagery, see Gayle Kimball "From Motherhood to Sisterhood: The Search for Female Religious Imagery in Nineteenth and Twentieth Century Theology," in *Beyond Androcentrism: New Essays on Women and Religion*, edited by Rita Gross (Missoula, Montana: Scholars Press, 1977), pp. 259-268. See also Susan M. Setta, "Denial of the Female-Affirmation of the Feminine. The Father-Mother God of Mary Baker Eddy" in the same volume.

[15] Nancy Cott, The Bonds of Womanhood: Woman's Sphere in New England, 1780-1835 (New Haven: Yale University Press, 1972), pp. 126ff.

[16] *Ibid.*, pp. 147-148.

[17] The General Association of Massachusetts (Orthodox) to the Churches Under Their Care, 1837, in *Feminist Papers*, ed. Alice Rossi, p. 305.

[18] Sarah Grimke, "Letter on the Equality of the Sexes and the Condition of Women" in *Ibid.*, p. 307. Both Grimke sisters were active women rights advocates (as well as abolitionists). They spoke out for the rights of women including the right to speak on any issue be it Negro or woman's suffrage. See also Angelina E. Grimke, *An Appeal to the Christian Women of the South* (New York: American Antislavery Society, 1836).

[19] Elizabeth C. Stanton, *Eighty Years and More (1815-1897): Reminiscence of Elizabeth Cody Stanton* (New York: European Publishing Co., 1898), p. 381.

[20] The interesting note about this action is that the National Woman Suffrage Association represented the radical contingent in the women's movement of the nineteenth century, having split (into National Woman Suffrage Association and American Woman Suffrage Association) over the issue of "the Negro Hour" vs. Woman Suffrage. The NWSA refusing to make the woman question secondary adopted a more radical agenda.However, as reflected in this resolution and argued by O'Neill, the NWSA became less radicalized with time. Eventually . . . NWSA "adopted the policies of compromise and experience that already dominated the American Suffrage Association. Increasingly the National focused on the comparatively safe, legal and political problem that it had once scorned the American for failing to see beyond. Soon only personal animosities separated the two. By 1890 these had sufficiently abated, so that the woman suffrage movement could be reunited in the cumbersomely titled National American Woman Suffrage Association. . . ." (O'Neill, *The Woman Movement*, pp. 28-29).

[21] Elizabeth Cady Stanton, "Introduction to *The Woman's Bible*," in *Feminist Papers*, ed. Rossi, p. 401. For complete history of Stanton's contribution to the woman's movement see Alma Lutz, *Created Equal, A Biography of Elizabeth Cady Stanton* (New York: John Day, 1940); *Eighty Years and More (1815-1897):*

Reminiscences of Elizabeth Cady Stanton (New York: European Publishing Company, 1898).

22 Rossi, *Feminist Papers*, p. 474.

23 Betty Friedan, *The Feminine Mystique* (New York: Dell Publishing Co., 1963).

24 Sheila M. Rothman, *Woman's Proper Place: A History of Changing Ideals and Practices, 1870 to the Present* (New York: Basic Books, Inc., Harper Colophon Books, 1978). In her history of changing ideals of women, Rothman names four era(s): (1) virtuous womankind; (2) educated motherhood; (3) wife-companion; and (4) woman as person. Virtuous womanhood "demanded that women embody and propagate an inherently feminine kind of morality, chastity, and sensibility in their families and throughout the society" (p. 5). The ideal of educated motherhood focused on the needs of the child, and consequently women were trained for their primary and sole duty—motherhood. Wife-companion shifted the emphasis from child to husband. In effect, women went from the nursery to the bedroom. In the 1950s there was a brief return to the wife-companion of the 1920s which gave way to the Women's Liberation Movement which brought the focus from "the other" (or "others") to the self—woman as person.

25 Friedan, *Mystique*, p. 325.

26 *Ibid.*, p. 336.

27 *Ibid.*, p. 353.

28 The sex clause was not originally a part of Title VII but was thrown in actually as an attempt to defeat Title VII itself which had to do with prohibiting racial discrimination in hiring practices. See Rothman, *Woman's Proper Place*, p. 323ff.

29 Rothman, *Ibid.*, p. 333.

30 Friedan, *Mystique*, p. 370.

31 *Ibid.*, p. 371.

32 *Ibid.*

33 *Ibid.*, p. 374. In the more recent book, *The Second Stage*, Friedan challenges women to move to the second stage. The first stage was concerned with equality of rights and "full participation, power and voice in the mainstream inside the party, the political process, the professions, the business world." (p. 27) Much of the first stage became anti-family, and in the eyes of some, anti-male. The second stage must correct some of the negative distortion of the

first stage and it must as well teach women how to live with the freedom acquired. Friedan says of the second stage the following:

The second stage cannot be seen in terms of women alone, our separate personhood or equality with men.

The second stage involves coming to new terms with the family—new terms with love and with work.

The second stage may not even be a women's movement. Men may be at the cutting edge of the second stage.

The second stage has to transcend the battle for equal power in institutions. The second stage will restructure institutions and transform the nature of power itself.

The second stage may even now be evolving, out of or even aside from what we have thought of as our battle.

The Second Stage (New York: Summit Books, 1981).

[34] Rothman, *Woman's Proper Place*, p. 236.

[35] *Ibid.*, p. 245.

[36] *Ibid.*, p. 246.

[37] After a seven-year battle, the ERA was defeated in the United States Congress in 1982. Ratification by three states was lacking which resulted in its failure. The move has begun to re-activate the struggle.

[38] For histories of women's involvement in the abolition movement, see Alma Lutz, *Crusade for Freedom: Women of the Antislavery Movement* (Boston: Beacon Press, 1968); Samuel Sillen, *Women Against Slavery* (New York: Massen and Mainstream, 1955). The split in the women's movement in 1869 resulted in some women remaining active in antislavery causes while advocating women's causes (AWSA) and others heralding the cause of (White) women only (NWSA).

[39] Rothman, *Woman's Proper Place*, p. 237.

[40] For example the December 15, 1980 edition of *Time* magazine contains a report of the work of Camilla Persson Benbow and Psychologist Julia C. Stanley. Following the trend of other studies, Benbow and Stanley argued that women are inherently inferior to men in mathematical skills. By and large they do not take into consideration socio-educational disparities between the sexes. Julie Matthaei speaks of this phenomenon as a part of the justification for sexual division of labor on "natural" grounds. She says:

"For example, society in the seventeenth and eighteenth centuries believed that women's brain were smaller than men's and hence less capable of study and learning. On the basis of this understanding, women were not admitted to the first colleges. And given that women were less educated than men, it indeed seemed that women had less intellectual capacity than men. (Similarly Black women and men, forbidden as slaves to learn to read or write, indeed appeared in-capable of reading.)

Julie A. Matthaei, *An Economic History of Women in America* (New York: Schocker Books, 1982).

For a discussion of studies advancing the notion of intelligence being related to size and weight of the brain and other psychological tests with sex and race differentials, see S. D. Porteus and Marjorie E. Babcock, *Temperament and Race* (Boston: Richard G. Badger Publishers, The Gorham Press, 1926).

[41] Sarah Evans, *Personal Politics: The Roots of Women's Liberation in the Civil Rights Movement and the New Left* (New York: Vintage Books, A Division of Random House, 1979).

[42] *Ibid.*, p. 57.

[43] *Ibid.*, p. 58.

[44] *Ibid.*, p. 57. A comparative analysis would show that the founders of the nineteenth century women's movement, Lucretia Mott and Elizabeth Cady Stanton shared a similar experience, much of which resulted from the more blatant act of barring women from delegation seats at the 1840 Anti Slavery Convention in London. Upon return to the United States these women began the work which culminated in the 1848 Women's Rights Convention at Seneca Falls. It was not until 1869 that the differences in opinions in the women's movement over the fifteenth amendment resulted in the actual split yielding the American Women's Suffrage Association (AWSA) and the National Woman's Suffrage Association (NWSA). See Eleanor Flexner, *Century of Struggle: The Woman's Rights Movement in the United States*, especially Chapter X, Bettina Aptheker, *Woman's Legacy: Essays in Race, Sex, and Class in American History* (Amherst, Massachusetts: The University of Massachusetts Press, 1982), chapter 2. Alma Lutz, *Crusade For Freedom*, chapter 18.

[45] A part of this struggle which predates this organization/ conference will be reflected further in the early works of Mary Daly which will be discussed in Chapter V.

Origins NC Documentary Service records much of the discussion centering around this issue. cf Biblical Commission Report, "Can Women be Priests?" Vol. 6, No. 6 (July 7, 1976), pp. 92-96. "Declaration on Women in Ministerial Priesthood" (Reaction by various Catholics), Vol. 6, No. 34 (February 10, 1977). Archbishop Joseph Bernardin of Cincinnati, Woman Priests: "Discovering Unreasonable Hopes," Vol. 5, No. 17 (October 16, 1975). "Women/Balancing Rights and Duties," Vol. 5, No. 35, (February 19, 1976). In this article as well as in other articles, Pope Paul VI affirms the equality of men and women and at the same time he claims almost in a Barthian sense sexual differentiation. The equalizing of rights must not degenerate into an egalitarian and impersonal leveling. Egalitarianism, which is blindly pushed forward by our materialistic society, is little concerned with the specific welfare of persons, and contrary to appearances, it takes no notice of what is suitable and what is not suitable for women (p. 552).

46 "Vatican Declaration," *Origins, N. C. Documentary Service*, VI (February 3, 1977), 522. Similar and many of the same words appeared a few months earlier.

47 *Ibid.*

48 For a synopsis of this history, see Maureen Dwyer, ed., *New Woman, New Church, New Priestly Ministry*, Proceedings of the Second Conference on the Ordination of Roman Catholic Women, November 10-12, 1978, Baltimore, Maryland (Rochester, New York: Kirkwood Press, 1980), pp. 11-12.

49 Priscilla Proctor and William Procter, *Women in the Pulpit: Is God an Equal Opportunity Employer?* (Garden City, New York: Doubleday & Company, Inc., 1976), p. 18.

50 Carter Heyward, *A Priest Forever: The Formation of a Woman and a Priest* (New York: Harper and Row Publishers, 1976).

51 *The Status and Role of Women in Program and Policy Making Channels of The United Methodist Church*, p. 2 (Report of the Study Commission to the 1972 General Conference and Actions of the General Conference on the participation of Women in Programs and Policy Making Channels of the United Methodist Church).

52 *Ibid.*, pp. 4-5.

53 *Ibid.*, p. 14.

54 *Ibid.*, p. 16.

55 *Ibid.*, p. 19.

[56] Elizabeth Howell Verdesi, *In But Still Out: Women in the Church* (Philadelphia: The Westminster Press, 1973).

[57] In spite of this gain, Verdesi argues that women in the Presbyterian Church have had no real power but have had two crucial opportunities to gain significant power. But for various reasons, e.g. cooptation, women were never successful at gaining power. The opportunities were in the area of Missions and Christian Education. It seems to me that Verdesi's argument is unconvincing. The evidence presented is insufficient to conclude that women ever had enough control in order to gain real power. Even she admits, in reference to Christian Education, that ". . . this center of power was never developed as a power base for women, even though potentially it might have been" (pp. 155-166). The question is, was this at all possible since control was never really out of the hands of men?

[58] *Ibid.*, pp. 17-18.

[59] The History Statement, from the 1976 Resource Kit. *Statements of History of the Task Force on Women and the Council on Women and the Church* (COWAC).

[60] Advisory Council on Discipleship of Worship, "Language About God 'Opening the Door'" (New York: The United Presbyterian Church in the U.S.A. 187th General Assembly, May 1975).

[61] Kathleen Bliss, *The Service and Status of Women in the Churches* (London: SCM Press LTD, 1952). This is the first world-wide study on the subject of women in church service. This study was sponsored by The World Council of Churches in 1952 and is primarily a survey of the status of women in various churches vis-a-vis ordination. See especially chapter 4 for a discussion of "Women and the Ordained Ministry."

[62] Susan Copenhauer Barrabee, "Education for Liberation: Women in the Seminary," in *Women's Liberation and the Church*, ed., Sally Bentley-Doely (New York: Association Press, 1970).

[63] *Ibid.*, p. 51.

[64] In Sheila Collins, *A Different Heaven and Earth*, p. 19.

[65] Seminary Quarter at Grailville, *Women United in Theologizing and Action*, (Summer, 1978), p. 1.

[66] The weakness of the program was that the presence of women was more of an illusion, because of the facts that the Research/Resource Associates of the first seven years of the program were all part-time and the program was really peripheral to

the main institutional structure. The new Women's Studies in Religion Program in the second seven years upgraded the previous programs by making the appointments full-time, one-year terms and focusing primarily on senior women scholars.

67 The Union approach in the long run provides more substance. There is a greater possibility that permanent full-time faculty could make more substantive change in theological education than transient part-time (or full-time) faculty as in the Harvard Program. There exists the potential for a greater consistency and continuity in curriculum reform and development.

68 "The Communique of the Council of Visioners of the Feminist Theological Institute, Inc.," October, 1981. (Photocopied.)

69 *Ibid.*

70 Feminist Theological Institute, Inc., "Statement" November, 1980. (Photocopied.)

71 See discussion in Chapter VII.

72 Church Women United felt that religion was constraining enough. Hoover says: "This fact alone was sufficiently limiting; there was no purpose to be served by further splintering ourselves along the lines of race." (Hoover, "Black Women and the Churches: Triple Jeopardy" in Gayrand Wilmore and James Cone, *Black Theology: A Documentary History* (New York: Orbis Books, 198), p. 382.

73 Racist attitudes, behaviours, and assumptions were examined by a group of Black and White women called the Cornwall Collective which met at the Grant Center in New York. The subject under discussion was women and theological education. They dealt with some of the racist structures which created oppressive conditions for women. Not only did they deal with sexist structures which created oppressive conditions for women, but they also spent considerable time on racist structures which give Black women a double dose of oppression in the context of theological education. The Cornwall Collective, *Your Daughter Shall Prophesy* (New York: The Pilgrim Press, 1980). See especially chapter 3, "Racism and the Responsibilities of White Women in Theological Education" and Appendix C, "Black Women in Ministry, Boston Theological Institute."

74 Marian Schneir, ed., *Feminism: The Essential Historical Writings* (New York: Vintage Books, 1972), p. xi.

75 Alice Rossi, ed., *The Feminist Papers*, pp. xii-xiii. This definition is taken from the unabridged Oxford dictionary.

[76] *Ibid.*, p. xii.

[77] Alison Jaggar, "Political Philosophies of Women's Liberation," in *Feminism and Philosophy*, eds. Mary Vetterling-Braggin, Frederick A. Elliston and Jane English (Totowa, New Jersey: Littlefield Adams & Co., 1977), pp. 5-21.

[78] Jane English, "Introduction," in *Feminism and Philosophy*, eds. Mary Vetterling-Braggin, Frederick A. Elliston and Jane English, p. 3. Also see A. M. Jagger and P. Rothenberg Struhl, *Feminist Frameworks: Alternative Theoretical Accounts of the Relations Between Women and Men* (New York: McGraw-Hill Book Company, 1978), pp. ix-xiv.

[79] Alison Jaggar, "Political Philosophies of Women's Liberation," p. 6.

[80] See Marabel Morgan, *The Total Woman* (Old Tappan, New Jersey: Fleming H. Revell Company, 1973). Phyllis Schafley is the Illinois Congressperson who is the champion of the anti-ERA movement.

[81] Ashley Montagu, *The Natural Superiority of Women* (New York: McMillan Co., 1953). Montagu based his claim in scientific, theological evidence having to do with women's IQ and strength. Encouched in his language of togetherness and a statement of equality, he articulates a traditional viewpoint of women: Human beings differ greatly in their abilities but practically not at all along sex lines; that is to say, abilities are not determined by sex. Abilities are functions of persons, not of groups or classes. Hence, so far as abilities are concerned both sexes should be afforded equal opportunities to realize their potentialities, and the judgement of their abilities should not be prejudiced by any bias of sex (p. 242). Women should no longer accept a state of permanent male patronage. They should no longer permit their world to be exclusively run by men. Women must be granted complete equality with men, for only when this has been done will they fully be able to realize themselves (p. 242). Yet he employs the principles of "complementarity of the sexes." The role of women is seen primarily as mother. The woman must serve as the true model of *love*. He says later: Women are mothers of humanity;. . . Women must assume the full birthright of motherhood. . . . Women are the carriers of the true spirit of humanity—the love of the mother for her child. The preservation of that kind of love is the true function of women. (p. 247-248).

82 Jaggar, "Political Philosophy of Women's Liberation," p. 9.

83 Jean Elshtain, *Public Man, Private Woman* (New Jersey: Princeton University Press, 1981), p. 228. For an extensive critique of liberal feminism see Zillah Eisenstein, *The Radical Future of Liberal Feminism* (New York: Longman, 1981). Eisenstein chalenges liberal feminists to grapple seriously with the contradiction "inherent in liberal feminism." (p. 5) She says: Until a conscious differentiation is made between a theory of individuality that recognizes the importance of the individual within the social collectivity and the ideology of individualism that assumes a competitive view of the individual, there will not be a full accounting of what a feminist theory of liberation must look like for western society. (p. 5) She further explicates her point by exposing the patriarchal bias of liberalism. (p. 6-7) See especially chapters 2, 9 and 10.

84 Friedrich Engels, *The Origin of the Family, Private Property and the State*, quoted by Jaggar, "Political Philosophy and Women's Liberation," p. 11.

85 Jaggar, "Political Philosophy and Women's Liberation" pp. 12-13.

86 *Ibid.*, p. 13. See discussion in Shulamith Firestone *Dialectic of Sex* (New York: Bantam Books, 1972), pp. 206-209.

87 *Ibid.*, p. 14, cited in Firestone, *Ibid.*, p. 209.

88 Mary Daly, *Beyond God the Father* (Boston: Beacon Press, 1973), Pissim. See also *Gynecology: The Metaethics of Radical Feminism* (Boston: Beacon Press, 1978), Passim.

89 Elshtain, *Public Man, Private Woman*, p. 205

90 Jaggar and Struhl, *Feminist Frameworks*, p. xiii. Socialist feminism is represented in the following works: Shulamith Firestone, *The Dialectic of Sex*; Juliet Mitchell, *Woman's Estate* (New York: Random House, 1973); Sheila Rowbotham, *Women, Resistance and Revolution: A History of Women and Revolution in the Modern World* (New York: Vintage Books, 1974); and *Woman's Consciousness, Man's World* (New York: Penguin, 1974).

91 A fifth group of women identified by Jean Bethke Elshtain in *Public Man, Private Woman*, is called "psychosanalytic feminism." It is a group in which "psychoanalysis is being deployed as a way to understand the individual, particularly the female individual, in society and to appreciate more richly than possible under perspectives that concentrate on 'externality' the inner connections between individuals and their social worlds within particular or

'universal' historical situations" (pp. 285-286). Psychoanalytic theory is being challenged and used for the advancement of women. Zillah Eisenstein divides the feminist political spectrum into nine categories. They are: Anti-feminist Traditionalists, Status Quo Liberal Feminism, Progressive Liberal Feminist Tendency, Radical Liberal Feminist Tendency, Anarchy Feminism, Radical Feminism, Lesbian Feminism, Socialist Feminism and Black Feminism (*The Radical Future of Liberal Feminism*, pp. 229-232).

[92] Susan Foh, *Woman and the Word of God* (Grand Rapids, Michigan: Baker Book House, 1979), passim.

[93] *Ibid.*, p. 1; cf p. 59.

[94] *Ibid.*, pp. 38-39.

[95] *Ibid.*, p. 39.

[96] Foh's position sounds remarkably Barthian. Karl Barth is noted for his notion that man is made in the image of God. However, as male and female, there exists within man sexual differentiation which cannot be transcended. Further, the relationship of the woman to the man is defined as subordinate. See discussion in Chapter III. Among others sharing this conservative view is Billy Graham who in the *Ladies Home Journal* article entitled "Jesus and the Liberated Woman" (December 1970,p. 42) said: The biological assignment was basic and simple: Eve was to be the child-bearer, and Adam was to be the breadwinner... Wife, mother, homemaker—this is the appointed destiny of real womanhood. Quoted in Donald Dayton "The Evangelical Roots of Feminism" in *Discovering an Evangelical Heritage* (New York: Harper and Row Publishers, 1976), p. 85. This perspective is further represented by Ruth Graham speaking on the question of the ordination of women. She said: I personally am "against it."... I believe that it basically goes against the principles of Scripture.... I think if you study you will find that the finest cooks in the world are men...; the finest courtiers... are men; the great politicians are men; most of our greatest writers are men; most of our greatest athletes are men. You name it, men are superior in all but two areas: women make the best wives and women make the best mothers. Ruth Graham, comment in "Others Say..." column, *Christianity Today*, June 6, 1975, p. 32, quoted in Dayton, *Discovering an Evangelical Heritage*, pp. 85-86.

[97] Carol Christ, "A Review of Feminist Literature," *Religious Studies Review*, III (October 1977), p. 203.

[98] *Ibid.*, p. 204.

[99] Elizabeth Fiorenza, "To Comfort or to Challenge: Feminist Theological Reflections on the Pre-Conference Process in *New Woman New Church New Priestly Ministry,* ed. Maureen Dwyer, p. 47.

[100] *Ibid.*, p. 50.

[101] *Ibid.*, p. 49

[102] Though these goals are especially true of reformist feminist theologians, they are true with certain qualifications or modifications of radical feminists. The reasons for this are implicit in Christ's definition of revolutionaries (radicals) and will become clear in the discussion in Chapter V of this dissertation.

[103] The three major religions are Islam, Judaism and Christianity. Others are Buddhism and Hinduism.

[104] This will be discussed further in Chapter II.

[105] For a brief discussion of these negative images see Vern L. Bullough, *The Subordinate Sex: A History of Attitudes Toward Women* (Baltimore, Maryland: Penguin Books, Inc., 1973), especially pp. 173-174 and 223.

[106] Collins, *A Different Heaven and Earth*, p. 60.

[107] *Ibid.*, p. 63.

[108] See discussion in Chapter V, especially endnote #39.

II

FEMINIST CHRISTOLOGY: THE PROBLEM STATED

Feminist theologians have not done overwhelmingly substantial amounts of work in the area of Christology. I believe that the reason is due primarily to the problematic nature of the doctrine itself. What is especially problematic for feminists regarding Christology? Why do arguments against women and for their oppression/subordination tend to be Christological? The latter question provides some insights into the first. The problem has centered in the indisputable fact that the historical Jesus was indeed a male. Some have attempted to retard (and others, with remarkable success, have retarded) the leadership of women, in the church and the larger society, because of this very fact.

What has Jesus Christ to do with the status of women in the church and society? It is this very question which serves as the basis of my Christological inquiry. It is my claim that there is a direct relationship between our perception of Jesus Christ and our perception of ourselves. (The very point can be made of God). Ludwig Feuerbach sheds some light on this relationship. He describes the content of this relationship as one of self-objectification: "The object of any subject is nothing else than the subject's own nature taken objectively."[1] With Jesus Christ as the object which the subject projects onto, it is important to discern who represents the subject. From the feminist perspective, Feuerbach unwittingly makes a significant point as he argued "man has given objectivity to himself, but has not recognized the object as his own nature"[2] Perhaps Feuerbach intended the generic use of the male language. However, it is the argument of feminist theologians that generic language is in fact no more than male language which represents a male perspective.[3] Man has, in fact projected himself as the subject with the authority to say who Jesus Christ is for us (men and women) yesterday, today and tomorrow.

Since man is limited by his social context and interests, Jesus Christ has been defined within the narrow parameters of the male consciousness. That is to say, the social context of the men who have been theologizing has been the normative criterion upon which theological interpretation have been based. What this has meant is that Jesus Christ consistently has been used to give legitimacy to the customary beliefs regarding the status of women. The critical question to answer at this time is what has the church (male theologian) taught about Jesus and how have these teachings functioned with regard to women? This chapter explores these two questions.

A. *The Classical Christological Formulation*

What does the church teach about Jesus or Who is Jesus Christ for the Christian Church?

> This selfsame one Jesus Christ is perfect [teleion] both in deity [theoteti] and also in human-ness [anthropoteti]; this selfsame one is also actually [alethos] God and actually man, with a rational soul [psyches logikes] and a body. He is of the same reality as God [homoousion to patri] as far as his deity is concerned and of the same reality as we are ourselves [homoousion hemin] as far as his human-ness is concerned; thus like us in all respects, sin only excepted.[4]

This excerpt of the christological definition which emerged out of the council of Chalcedon in 451 AD essentially represented what the church taught about Jesus Christ. Though it may appear as a neatly wrapped package, the process towards its formulation was long and rugged.[5] Even though the council of Nicea of 325 AD had settled the question of who Jesus was in relation to God by condemning Arianism,[6] all of the problems were not yet solved. It was established that Jesus was *homoousion to Patri*. Jesus was not of the created order, but of the same essence or substance as God. Jesus was in fact "God from God, Light from Light, true God from true God, begotten not created, of the same reality as the Father. . . .[7] Having settled on the relationship what remained was to clarify how it was possible.

The Council of Chalcedon set about the task of clarifying this issue, for several persons in the years following Nicaea had attempted to articulate this relationship. Three of the major points of views were put forth by Apollinaris,[8] Nestorius,[9] and Eutyches.[10] These persons, primarily concerned with the unity or purity of God, proposed positions which protected the divine reality. The points of controversy centered around the use of such terms as "rational soul" (against Apollinarius), *"theotokos"* (against Nestorius) and "in two natures" (against Eutyches), which the Chalcedonian bishops employed. By this action these persons were eventually deemed heretics, because they essentially emphasized one aspect of the two natures to the exclusion of the other. Alan Richardson says the following of these attempts in relation to the Chalcedonian solution:

> It is evident that the Chalcedonian Fathers... were... concerned with removing the false limitations of the subject in the one-sided theories of the heretics. It was the heretics who were one-sided, not the Chalcedonians; it was the heretics who emphasized one aspect to the exclusion of the other, whereas the Catholic bishops merely insisted that both aspects should be given full and equal consideration. Thus the Chalcedonian Definition does not prescribe a theory of how Godhead and manhood were united in the one Christ, but contents itself with insisting that they actually were united–a fact which each of the three main types of heresy had denied. The Chalcedonians stand for equal emphasis on both the Godhead and the manhood

in Christ as against the heretical emphasis of
the one to the exclusion of the other.[11]

The language conveys that Jesus Christ is just as much God as
he was man and just as much man as he was God. For the
Chalcedonian bishops this was a nonnegotiable claim which
was to be a basic presupposition of the Church forever.
Fifteen centuries after Chalcedon, Karl Barth puts the same
idea this way: "that God's Son or Word is the man Jesus of
Nazareth is the one christological thesis of the New
Testament; that the man Jesus of Nazareth is God's Son or
Word is the other."[12] Indeed, Jesus Christ is *vere Deus vere
homo*.

But unlike Barth, Richardson goes on to describe this
statement as the christological principle, as opposed to a
theory. Whereas a theory is changeable with time, a
principle applies for all times.

> Thus the Definition stands for a principle rather
> than a theory; and it permits the formulation of
> theories provided that the principle is
> safeguarded in them. We are free to suggest any
> theory about the mode of the Incarnation which
> commends itself to us, provided that we do not
> lose sight of the fundamental truth that God and
> man are brought together in the Person of Jesus
> Christ. The Definition provides us with the
> postulates or data of Christological theory: it
> does not attempt to give us a theory of its own.
> This is the reason why the Definition may
> remain for those who accept the fundamental
> claim of the Church—that God himself is in-
> carnate in Jesus Christ—the classic expression of
> Christological truth; had the Chalcedonian
> Fathers attempted to formulate a theory, their
> work would by now be out of date, for theories
> must be altered by each generation as the bounds
> of our knowledge extend. But because they were

> content merely to enunciate a principle, the Chalcedonians handed down to all succeeding ages a standard by which every theory might be tested and judged. It is in this sense, and this sense only, that the Chalcedonian formula may be said to be "final."[13]

The principle then lives forever. In Richardson's view herein lies the once-and-for-allness of the Chalcedonian definition. Richard Norris sees this once-and-for-allness in a different way. He speaks of the significance of this definition as having established a "rule of christological language." The formula of a definition does not give us the intricate and technical details of how, in the sense of the way Jesus Christ is "put together," but it explains the proper way to speak of Jesus Christ. The value in the Council of Chalcedon then lies not in the notion that it provides a Christology, but rather that it provides "formal outlines of an adequate christological language."[14]

Their differences not withstanding, both Richardson and Norris speak of a certain finality of the Chalcedonian definition. In more traditional terms, Jesus Christ represents a decisive and definitive event of all Christianity. As acknowledged by one thinker, this traditional view holds that ". . . to speak of the meaning of Jesus Christ is to speak of what is most distinctive and most decisive in Christian life and faith. The Christian religion . . . finds its center and . . . its circumference also in Christ."[15] Without this Jesus Christ who is both divine and human, Christianity would have no content. With this Jesus Christ, as affirmed at Chalcedon, Christians have both a Lord and a Saviour.

Grillmeier observed that the (Nicene and) Chalcedon creeds clarified "only one, albeit the decisive, point of belief in Christ: that in Jesus Christ, God really entered into human history and thus achieved our salvation."[16]

What could it mean to say that God became incarnate in the man, Jesus? In no other human being did this miraculous event occur. This occurrence was not one only to be marvelled at by Jesus' contemporaries, but it is the critical event (reality) in all of Christian history. This being the case, feminists ask what can be said about a religious expression which make its supreme deity totally represented in one male figure through whom everyone must pass in order to be saved? The social context in which this religious perspective emerged provides some insights into this question.

B. *Christology and its Social Context as Related to Women*

What is this social context in which Christology emerged and developed? More specifically, what has Christology to do with the status of women within this social context? First of all, the social context in which orthodox theology arose can be characterized by the term "patriarchy."

Patriarchy represents a condition in which men dominate women. In it reality is defined from the perspective of men and women are always relegated to secondary subordinate roles. But patriarchy "refers to more than a socially prescribed hierarchy of sex roles," says Sheila Collins. The term connotes "the whole complex of sentiments, the patterns of cognition and behavior, and the assumptions about human nature and the nature of the cosmos that have grown out of a culture in which men have dominated women."[17] Patriarchalism apparently is a way of looking at all of reality so that roles are not assigned to women and men arbitrarily but they represent "systematic," "objective," "ordered," "logical," and "rational" analyses. In Collins' words, "Patriarchalism, then, refers to a metaphysical world view, a mindset, a way of ordering reality which has more often been associated with the male than with the female in Western culture."[18] It is a "social system maintaining male dominance and privilege based on female submission and marginality."[19]

Having been described as a conceptual trap[20] which is pervasive, patriarchy is evidenced not only throughout history,[21] but also within all aspects of our existence. "The fact is evident at once if one recalls that the military, industry, technology, universities, science, political office, and finance—in short, every avenue of power within the society, including the coercive force of the police, is entirely in male hands. . . .the Deity, "His" ministry, together with the ethics and values, the philosophy and art of our culture—its very civilization . . . is of male manifestation."[22] It is only consistent then that Patriarchy is undergirded by ideology, biology, sociology, education, economics, force, psychology, anthropology, myth and religion.[23]

What has been the effect of patriarchy upon women? In the "95 Theses on Patriarchal Oppression of Women," Judy Gere and Virginia Mills described what happens to women in patriarchy (tradition) in the following manner:

> The experience and contributions of women throughout *history* [italics mine] have been ignored, distorted, and repressed, and a patriarchal bias substituted.[24]

Further, and more directly,

> The experience and contributions of women to *Christianity and Church History* [italics mine] have been ignored, distorted and repressed with a patriarchal bias substituted.[25]

Concretely, this means that in patriarchy women's lives are carefully controlled and contained so that, though socialization, human personality is guided along lines of sex category (the masculine and the feminine) producing sex roles that are virtually mutually exclusive.

Theology and Christology have developed in this context. Characteristically then, in theology and Christology, the male-masculine is projected as the valued entity and the female-feminine is projected as devalued entity. In effect, there is the institutionalization of dual existence.

Rosemary Ruether discusses the matter in the following way:

> The psychic organization of consciousness, the dualistic view of the self and the world, the hierarchical concept of society, the relation of humanity and nature, and of God and creation all these relationships have been modeled on sexual dualism. Therefore the liberation of women attacks the basic stereotypes of authority, identity and the structural relation of "reality." The male ideology of the "feminine" that we have inherited in the West seems to be rooted in a self-alienated experience of the body and the world, projecting upon the sexual other the lower half of these dualisms. As Simone de Beauvoir pointed out many years ago in her classic study, *The Second Sex*, in male-dominated societies, it is always woman who is the "other," the antithesis over against which one defines "authentic" (male) selfhood.[26]

More concretely, some feminists explicitly are locating the problem as patriarchy and its inherent dualisms and identifying them as a primary source of human sinfulness. In doing just that, Collins discovers that "we are able to find metaphors which help to explain and to connect the various manifestations of sin, both personal and corporate, in a way that was not possible before."[27]

Collins continues:

> Such metaphors are summed up in a series of dualisms, the two halves of which are related to each other as superior to inferior, superordinate to subordinate. Male/female, mind/body, subject/object, man/nature, inner/outer, white/black, rational/irrational, civilized/primitive — all serve to explain the way in which the

patriarchy has ordered reality. As we have seen, the left-hand side of each equation has assumed a kind of right of ownership over the right. The relationship is one of owner to owned, oppressor to oppressed rather than one of mutuality.[28]

In other words, the active, strong, independent traits are associated with men and the passive, weak, dependent traits are associated with women.

This dualism or dichotomy is carried over and maintained in theology proper. In the eyes of some feminists, for example, Karl Barth's theological system represents the epitome of theological (and social) dualism. The qualitative distinction between God and man which he borrows from Soren Kierkegaard is transferred to the qualitative (sexual) distinction (differentiation) between man and woman. This is essentially Joan Romero's critique of Barth's theology.[29] According to Barth, any attempt to eradicate this basic inherent sexual differentiation is to engage in "gnosis"—false spirituality.[30]

Barth's concept of *"Ordnung"* (order) further illustrates the qualitative distinction.

The disjunction and the conjunction of man and woman, of their sexual independence and sexual interrelationship, is controlled by a definite *order*. As the attitude and function of the man and those of the woman must not be confused and interchanged but faithfully maintained, and as on the other hand they must not be divorced and played off against each other but grasped and realized in their mutual relatedness, so they are not to be equated, nor their relationship reversed. They stand in a *sequence*. It is in this that man has his allotted place and woman hers. It is in this that they are orientated on each other. It is in this that they are individually and together the human creature as created by God. Man and

woman are not an A and a second A whose being
and relationship can be described like the two
halves of an hour glass, which are obviously two,
but absolutely equal and therefore interchangeable. Man and woman are an A and a B, and
cannot, therefore, be equated. In inner dignity and
right, and therefore in human dignity and right,
A has not the slightest advantage over B, nor
does it suffer the slightest disadvantage. What
is more, when we say A we must with equal
emphasis say B also, and when we say B we must
with equal emphasis have said A. . . . [Italics
mine.][31]

Note that although man and woman are not the same, they
are equal. Yet they are not equal as we simplistically
understand equality, but they are equal in a deeper sense.[32]
However, two critical words for understanding Barth's
meaning are *order* and *sequence*. It seems clear that order here
is used in the sense of sequence. Because man and woman are
not both A's there must be some order in the relationship of A
and B. Man and woman are not the same and sequentially
man comes before woman. However, because one is not better
than the other, there is mutual human dignity and right.

Next, Barth proceeds to explain the notion of order in the
relationship which he has just described.

Man and woman are *fully-equal* [italics mine]
before God and therefore as men in respect of the
meaning and determination, the imperilling, but
also the promise, of their human existence. They
are also equal in regard to the necessity of their
mutual relationship and orientation. They stand
or fall together. They become and are free or
unfree together. They are claimed and sanctified
by the command of God together, at the same
time, with equal seriousness by the same free
grace, to the same obedience and the reception of

the same benefits. Yet the fact remains—and in this respect there is no simple equality—that they are claimed and sanctified as man and woman, each for himself, each in relation to the other in his own particular place, and therefore in such a way that A is not B but A, and B is not another A but B. It is here that we see the order outside which man cannot be man nor woman be woman, either in themselves or in their mutual orientation and relationship.[33]

One writer explains in Barth's behalf that *"Ordnung"* has significance of sequence, not hierarchy. Clifford Green, after explaining the idea of *"Ordnung"* as *"sequence"* in terms of the superordination of man and the subordination of woman; the initiative of man and the responding of woman; the Christ-like nature of man; and the disciple-like nature of woman, finally admits "the sequence, male-female, initiative-following, simply will not do, no matter how many qualifications Barth offers."[34] If sequence rather than hierarchy is intended, these strong/weak dualisms simply are inadequate or inappropriate because they in fact do promote hierarchy.

In light of the foregoing explanations, it is the feeling of some feminists that this kind of qualitative distinction and the idea of orders (of creation) flow naturally into a hierarchy which is simple and rigid. The order of creation is as follows according to Sheila Collins:

God = Goodness, order
Angels
Jesus
Men
Women
Children
Beasts
Plants

Earth
Evil, Chaos[35]

Collins locates the origin of this scheme in the period following the death of Christ. Her analysis follows the line of Romero's argument regarding the interrelationship between God, Man and Woman. Collins puts it this way: "God is the ruler and creator of his world so man is to rule woman who is beneath him. She, in turn, rules children who are beneath her."[36] The hierarchical images of the ruler as the superior over against the ruled as the subordinate are clearly demonstrated in Paul's letter to the Corinthians and Ephesians.[37] This hierarchy is a peculiar characteristic of patriarchalism.

It is not surprising then that the development of theology and Christology in this context of patriarchalism has meant that Jesus Christ has been interpreted to fit into the *weltanschauung* of patriarchy. Because of this, much of Christological interpretations have undergirded the oppression of women in the church and society. The question posed at the beginning of this section, "what has Jesus Christ to do with the status of women in church and society", can be answered tentatively at this point. For some theologians, Jesus Christ provided normative evidence for legitimation of the oppression of women,[38] as we shall see in the following section.

C. *Christology and the Oppression of Women*

The second question must be taken up and examined. Why do many arguments supporting the oppression of women tend to be Christological? Because Jesus Christ represents the essence of the Christian faith, it is important that theologians ground their interpretations in the very nature of the faith. In this way, their analysis is believed to have greatest authenticity and authority for defining the meaning of Christianity. If we could determine that the status of women in the society was condoned by Jesus, then we could believe that the same status must be maintained now, hence-forth and forevermore.

How have Christological arguments been used to support the subordinate status of women in contemporary church and society? This question can best be answered by focussing on the issue of leadership. If we look at the question of leadership in the society in general, we discover that women have been and still are systematically excluded from leadership positions in the society.[39] It is reasoned that women are the weaker sex and are psychologically, not to mention politically, unequipped for leadership. The "woman's sphere" traditionally has been defined as the family, her roles being those of mother, wife and housekeeper. Women serve as the support structure for the leadership of men, be it in the areas of business, politics or religion.

The struggles described in Chapter I indicate that this argument is also operative in the church. Women are systematically excluded from positions of leadership for basically the same reasons as in the larger society, but with historical, biblical, and theological justifications. Although the issue of leadership is a broader one, the arguments against women in leadership are similar, if not the same, as those specifically against the ordination of women. There are churches who allow and provide for the ordination of women, yet their overall leadership privileges are stifled by various means and for the same or similar reasons that other churches do not ordain them.[40] Reginald Fuller, in discussing the pros and cons of the ordination issue, gives one argument which is often used by antagonists:

> The recorded calls of disciples were all of men....
> Jesus in his earthly life choose Twelve for a
> particular role—to be signs of the New Israel
> that would come into being with the advent of
> God's Kingdom. The Twelve were men. If Jesus
> intended his church to have women ministers
> (leaders), it is argued, he would have included
> women among the Twelve.[41]

An episcopal priest writing under the pseudonym David R. Stuart brings together the Christological, the historical, the psychological, the secular and the ecclesiastical arguments against the leadership of women:

> Christ himself chose men to be apostles, the early church ordained men to be priests and consecrated men to be bishops. For generations the worshipper has heard the sounds of a male voice reading the prayers of consecration, for centuries the priest-confessor has been a man. Men were and continue to be the leaders, the initiators, the heads of households familial and eccelesiastical and it would be psychologically confusing as well as historically disruptive to substitute women for that office. The long history of the Holy Catholic Church has been that of a male priesthood—this tradition is not hastily or lightly to be broken.[42]

Implicit in this argument is not only the primary question of whom Jesus chose, but who or what he, Jesus was. The political question of Jesus' choice of twelve male disciples and later apostolic succession, is magnified by the ontological question of who/what Jesus was. As John Paul Boyer aptly puts it:

> Being a Jew, being a Palestinian, being a first century man—all these are what we might call, in the language of Aristotelian metaphysics, the "accidents of Christ's humanity"; but his being a man rather than a woman is of the "substance" of his humanity. He could have been a twentieth-century Chinese and been, cultural differences notwithstanding, much the same person he was; but he could not have been a woman

without having been a different sort of personality altogether.[43]

Taking this idea a bit further, some scholars and church
leaders have used the doctrine *in persona Christi* and the
sacramental nature of the office of priest to concretize the
issue.

Perhaps the most significant use of this argument comes
from or through Rome. Pope Paul VI, on October 15, 1976,
approved and ordered published a declaration on the
question of women and the priesthood, which was presented
by Franjo Cardinal Seper. In the declaration, Seper made it
perfectly clear that the *imago dei* is a central issue in the
ordination question:

> The Christian priesthood is therefore of a
> sacramental nature: the priest is a sign, the
> supernatural effectiveness of which comes from
> the ordination received, but a sign that must be
> perceptible and which the faithful must be able
> to recognize with ease. The whole sacramental
> economy is in fact based upon natural signs, or
> symbols imprinted upon the human psychology:
> "Sacramental signs", says Saint Thomas,
> "represent what they signify by natural
> resemblance." The same natural resemblance is
> required for persons as for things: when Christ's
> role in the Eucharist is to be expressed
> sacramentally there would not be this "natural
> resemblance" which must exist between Christ
> and his minister if the role of Christ were not
> taken by a man. In such a case it would be
> difficult to see in the minister the image of
> Christ. For Christ himself was and remains
> man.[44]

Later the Catholic Church declared that because the priest
represents Christ himself, he is actually *in persona*

Christi.[45] As applied here, the argument is that because Jesus was male, his representatives, in turn, must be male also. Women do not represent that image. This is a nonnegotiable item. As Stuart asserts, "To change the sex of the priest alters the image of God. . . ."[46] With varying theological sophistication, the same line of argument has undergirded the resistance to the leadership of women in other churches as well.[47]

As we can see in this ecclesiastical controversy, the question of leadership or ordination of women is directly xrelated to the maleness of Jesus. Theologians and Christians alike utilize christological arguments encouched in larger theological concepts as mechanism for legitimating the primacy of the maleness of Jesus. It has become critical not only that God became human, or Jesus Christ was both divine and human, but more importantly that functionally God became man, therefore Jesus was both divine and man. Consequently, it is Jesus' maleness which is the primary characteristic which defines who is Jesus Christ—the Christology question. For this reason, Ruether is on target when she asks the question, "Can a male Jesus help woman?"[48] If it is primarily the male Jesus which has been used as the criterion for oppressing women, can women look to this same male Jesus as the source of their salvation?

This question focuses us on the discussion of the relationship between Christology and Soteriology. When Christology is done in the context of patriarchy, can this person of Jesus Christ (Christology), maleness and all, provide women with a fair share of the "benefits" of the work of Jesus Christ (Soteriology)?

D. *Christology, Soteriology and Women*

Reginald Fuller is consistent with traditional belief when he says that:

> Christology is the doctrine of the 'person' of Jesus Christ. In traditional dogmatics, Christology

(the doctrine of Christ's person) precedes soteriology (the doctrine of Christ's work). Logically this is true order. It was because he was who he was that Jesus Christ did what he did."[49]

Theologians are often unclear on the relationship between Soteriology and Christology. While trying to claim equal importance of both, Christology so defined, seems to gain an edge on Soteriology. For example, Dietrich Bonhoeffer says that Christology is not Soteriology, and Soteriology can not lead us to Christology.[50] He explains that "The attempt to understand the person from the work is doomed to failure because of the ambiguity of the work."[51] Bonhoeffer makes an important point when he observes that the work can only be understood in light of the person—Soteriology can be understood in the light of Christology. If the "who" is known the "what" follows. Yet, after making the separation, Bonhoeffer affirms that it would be incorrect "to conclude from this that the Person and the Work can be separated." Still the one-sided importance which Bonhoeffer has placed on Christology as reflected in the earlier part of his discussion makes it impossible not to separate the Person from the Work of Christ. It is clear that the Person holds primary importance for some theologians who make this dichotomy, even though it is claimed that the dichotomy is for the sake of convenience. George Hendry writes that "It is convenient for purposes of inquiry to distinguish the question, who he is, from the question, what he does.[52]

The traditional split between Christology and Soteriology accents other such dichotomies, as for example, the separation between being and doing, faith and action, theory and practice. The basic question regarding the separation is, can we know the being apart from the doing? or, can we know the "who" apart from the "what"?

In a little book entitled, *What Are They Saying About Jesus?* Gerald O'Collins, in discussing the Christology of several contemporary theologians, located this split between

Christology and Soteriology at the point of Chalcedon: ". . . Much theology that took its inspiration from Chalcedon managed to separate Christology from Soteriology, and felt happy to consider the person of Christ apart from his saving 'work'."[53] Chalcedon seemingly "represents Christ to us merely as an object of knowledge," even though careful study will reveal soteriological themes undergirding the christological statements. Many theologians today would argue that there needs to be a bridging of the person and the work of Jesus Christ or what O'Collins calls ontological and functional Christology.[54] That is to say, speculations about the person of Jesus Christ have to be related directly to the historical work of Jesus.

Wolfhart Pannenberg also attempts to address this in his christological method. In Pannenberg's view, there are two approaches to Christology—"Christology from above" and "Christology from below—." Christology from above is the type of Christology which is described earlier and which O'Collins criticizes.[55] Indeed, this was the approach to Christology which was prevalent at the Council of Chalcedon, through the position of Cyril of Alexandria. Pannenberg thinks that this method is not feasible for three reasons. First, this approach to Christology presupposes the divinity of Jesus. However, it is Christology which must present the reason for confessing the divinity of Jesus. Second, in this approach the historical Jesus is not as important as he should be. Third, this approach is possible only if the theologian is able to "stand in the position of God in order to follow the way of God's Son into the world."[56] Pannenberg's designation, "Christology from below," emphasizes the historical Jesus. This does not mean that the divinity of Christ is ignored. Though Pannenberg attempts to make a close connection between the christological question and the soteriological question, for him the christological question, that is, the "person" of Christ, is a prior one: ". . . The relationship of Jesus to God must be discussed first, and only then can Jesus as man and as the fulfillment of human existence in general be discussed."[57] In the "total characterization of (Jesus's) appearance, the decisive point lies in his relationship to God."[58]

Liberation theologian Jon Sobrino acknowledges that Pannenberg's intention "is to understand Christ in his divinity so that one may better understand the whole of reality. In the actual working out, of course, the two aspects interact with each other."[59] Sobrino more consistently emphasizes Christology from below as he develops a Christology in the context of Latin American theology of liberation. Here, he defines Jesus as a part of the historical reality in the struggle of poor people for liberation. In employing this approach, he uses the historical Jesus as the primary focus. Early in his work, Sobrino explains why he and the Latin American liberation theologians choose to adopt the historical Jesus as the starting point for doing Christology:

> Our Christology will (by starting with the historical Jesus) avoid abstractionism, and the attendant danger of manipulating the Christ event. This history of the church shows, from its very beginnings as we shall see, that any focusing on the Christ of faith will jeopardize the very essence of the Christian faith if it neglects the historical Jesus. Finally, we feel that the historical Jesus is the hermeneutic principle that enables us to draw closer to the totality of Christ both in terms of knowledge and in terms of real-life praxis. It is there that we will find the unity of Christology and soteriology.[60]

As reflected in Sobrino's work, we see that liberation theology has brought about a shift in the approach of Christology. Christology and Soteriology are seen as inseparable. What Jesus did is inseparable from who he was in first-century Palestine. How, then, can the specific aspects of Jesus Christ be separated from claims regarding who Jesus was? For women involved in liberation, the implication of this question is far-reaching. Since Christology has been done in the context of patriarchy, what is the significance of the person of Christ, that is the maleness of Jesus, in a patriarchal society?[61] Does the person assume male personality as we understand what it means to be male in a patriarchal society?

In the light of feminist questions about patriarchy itself, feminist Christology has two tasks. First, feminist Christology must show how traditional male articulated christologies have been used "to keep women in their place," rather than to save women. And second, feminist Christology must provide constructive means for the liberation of women by way of the liberation of Jesus from oppressive and distorted interpretations.

In executing these tasks, I would suggest that Christology and Soteriology must be held in dialectical tension; one cannot be conceived without the other. To talk about salvation or deliverance of human beings (Soteriology) apart from God's action in Jesus (Christology) leads to total secularization. Conversely, to talk about Christology apart from Soteriology leads to total spiritualization (abstract God-talk).

The soteriological question remains before us: "How shall humans (and women in particular) be saved"? Since I concur with liberation theologians that Christology and Soteriology are inseparable, a given Christology must function to answer this question. Feminist Christology functions to answer this question with particular reference to women. Feminist theologians, holding that 'experience is the crucible for doing theology"[62] would argue that women's experience is the crucible for doing feminist Christology. It is as Jesus (Christology) acted (Soteriology) in the lives/experiences of women that we are able to know the salvific significance of Jesus Christ for women today.[63] The new question, a variation of the old, is, "who do [wo]men say that I am"? (Mark 8:27) Because for the most part men's responses to the question, "whom do men say that I am"? have been tainted by patriarchalism, women must respond to the question in light of their critique of patriarchalism. Their critique has taken them back to re-thinking, re-evaluating and re-writing their own experiences as women. It is only when Christology is grounded in the experience of women that we can arrive at a perspective which is equally salvific for women and for men.

E. *Summary*

The doctrine of Christology, from its initial formulated inception has been problematic for women. Whether taken as a basic christological principle (Grillmeier), or as "outlines of christological language" (Norris), the fact that the church teaches that God's incarnation is uniquely represented in the historical male figure Jesus, provided for the predominance of the one-sided christological interpretation throughout the history of theology. Providing the social context for the development of Christology, patriarchy virtually insured that women's questions would be irrelevant to christological concerns. If women are indeed to be saved they must begin to re-articulate Christology starting from the questions which arise out of their experiences. Some women have begun the process of rethinking Christology. I turn now to examine three emergent perspectives.

NOTES

[1] Ludwig Feuerbach, *The Essence of Christianity* (New York: Harper and Brothers, 1975), p. 12.

[2] *Ibid.*, p. 13.

[3] The language issue has attracted much attention over the past few years. It is the feminist belief that language is political. Some churches have demonstrated concern for this through study on the matter (cf. Presbyterian Church, "Opening the Door.") The National Council of Christian Churches has published *Inclusive Language Lectionary: Readings for Year A* (Philadelphia: Westminster Press, 1983). The Consultation on Church Union has participated in this study (cf. "Consultation on Liturgy and Language" held at Scarritt Seminary, Nashville, Tennessee, Nov. 1981). Also see Letty Russell,

ed., *The Liberating Word: A Guide to Non-Sexist Interpretation on the Bible* (Philadelphia: The Westiminster Press, 1976), passim. Certainly this is related to the earlier discussion in Chapter I on male experience as universal experience. As women challenge that general category so also they challenge the specific issue of language.

[4] From "The Definition of Chalcedon (451)" in John Leith's *Creeds of the Churches* (New York: Anchor Books, 1963), pp. 35-36.

[5] For brief histories of the developments see Richard A. Norris, Jr., *The Christological Controversy* (Philadelphia: Fortress Press, 1980) and Bernhard Lohse, *A Short History of Christian Doctrine: From the First Century to the Present* (Philadelphia: Fortress Press, 1966). For more extensive histories see Aloys Grillmeier, *Christ in Christian Tradition* (New York: Sheed and Ward, 1964); J. N. D. Kelly, *Early Christian Doctrine* (New York: Harper and Row, 1960) and R. V. Sellers, *The Council of Chalcedon: A Historical and Doctrinal Survey* (London: S.P.C.K., 1953).

[6] Arianism was named for its leader Arian, an Alexandrian presbyter, who (primarily concerned with the unity, the uniqueness and the transcendence of God) argued that Jesus Christ was among the created order, superior to other creatures but inferior to God. See Norris, *Christological Controversy*, pp. 17-21 and Lohse, *Christian Doctrine*, pp. 48-50. Arius said: "we confess one God who alone is unbegotten, alone eternal, alone without beginning, alone true, alone immortal, alone wise, alone good, alone Lord, alone the judge of all." (quoted in Lohse, *Christian Doctrine*, p. 48).

The Nicene Creed not only condemned Arianism, but it also condemned other heresies which advocated any form of subordinationism or inequality—the notion that Jesus was less than or different from God, e.g., Marcionism, Originism, Dynamic Monarchianism, and Docetism. See Grillmeier, *Christ in Christian Tradition* and Lohse, *Christian Doctrine*, p. 265).

[7] From "The Creed of Nicaea (325) in John Leith, *Creeds of the Churches*, pp. 30-31.

[8] Apollinaris of Laodicea in an early period taught that Jesus did not have a human soul, yet he was a mixture of God and man (Lohse, *Christian Doctrine*, p. 83).

[9] An Antiochene Monk and Bishop of Constantinople, Nestorius challenged the use of *Theotokos* and proposed that it should be supplemented with the term *Anthropotokos* but preferred the term

Christotokos in reference to Mary (Lohse, *Christian Doctrine*, pp. 87-88).

[10] Eutyches argued that there were two natures before the union and one nature after the union (Norris, *Christological Controversy*, p. 28).

[11] Alan Richardson, *Creeds in the Making: A Short Introduction to the History of Christian Doctrine* (London: Student Christian Movement Press, 1951, first printed in 1935), p. 84.

[12] Karl Barth, "Church Dogmatics", Vol. I/2, p. 15, quoted in William Anderson's *Aspects of the Theory of Karl Barth* (Washington, D.C.: University Press of America, 1981), p. 119.

[13] Richardson, *Creeds in the Making*, pp. 84-85.

[14] Norris, *Christological Controversy*, pp. 30-31.

[15] John Knox, *Jesus Lord and Christ* (New York: Harper and Brothers Publishers, 1958), p. 193.

[16] Grillmeier, *Christ in Christian Tradition*, p. 493.

[17] Sheila Collins, *A Different Heaven and Earth*, p. 51.

[18] *Ibid.*, p. 52.

[19] Elizabeth S. Fiorenza, "To Comfort or to Challenge . . .," p. 43n.

[20] Elizabeth Dodson Gray, *Patriarchy as a Conceptual Trap* (Wellesley, Massachusetts: Roundtable Press, 1982). For Gray, "a conceptual trap is a way of thinking that is like a room which—once inside—you cannot imagine a world outside." (p. 17)

[21] See *Ibid.* for a discussion of the pervasiveness of patriarchy (pp. 19ff). Also note that several feminist anthropologists are arguing not only for the contemporary, but also for the historical pervasiveness of patriarchy. See Michelle Zimbalist Rosaldo and Louise Lamphere, editors, *Women, Culture and Society* (Stanford, California: Stanford University Press, 1974). See especially Sherry B. Ortner's "Is Female to Male as Nature is to Culture"? and Joan Bamberger's "The Myth of Matriarchy." Ortner argues that the second-class status of women is a universal fact and the devaluation of women is associated with the devaluation of nature. Bamberger argues that "a clearcut and indisputable case of matriarchy" cannot be made given current evidence. (p. 265)

[22] Kate Millett, *Sexual Politics* (New York: Equinox Books Published by Avon, 1970), p. 25.

[23] *Ibid.*, pp. 23ff. In *Public Man, Private Woman* Jean Bethke Elshtain challenges the existence of an actual patriarchy particu-

larly as employed by radical feminists. She explains the conditions of patriarchy.

> The following were conditions for patriarchy historically:
>
> 1. The father's power was absolute and, sanctioned by religion or official authority, "political" in its essence;
>
> 2. Women and children were (said) to be dutiful and obedient subjects;
>
> 3. Male children alone could inherit property, be educated, and have a public role;
>
> 4. Female children were told when they could be married, and to whom, even as they were kept uneducated, disinherited, and privatized;
>
> 5. This patriarchal structure was kept in place through a reinforcing ideology which permeated all levels of society, up to and including its absolutist monarchy.

It is Elshtain's view that not one of these conditions exist in contemporary American society. One must then distinguish between absolute patriarchy and male dominance. However, each may be a concomitant of the other. Contrarily, others argue not only that patriarchy exists, but also that it is inevitable. Steven Goldberg posits that because of biological determinism, women are forever doomed to submission, and men are forever bearer of authority and domination over women. Steven Goldberg, *The Inevitability of Patriarchy* (New York: William Morrow Co. Inc., 1973/74), passim.

[24] Judy Gere and Virginia Mills, "95 Theses on Patriarchal Oppression of Women," compiled by the Task Force on Women in the Presbyterian Church, *Moving Toward Full Personhood: A six-session seminar on the Changing status of women.*

[25] *Ibid.*

[26] Rosemary Reuther, *New Woman/New Earth* (New York: The Seabury Press, 1975), pp. 3-4.

[27] Collins, *A Different Heaven and Earth*, p. 166.

[28] *Ibid.*, pp. 166-167.

[29] Joan Romero, "The Protestant Principle: A Woman's-Eye View of Barth and Tillich," in *Religion and Sexism*, ed. Rosemary Ruether (New York: Simon and Schuster, 1974), pp. 319-340.

30 *Ibid.*, p. 324, cited in Karl Barth, *Church Dogmatics*, vol. III part 4 (Edinburgh: T. & T. Clark, 1961), p. 157. In his *Church Dogmatics* Barth comments on the move to change this basic reality. Attempted violations have not only been at the level of assuming the characteristic of the opposite sex but have moved to another level—"a third and supposedly higher mode of being, possible to both sexes and indifferent to both." He continues: What is sought is a purely human being which in itself and properly is semisexual and therefore, in relation to its apparent bio-sexuality, sexless, abstractly human, and to that extent a third and distinctive being as compared with male and female. There can be no doubt that what we have here is a more sublime and lofty and spiritualized form of that movement of escape. It is no accident that this type of consciousness has been traditionally impregnated with the magic gnosis. It is a movement in which man and woman aspire to overcome their sexual and separated mode of existence and to transcend it by a humanity which is neither distinctively male nor female but both at once, or neither. Barth goes further to state: "Outside their common relationship to God, there is no point in the encounter and fellowship of man and woman at which even as man and woman they can also transcend their sexuality" (Barth, p. 157). Clearly, for Barth, neither women nor men have any way of moving beyond socially prescribed roles, which for him are divinely ordained.

31 Barth, *Church Dogmatics*, III/4, pp. 168-169.

32 *Ibid.*

33 *Ibid.*

34 Clifford Green, "Liberation Theology: Karl Barth on Women and Men," *Union Theological Seminary Quarterly*, XXIX (Spring/Summer, 1974), pp. 228-229.

35 Collins, *Different Heaven*, p. 66. See also Elizabeth Dodson Gray, *Green Paradise Lost* (Wellesley, Massachusetts: Roundtable Press, 1979). In chapter one she graphs a pyramid of dominance and status which begins with God above the pyramid, followed within the pyramid from top to bottom, by men, women, children, animals, and plants. Nature appears below the pyramid. (p. 4).

36 *Ibid.* Romero in the previously cited article also relates this line of argument to the church's leadership. The preacher (man) is to the church (woman) what God is to Man. As God is the highest leader, man, the preacher is the leader of woman (the congrega-

tion). The same idea is expressed by Tine Govaart-Halkes as he criticizes the argument of opponents of the ordination of women saying: They derive from the fact that Jesus of Nazareth was a man and from his mandating twelve Jewish men to continue his task, that only the men of all ages can express the ministry of Jesus Christ in a more or less official and recognized way. . . . Woman expresses the congregation, the parish; and the man may express the minister, and so Jesus Christ. Tine Govaart-Halkes, "Developments in the Roman Catholic Church Regarding the Question of the Ordination of Women," in *What is Ordination Coming to?*, edited by Brigalia Bam (Geneva: World Council of Churches, 1971).

37 "But I want you to understand that the head of every man is Christ, the head of a woman is her husband, and the head of Christ is God." (I Corinthians 11:3). "Wives, be subject to your husbands, as to the Lord. For the husband is the head of the wife as Christ is the head of the church his body, and is himself its Savior." (Ephesians 5:22-23).

38 The Maleness of Jesus as normative will be discussed later.

39 This exclusion can be seen as we look at the numbers of women in leadership in both areas. In the society it is still virtually unheard of that a woman could be leader of a country (with few exceptions, India, Israel, England). Within countries, as for example the United States it is still an oddity when women are Governors, U.S. Congresspersons and Mayors, and more recently a serious Vice-Presidential candidate. Within the Church, unless founded by women, they are generally not in the top leadership. In both arenas, women make up a majority of the populace and a minority of leadership.

40 See Chapter I for an account of struggles towards ordination or full participation, usually meaning leadership in various churches.

41 Reginald Fuller, "Pro and Con: The Ordination of Women in the New Testament" in *Toward a New Theology of Ordination: Essays on the Ordination of Women*, eds. Marianna H. Micks and Charles P. Price (Somerville, Massachusetts: Greeno, Hadden & Company LTD, 1976), p. 1.

42 The Rev. David R. Stuart (Pseud.), "My Objections to Ordaining Women," in *The Ordination of Women: Pro and Con*, eds. Michael P. Hamilton and Nancy S. Montgomery (New York: Morehouse-Barlow Co., 1975), pp. 47-48.

[43] John Paul Boyer, "Some thoughts on the Ordination of Women," *A Monthly Bulletin of the Church of St. Mary the Virgin,* New York City, vol. XLI, No. 5 (May 1972), p. 73, quoted in Emily C. Hewitt and Suzanne R. Hiatt, *Women Priests: Yes or No?* (New York: The Seabury Press, 1973), p. 62.

[44] Franjo Cardinal Seper, "Vatican Declaration," *Origins, N.C. Documentary Service* (February 3, 1977):6.

[45] *The Order of Priesthood, Nine Commentaries on the Vatican Decree Inter Insigniores,* pp. 14-15. Referred to in Jewett, *The Ordination of Women* (Grand Rapids, Michigan: William B. Eerdman's Publishing Company, 1980), pp. 80-81.

[46] Stuart, "My Objections . . .," p. 48.

[47] For discussions of the leadership/ordination issue from inter-denominational, interdisciplinary and international perspective see the following sources: Brigalia Bam, ed., *What is Ordination Coming to?* (Geneva: World Council of Churches, 1971); See also Margaret Sittler Ermarth, *Adams Fractured Rib* (Philadelphia: Fortress Press, 1970); For an episcopal view, Emily C. Hewitt and Suzanne R. Hiatt, *Women Priests: Yes or No?* (New York: The Seabury Press, 1973); for a Catholic view with theological and historical perspectives, see Haye van der Geer, SJ, *Women Priests in the Catholic Church?* (Philadelphia: Temple University Press, 1973), translated and with a foreword and afterword by Arlene and Leonard Swidler; for objections to the ordination of women, see Michael Bruce and G. E. Duffield, eds., *Why Not? Priesthood and the Ministry of Women: A Theological Study* (Sutton Courtenay: Marcham Manor Press, 1972); for objections to women's ordination based on the social roles of men and women see Stephen Clark, *Man and Women in Christ, An Examination of the Roles of Men and Women in Light of Scripture and Social Science* (Ann Arbor, Michigan: Servant Books, 1980).

[48] Rosemary Ruether, "Christology and Feminism: Can a Male Savior Help Women," *An Occasional Paper* of the Board of Higher Education and Ministry of the United Methodist Church, I (December 25, 1976).

[49] Reginald Fuller, *The Foundations of New Testament Christology* (New York: Charles Scribner & Sons, 1965), p. 15.

[50] Dietrich Bonhoeffer, *Christ the Center* (New York: Harper and Row, 1960), p. 37.

[51] *Ibid.,* p. 38.

[52] George Hendry, "Christology" in *The Dictionary of Christian Theology*, ed. Alan Richardson (London: SCM Press Ltd., 1976), p. 51.

[53] Gerald O'Collins, *What Are They Saying About Jesus?* (New York: Paulist Press, 1977), p. 10.

[54] *Ibid.*

[55] *Ibid.*, p. 12.

[56] Wolfhart Pannenberg, *Jesus, God and Man* (Philadelphia: The Westminster Press, 1974), p. 33.

[57] *Ibid.*, p. 49.

[58] *Ibid.*, p. 56.

[59] Jon Sobrino, *Christology at the Crossroad* (New York: Orbis Books, 1978), p. 27.

[60] *Ibid.*, p. 9.

[61] It should be noted that the term used in the Chalcedon definition with respect to the human-ness of Jesus is anthropoteti. However feminists charge that functionally (and ontologically) the church has come to understand this as man (rather than human).

[62] Sheila Collins, *A Different Heaven and Earth*, Chapter 1, Passim.

[63] Just how Jesus acted in the lives of women will be discussed later, especially in Chapter 3.

III

BIBLICAL FEMINIST CHRISTOLOGY: JESUS, THE FEMINIST

As I have suggested, the "reformist" position among white Christian feminists is best illustrated by those who have accepted a basic core of Christian teachings. This core includes use of and sometimes emphasis on scripture as a source of Christian theology and Jesus Christ as a critical reference point. The perspective of Biblical feminists is first, forged in dialogue with the Bible and second, centered in Jesus Christ. Biblical feminists emerged in the evangelical community in which these two elements–the Bible and Jesus Christ–are critical in theological and faith validity.[1] That is to say, neither theology nor faith is valid or possible without the Bible and Jesus Christ. Among evangelical Christians, not only women, but men have engaged feminist criticism and responded. Virginia Mollenkott credits Paul Jewett for inspiring her to pursue further her feminist line of thinking in a hostile community–the evangelical Christian community.[2] It was in 1975 that Paul Jewett published his book, *Man as Male and Female*[3] in which he puts forth the notion of "Partnership" which is grounded in the Christian concept of imago dei. Interestingly enough, this contribution was the ground-breaking work among evangelicals which encouraged a feminist option for many in that circle. Jewett did this by providing the theological and Biblical rationale for partnership. Another angle which was attractive to evangelical feminists was advanced by another male writer, Leonard Swidler, who pioneered in providing significant interpretations of old data which evidenced Jesus' radical departure from traditional customs and norms, especially with respect to women. Arguing that Jesus was a feminist, he looked too at relationships–this time Jesus' relationships with women in the Bible.[4]

It is not that women such as Virginia Mollenkott were not dealing with these issues prior to male initiative on the question. However, they had no real public support in the evangelical world. The perspective of Mollenkott and others evolved out of their evangelical up bringing and developed into a more liberal and eventually feminist viewpoint. Like Jewett, Mollenkott located the problem at the point of relationships.[5] Still focusing upon relationships, the partnership theme is explored again by Letha Scanzoni and Nancy Hardesty.[6] Their approach to the subject matter is readable and practical, though at the same time profoundly theological.

These evangelical women and men have survived the severe criticisms of their community and have begun to make a contribution to evangelical thought, particularly on the subject of women. I shall discuss the theological context in which Christology of biblical feminists was nourished. From there, a discussion of the use of the Bible will precede a discussion of the Christology of these feminists.

A. *The Context of the Christology of Biblical Feminist Theology*

Jewett's discussion provides a background for the position of evangelical feminists. Jewett operates from an undertanding of man [sic] as male and female in "mutual relationship to each other and to God."[7] Any other kinds of relationships, hierarchical, or other unequal relationships are not "Christian" ones. The matter of relationship as spurred on by the recent raising of the "woman question" must be viewed with greater theological understanding. This is why Jewett claims that "the woman question" is a "man/woman" question which has its roots, theologically speaking, in the doctrine of the *"imago dei."* Just as God's relationship is essentially fellowship in himself (as in the Trinity), so man's relationship is essentially fellowship in himself (male and female). Borrowing from Karl Barth's treatment of the Trinity–God being in fellowship with Godself, and man

[sic] being the image of God,–Jewett interprets *Man* as being in fellowship with *himself* (italics mine). Because Barth, in articulating this trinitarian fellowship, emphasizes the singular essence of God, confusion may result when this same idea is applied to human beings. Jewett explains Barth's thoughts:

> In using the term "Person" to describe the members of the Godhead, the doctrine of the Trinity affirms that God in himself is a fellowship like that of three human persons; but such a fellowship of persons at the human level is only a reflection of the divine fellowship. Humans are so distinct from each other that even in the most intimate fellowship they are not one as God is one. They always remain "they" even when united as one flesh in marriage. God, on the other hand, always remains, "he," even when distinguished as the three persons of the Trinity. Hence some Theologians prefer the so-called "individual" analogy of the Trinity; others, the "social" analogy.[8]

Barth exercises caution in drawing an analogy between the fellowship of male and female and the fellowship of the Godhead. Again, Jewett explains Barth's position as follows:

> In God's own being there is a radical distinction; God is Father, Son and Holy Spirit. Hence God is himself a God who is in fellowship with himself. So also in Man's being there is a radical distinction. Man is male and female, hence Man too is a being who is in fellowship with himself. But it is an abstraction to talk of this fellowship, in Man's case, as simply a fellowship of persons, because there are no such persons in the abstract, but only persons who are men and persons who are women. At our creaturely human level the most

elemental form of fellowship we know is the
fellowship of male and female, and we never
know fellowship in any other way than as men
and as women. Therefore, man's existence in the
fellowship of male and female is the mode of his
existence as created in the image of God.[9]

Still Barth goes a bit too far for Jewett as he tends to discuss
Man as male and female, and man as husband and wife in the
institution of marriage, as synonymous, although in reality
Barth is cognizant of the distinction. Jewett's concern put differently is that the Christian view of human sexuality and
the Christian view of marriage are treated as though they
were one and the same. And this cannot be. Putting quite a bit
of weight upon this distinction, Jewett interprets human sexuality as something much broader than marriage which traditionally was for the sole purpose of biological
reproduction. Because Barth adheres to traditional
interpretations of male/female relationship, he invokes
sexual hierarchy as the norm for such relationships, though
in actuality, his theology itself does not necessarily lead to
sexual hierarchy nor does it inherently mean superiority and
inferiority "but only means that some are *over*, others are
under; some *exercise* authority, others *submit* to it."[10]
However, Barth's use of the idea of woman as subordinate
implies also woman as inferior. Therefore, sexual hierarchy
is the result of Barth's anthropology of man as male and
female.

    This theology of man as male and female involves
essentially three steps: 1) Because man is created either male
or female, one's sex must be accepted; 2) relationship to one's
sexual partner is a function of life; and 3) this relationship
contains a definite order of preceding and following, of
super—and subordination. It is this third step which serves
as the basis of sexual hierarchy. Jewett, one might say,
makes an internal criticism of Barth's theology of man as
male and female. Although agreeing with the first two

steps, Jewett fails to see how and why Barth arrives at step three.

> One wonders, in all this, why Barth does not work through to the clear conclusion which follows from his own theology of man as male and female. Man and woman are partners in life, significantly different from each other but definitely equal to each other; so related to each other as to be a fellowship like God himself; the very image of him who is the Father, the Son, and the Holy Spirit. How then can he escape the conclusion that there is no absolute, invariable *super-*/and subordination between the sexes at the human level.[11]

In the theology of man as male and female, Jewett argues for fellowship rather than sexual hierarchy. He explains that "The theology of man as male and female, which [Barth] has espoused, is inimical to a doctrine of sexual hierarchy. The basic thrust of that Theology is rather one of a fellowship of equals under God."[12]

In *The Ordination of Women*,[13] Jewett shows how sexual hierarchy has been translated into concrete discriminatory and oppressive practices. Sexual hierarchy provides the basis for oppression of women in many areas. It is the belief that women are subordinate, and it justifies the second class citizenship of women. This second-class citizenship is expressed especially in the area of the ministry of the church. The concept of the superordination of males and the subordination of females has resulted in men being God's inner circle and women being God's outer circle.[14] Because of this distinction women are barred from serving as ministers of God. In other words, ". . . an affinity between maleness and divineness remains the basic assumption behind every argument from the nature of God for the exclusion of women from the office of the ministry."[15] Jewett's solution to the problem is to recognize the male and female as the image of God.

B. *The Bible as Employed by Biblical Feminists*

Women, Men and the Bible is the book in which Mollenkott attempts to redefine the nature of male/female relationships, based on her reading of the Bible and her understanding of Jesus Christ. Responding to traditionalists, especially Marabel Morgan who advocates what is actually a "carnal way of relating" often misrepresented as Christian, Mollenkott proposes what she considers to be the character of the true "Christian way of relating." The carnal way of relating, one which promotes power games, domination and submission is structured not only into private relationships but also into public ones. Any position which holds that women must be submissive or manipulative is unchristian. On the other hand the Christian way of relating is one of mutual partnership. Mollenkott explains that ". . . Christian equality is never a matter of jockeying for the dominant position. Christian equality is the result of mutual compassion, mutual concern, and mutual and voluntary loving service."[16]

Mollenkott grounds this relationship of mutuality and partnership in her concept of God and Jesus Christ as emerged out of her reading of the Bible. Contrary to the traditionalist who masculinizes God, Mollenkott believes that God does not merely possess masculine qualities but feminine ones as well. Based on her discussion of the creation story in Genesis 1, she believes that since the text uses the word "anthropos" (human) rather than "aner" (male) then both human, male and female were created in God's image. To clarify, she writes that ". . . If both male and female are made in God's image, then in some mysterious way the nature of God encompasses all the traits which society labels feminine as well as the traits society labels masculine."[17]

After quoting or referring to several Old Testament passages which picture God in feminine imagery[18] or doing womanly things, the passage in Isaiah 46:3-4 is used to show that God is an androgynous God. The passage makes clear that the use of male pronouns for God does not mean that God is literally masculine. For in spite of the male pronoun, God is pictured as a midwife and a nurse maid.

The fact that the Bible speaks of God in both feminine and masculine imagery is evidence that the traditionally accepted masculine imagery of God must be rejected.

In terms of her approach to the Bible as a source for theology, Mollenkott describes herself as "marginal." This marginality is evidenced by her use of the Bible. As she puts it, she is "'too radical' for most evangelicals, too 'addicted to the Bible' for many people in the mainline churches."[19] For most of Mollenkott's life she was restrained by Church tradition in general and her church tradition, the Plymouth Brethren, in particular. In spite of this restraint, she credits this church experience as responsible for her being "thoroughly grounded in the surface facts (the words themselves) of the Bible."[20] Studying the Bible for herself radicalized her to the point of being committed to reading the Bible from a liberation perspective. No longer does she read merely the words of the Bible, as if it were possible to do so in a vacuum, but her study of the Bible is informed by other disciplines such as sociology, anthropology, psychology, and history, all of which enable her to bring new questions to the Biblical table. In so doing, the Bible is viewed differently. It is not the static sacred (untouchable) book which is read literally at convenient points by traditional interest groups (conservative churches); rather it is a dynamic, living, liberating book which must not be chopped up to serve narrow personal interests but must be read holistically.

In the interview by John Alexander in *The Other Side Magazine*, Mollenkott shares thoughts on how she uses the Bible.[21] Unlike the evangelical community in which she was "nurtured" Mollenkott rejects the notion of the inerrancy of Scripture. Two significant points about Scripture are central to her thoughts: (1) Scripture is culturally limited and (2) Scripture is subject to internal contradictions.

What does it mean to say that Scripture is culturally limited? One has to distinguish between those portions which are culturally limited and those which are normative. Culturally-limited passages are those which apply specifically to the times in which they were written. These passages, therefore, are not for all times but they are bound by and to the particular political and social, time, and space. Evangelicals and other traditionalists have made these time-bound, culturally conditioned aspects of the Bible normative. In view of this thrust, feminists "must de-absolutize the biblical culture as we have already done for slavery and monarchy."[22] Feminists have to apply the "de absolutizing" process, which has already been done in other areas, to women's concerns.

Additionally, rather than accepting the Bible as a whole as "The Word of God," Mollenkott sees an internal critique which the Bible itself possesses. She argues for her approach in this way:

> The case for an all-inclusive, egalitarian, nondualistic, global Body of Christ–the single organism of the New Humanity–can be made from numerous passages in the Bible. It is of course important to avoid the "supermarket approach" of proof-texting from a single remark wrenched out of its context and possibly faulty in its English translation. We have had enough of that in sexist plucking out of context such passages as Ephesians 5:22 (wifely submission) or I Timothy 2:13: "I suffer not a woman to teach" (KJV). If the case for organic unity is to be honest as well as convincing, we need to make it from a holistic reading of the Bible, which not only places each passage against its primary historical context but also allows other

Scriptures to provide commentary on its meaning.[23]

A wholistic approach to the Bible allows this self-critical mechanism in the Bible itself to be manifested.[24] The normative scriptures are used to interpret the culturally bound scriptures. That is, insights into the interpretation of one passage may be obtained from another passage. Just as the Bible cannot be divorced from the context in which it was written or is read, social context having its bearings, individual scriptures cannot be taken out of the larger Biblical context. Consequently, a more adequate interpretation of the Bible is possible when it is viewed wholistically. The inevitable questions are these: How do we justify differentiating between scriptures in this way? How do we know which scriptures are normative and which are culturally bound? By what criteria do we distinguish the two? Mollenkott uses the Bible as a basic source of her perspective. Taking her cue from John Milton in his essay, "Of Education," she tests her beliefs and interpretations by the "determinate sentence" of Scripture. ". . . I adhere firmly to the practice of subjecting everything that I learn to what for me will always be the 'determinate sentence' of Scripture."[25] This means that Mollenkott is not restricted by the narrow confines of fundamentalistic interpretations of the Bible. The "determinate sentence" principle has brought Mollenkott from the fundamentalism and narrow views of her Plymouth Brethren upbringing to an ecumenistic and universalistic vision of the church and world. Her theological journey could be seen as an experience in liberation. "I think my own experience," says Mollenkott, "suggests that teaching the Bible from a liberating perspective is an excellent tool for ecumenists to use in the attempt to stimulate in people an all-inclusive, global vision of human justice, dignity, and oneness."[26]

While exercising this process of internal criticism, Mollenkott affirms the authority of scripture. Matthew 19 provides the basis for her approach: The Pharisees came to

Jesus and tried to trap him about divorce. If he agreed with the Mosaic law that men could divorce women rather easily, then they had caught him in a double standard. Of course, he did pit himself against the Mosaic law. He says, Moses gave you that law because of the hardness of your heart, but from the beginning it was not so. Then he quotes Genesis 1 and 2 to prove his point. Even the most intrepid traditionalist isn't going to say Jesus was doing away with the authority of Scripture. So why can't we cite Galatians 3:28 and the many passages about the new creatures to refute I Corinthians, II and I Timothy 37? That's what Jesus did.[27] How does one verify accuracy in this approach to scripture. Mollenkott relies on "scholarly exegesis" for this verification. In order to interpret scripture accurately, she claims, "we have to pay attention to word choice, literary forms, who is speaking, and ideas we aren't used to . . . tools of scholarly knowledge must be brought into play. . . . Then we can tell which passage are God's ideal for all times and places and which are associated with individual church problems."[28] For example, specific passages regarding women related to specific church problems which were cultural and time-bound, whereas Galatians 3 is theological, having to do with no particular church problem; therefore it is normative.

Contradictions do exist in the Bible. In the New Testament, they occur primarily in Paul's writings, particularly with reference to women. There are instances in which Paul contradicts Jesus. In these instances Paul, a mere human being, became a victim of his culture yet struggling to work out his human conflicts. Using again the creation stories, Mollenkott explains:

> The rabbinic position is that since Adam was created first, he is superior. Now Genesis 2 does not come to that conclusion. In fact it says that because woman was created from man, the two are one flesh. It doesn't say they are two fleshes, one of which is inferior....

> Some think that Genesis 2 teaches that women
> are inferior because it says that women are men's
> "helps." But the more you know about the
> Hebrew word for help and the way it is usually
> used for God the more you could almost argue, for
> the superiority of women as "helps."[29]

The conversation now moves specifically to Paul's errancy by
virtue of his cultural limitations:

> So Genesis 2 does not teach subordination. Paul is
> here clearly following the rabbinic tradition he
> has been taught.
>   Paul's interpretation also leads to serious
> trouble for anyone who believes in inerrancy. If
> you interpret Genesis 2 literally that Eve was
> created after Adam, then you have to harmonize
> that with Genesis 1. Genesis 2, if taken literally,
> teaches that Adam was created, then plants,
> then the animals, and then Eve, while Genesis 1
> says that plants were created, then animals, and
> the man and the woman were created in the
> image of God simultaneously. Jesus by the way,
> puts his authority behind Genesis 1–from the
> beginning God made them, male and female. So
> Paul is in a way contradicting Jesus here.[30]

Mollenkott goes on to say that Paul's position was not an
"error in Scripture" but an accurate recording of actions of a
human being in struggle and conflict. The Bible, then, is not
devoid of human weakness.
    For Letha Scanzoni and Nancy Hardesty the Bible is
likewise central. However, though the Bible is basic for
them, they are not biblical literalists. Rather than holding
fast to one strictly literal interpretation of scripture, they see
that scriptures can be interpreted in two ways:

We view certain passages as allegorical. We understand certain instruction to be addressed to a particular person or group (e.g., II Tim. 4:21; I Tim. 5:23). To interpret other instructions, we must know the custom of the times in which they were given. The teachings on meats offered to idols (I Cor. 8 and 10) for example, require some understanding of the situation in Corinth when Paul was writing. From this understanding we go on to find principles of Christian liberty that can be applied in today's world.[31]

Their interest is in getting at the "spirit of the law" not being confined to the "letter of the law." In Scanzoni and Hardesty's view, theology aids in this task. It functions to enable us to understand the Bible. We must understand that some passages are not only the figurative/literal breakdown of scripture but also the theological/doctrinal breakdown of scriptures. In other words, "Passages which are theological and doctrinal in content are used to interpret those where the writer is dealing with practical local cultural problems."[32] Thus, as does Mollenkott, Scanzoni and Hardesty argue that the Bible contains some culturally-limited passages.

C. *The Christology of Biblical Feminists*

The crux of Biblical feminists' argument is really Christological. That is, for them Jesus is the beginning and the end. Their view of Jesus Christ as the example and model for the Christian way of relating provides the basis of all their arguments. This is verified in the New Testament's recording of the teachings of Jesus.

1. *Jesus, the Non-Conformist*

Christology provides a central focus and source for the understanding of the Christian way of relating. Jesus' teachings were significant and must be seen against the backdrop of cultural conditions of Biblical times. Recognizing the problematic resulting from the fact that Jesus did not sharply and directly renounce beliefs regarding women's place in society as he did in the case of other teachings, Jewett points out that "we never read in the Gospels: 'it has been said of old time, women shall not read the law in the synagogue; but I say unto you, woman shall have the same privileges as men in this regard'."[33] But in order to get an accurate and radically different picture of what Jesus felt about women, we must look at his actions toward them:

> It was not so much in what he said as in how he related to women that Jesus was a revolutionary. In this relationship his life style was so remarkable that one can only call it astonishing. He treated women as fully human, equal to men in every respect; no word of deprecation about women, as such, is ever found on his lips.[34]

With this observation, Jewett proceeds, as other Biblical feminists, to examine the actions of Jesus, especially as he related to women in the light of cultural conditions of biblical times. When this is done, the radical character of Jesus is revealed. Likewise, "the more we find out about the cultural conditions of rabbinic Judaism, the more we realize that in situations like the conversations with the Samaritan woman, Jesus was deliberately breaking rabbinic customs that were degrading to the self-concept of women. He was providing object lessons for his disciples–and for us all."[35]

Mollenkott cites specific activities of Jesus which illustrates that Jesus in spite of his knowledge of rabbinic customs, intentionally violated them. The case of the Samaritan woman, the hemorrhaging woman, the adulterous woman, the mistaken woman (Luke 11:27), the practical and theoretical women (Luke 10:41-42), the messenger woman (John 20:17) all represent some evidences for Jesus' rejections of his contemporary norms and customs. In addition to these,

On many occasions during his earthly ministry, Jesus spoke specifically of how his followers were supposed to relate to one another. Very often, Christ's statements were made in response to squabbles among male disciples concerning who among them was the greatest. Repeatedly, Christ defined greatness in terms of humility and servanthood. For instance, when the disciples asked who was the greatest in the kingdom of heaven (Matthew 18:1), Jesus called a little child into the middle of the group and commented that "whoever welcomes a little child like this in my name welcomes me" (Matthew 18:4-5 NIV). This was, of course, a deliberate reversal of all the values in the world in which Jesus and his disciples were living. And it remains a complete reversal of worldly values here in the twentieth century. The fact is that very few people have ever believed or acted upon Christ's definition of greatness.[36]

Many of our notions of greatness are peculiar to those who buy into the domination/submission way of relating. Clearly, Jesus was a nonconformist who rejected many of the rules and regulations regarding relationships between men and women.

2. *Jesus, the Model of Androgyny*[37]

Because Jesus was not afraid to defy established codes of his time some scholars have been prompted to re-examine the character of Jesus himself, to determine if there is a relationship between who he was (his psychological make-up) and what he demonstrated regarding women. In this vein Leonard Swidler affirms the Nicene Creeds statement that Jesus became *human*. He argues that the composers of the creed wrote "et *homo* factus est," meaning "and he became human." They did not say "et *vir* factus est" meaning "and he became *male* (virile)."[38] Because to be human is to be male and female, Jesus must have, in some sense, become both male and female. Here, Swidler is not advocating that Jesus was some "circus freak" with physical characteristics of both male and female, but he had reference to psychological traits, both masculine and feminine, which were possessed by Jesus. Discerning from the surrounding culture those traits which are considered masculine and those considered feminine and searching the scripture for Jesus' actions, Swidler discovered that Jesus was not limited by the cultural norms of masculinity (or femininity). In western culture, men and women are categorized in the following ways:

MEN	WOMEN
- reasonable and cool (Lk 20:20-26 & Lk 4:28-30)	- feeling and emotions (Lk 7:11-15 & Jn 11:33-36)
- firm, aggressive (Mk 8:33 & Lk 12:49)	- gentle, peaceful (Lk 13:34, Mt 5:4 & Lk 2:14 & 7:50)
- advocates of justice (Mt 5:17-19, 5:6)	- advocates of mercy (Mt 9:13, 5:7)
- pride and self-confidence (Mt 21:8-10 & Jn 18:33-37, 19:10)	- humility and reserve (Lk 14:7-11 & Mt 6:1-6)
- providers of security (food, clothing, shelter) (Jn 6:67, 35 & Lk 12:22)	- need security (Mt 15:34)
- concerned with and especially children.[39] (Lk 22:30)	- concerned with persons, organization structure (Lk 19:1-6, 7:36-50 & Jn 8:1-11)

The indicated Scriptures, among others, were cited by Swidler to demonstrate that Jesus possessed both types of traits–masculine and feminine. For example, Jesus was not only a reasonable person as masculine persons are said to be, but he also had feelings and emotions. In Luke 20:20-26, his

response to the men who asked if they should pay taxes to
Caesar, Jesus cunningly said ". . . give back to Caesar what
belongs to Caesar–and to God what belongs to God." Swidler
reasons:

> They were a clever lot, for Israel was occupied by
> Roman troops and the Jews in general
> consequently hated everything Roman with a
> passion, and especially the publicans (native tax
> collectors for Rome). If Jesus had said . . . to pay
> Roman taxes, he would have immediately lost
> his influence with the people, which would
> have suited his enemies. But if he had said not to
> pay taxes, he would have immediately ended up
> in a Roman jail, or perhaps worse, which also
> would have suited his enemies.[40]

At other times Jesus expressed such emotion caring, feeling
and weeping as when he ministered to Martha, Mary and
Lazarus. (Jn 11:33-36)[41] The conclusion made is that Jesus was
an androgynous being.

> . . . In all the traditional categories of so-called
> feminine and masculine traits the image of Jesus
> that is projected is very strongly both; it is
> emphatically androgynous. The model of how to
> live an authentically human life that Jesus of
> the Gospels presents is not one that fits the
> masculine stereotype, which automatically
> relegates the "soft," "feminine" traits to women
> as being beneath the male–nor indeed is it the
> opposite stereotype. Rather, it is an egalitarian
> model. Thus the same message that Jesus (and the
> Gospel writers and their sources) taught in his
> words and dealings with women, namely,
> egalitarianism between women and men, was also
> taught by his own androgynous life-style.[42]

3. *Jesus, the Feminist*

In his article entitled "Jesus was a Feminist," Swidler
gave evidence of his contention that Jesus advocated in his
action and indirectly in his words that women are not inferior
to men. Swidler defends his thesis by setting up the context in
which Jesus lived and worked. Against this background he
examines the words and deeds of Jesus.

The context described is Palestine during the time of
Jesus. Briefly considered, women were private persons to be
hidden–not seen and not heard. Women could not study the
Scriptures (Torah); they could neither pray (at morning
prayers or meals) nor pray in public; they could be seated
only in certain, out-of-the-way areas of the synagogues, and
as reflected by these seating arrangements they could not
serve in leadership capacities. Because women were private,
uneducated entities, they were not to be associated with in
public, in any way. The views towards women in that society
was summarized in the following way:

> Rabbinic sayings about women also provide an
> insight into the attitude toward women: 'It is
> well for those whose children are' male, but ill
> for those whose children are female. . . . At the
> birth of a boy all are joyful, but at the birth of a
> girl all are sad. . . . When a boy comes into the
> world, peace comes into the world: when a girl
> comes, nothing comes. . . . Even the most virtuous
> of women is a witch. . . . Our teachers have said:
> "Four qualities are evident in women: They are
> greedy at their food, eager to gossip, lazy and
> jealous."[43]

Against this background stands the liberative views of
Jesus, as elevated by Swidler. Contrary to popular and
scholastic belief, there were women disciples of Jesus, both
named and unnamed: "Women became disciples of Jesus not
only in the sense of learning from him, but also in the sense of

following him in his travels and ministering to him" and even proclaiming the message. Examining various specific passages, Swidler advances non-traditional interpretations. For example, because women then, as now, were seen as sex objects, they were treated as such. But Jesus was receptive to the deeds of the woman of questionable character (Luke 7:36ff), to the surprise of the Pharisees, and hailed her human and spiritual qualities.[44] The woman with a flow of blood (Matthew 9:20ff; Mark 5:25ff; Luke 8:43ff) was not only healed by Jesus but was given public attention–a far cry from the untouchable unclean character of a menstruating woman. Similarly, Jesus' relationship with the woman at the well (John 4:5ff) resulted in his commissioning a woman to bear witness. In a society in which women for the most part were uneducated, the encounter with Martha and Mary (Luke 10:38ff) gave intellectual options for women. The ultimate challenge to the existing customs was the fact that Jesus chose to reveal, first to women, that event without which there would be no Christian faith–the resurrection (John 20:11ff; Matthew 28:9f; Mark 16:9ff). Feminists have interpreted these and other actions of Jesus as a rejection of patriarchy and an affirmation of women's experience.[45] Swidler concludes his analysis by reiterating that

> . . . it should be clear that Jesus vigorously promoted the dignity and equality of women in the midst of a very male dominated society; Jesus was a feminist, and a very radical one. Can his followers attempt to be anything less–*De Imitatione Christ?* [Italics mine.][46]

Swidler expanded his thesis that Jesus was a feminist in the previously cited work entitled *Biblical Affirmation of Women* (1979). In this work, Swidler does a substantial survey and analysis of Biblical, Post-Biblical and early Christian traditions. In the same tradition of Jewett, Mollenkott and other Biblical feminists, Swidler elevates the various passages of scriptures and Post-Biblical writings which employ feminine imagery for God.[47] Careful analysis and study have yielded the conclusion that the authors of the gospels, to varying degrees, were sensitive to the "feminist" attitude of Jesus.

D. *Contributions and Problems of Biblical Feminists*

Biblical Feminists' greatest contribution to feminist Christology is twofold. On the one level they are biblically focused. They have taken the very instrument which has been used against women and made it the basis of their egalitarian thoughts. On the other level, they have made a significant connection between human relationships and our notion of Jesus Christ. As Jesus Christ presented and represented a model of mutuality, we are commended to mutuality in our human relationships.

Consciously remaining within the evangelical camp, some Biblical feminists have shaken the foundation of many of the narrow views of that community, especially regarding women. Employing the same primary source, the Bible, and the same norm, Jesus Christ, Biblical feminists as other feminists have shown that Jesus has been viewed through the narrow spectacles of a patriarchal society. It is only as we are able to arrive at different and more equitable understanding of human relationship that the "deviant" behaviors of Jesus can be recognized.[48] This recognition is necessary because it is at the level of human experience that theological and christological questions are formulated and interpretations offered.

In the work of biblical feminists we find little interstructuring of oppression but rather a single line of argument geared to the elimination of sexism from theology and Christology. The lack of a broader analysis leads to proposals which are too simplistic in nature and inadequate in scope. Certainly it is too narrow and simplistic to adequately embrace the multi-dimensional critical needs of Black women's traditions. Chapter VI contains an analysis of this perspective.

Additionally, much attention of Biblical feminists has been concentrated upon the Bible which has encouched and perpetuated patriarchal and sexist attitudes regarding women. These thinkers have not focused substantially upon tradition as a central problem.[49] Other feminists, particularly those in the liberation camp, have brought the critique of the Bible to another level. They have continued the exploration of the function of human experience in theological and christological investigations. In addition, liberation reformists have looked at tradition more deliberately as a source of the problem for women.

NOTES

[1] One of the leading spokespersons for the evangelical movement today is Carl Henry. See his six volume work, *God, Revelation and Authority* (Waco, Texas: Word Books). Bob E. Patterson in his study of Carl Henry says of Henry and evangelicals: . . . Protestant orthodoxy still characterized the theological out-look of the evangelicals. This included a belief in the doctrine of the Trinity, the two natures of Christ, the Virgin Birth, the bodily resurrection and second coming of Christ, salvation by grace through faith, the sinfulness of man, the sacrificial death of Christ for sin, the Bible as the inspired Word of God and the final norm for doctrine, evangelism as the main task of the church, and the Christian life as one of holiness and godliness. Bob E. Patterson, *Carl F. H. Henry* (Waco, Texas: Word Book, 1983), p. 27. See also John Jefferson Davis, *Foundations of Evangelical Theology* (Grand Rapids, Michigan; Baker Book House, 1984); and Kenneth S. Kantzer and Stanley N. Gundry, etc., *Perspectives on Evangelical Theology* (Grand Rapids, Michigan; Baker Book House, 1979).

[2] John Alexander, "A Conversation with Virginia Mollenkott," *The Other Side Magazine* (May-June 1976). At a meeting in 1974 at which both Mollenkott and Jewett were present, Mollenkott said of Jewett, "he was the first male evangelical I had met who was willing to be honest about the Bible and when I was attacked at the meeting for my views on women he supported me." (p. 25). Jewett helped her to take her secular feminism into the church.

3 Paul Jewett, *Man as Male and Female* (Grand Rapids, Michigan: William B. Eerdmans Publishing Company, 1975).

4 Leonard Swidler, "Jesus was a Feminist," *Southeast Asia Journal of Theology*, XIII (1971), pp. 102-110.

5 Virginia Mollenkott, *Women, Men and the Bible* (Nashville: Abingdon, 1977).

6 Letha Scanzoni and Nancy Hardesty, *All We're Meant To Be: A Biblical Approach to Women's Liberation with Study Guide* (Texas: Word Books, 1977), p. 19.

7 Jewett, *Man as Male and Female*, p. 15.

8 *Ibid.*, pp. 44-45.

9 *Ibid.*, p. 45.

10*Ibid.*, p. 71. See Clifford Green who argues that Barth's explanations are insufficient and his system does indeed mean inequality and hierarchal subordination for women.

11 *Ibid.*, p. 85.

12 *Ibid.*

13 Jewett, *The Ordination of Women* (Grand Rapids, Michigan: William B. Eerdman's Publishers, 1980).

14 Cf. George Kelsey, *Racism and the Christian Understanding of Man* (New York: Charles Scribner's Sons, n.d.). A similar race analysis is employed by Kelsey in this book. Whites, the oppressors, are those in the in-house and blacks, the oppressed, are those in the out-house.

15 Jewett, *The Ordination of Women*, p. 35.

16 Mollenkott, *Women, Men and the Bible*, p. 33.

17 *Ibid*, p. 56.

18 Nehemiah 9:21; Numbers 11:12; Psalm 22:9, 71:6, 131:1-2; Job 3:2; Isaiah 66:9, 42:14, 49:15.

19 Mollenkott, *Speech Silence, Action! The Cycle of Faith* (Nashville: Abingdon, 1980), p. 25.

20 *Ibid.*, p. 22.

21 Alexander, "A Conversation . . .", passim.

22 *Ibid.*, p. 30. Cf. Sheila Collins, *A Different Heaven and Earth*, passim.

23 Mollenkott, *Speech, Silence, Action! . . .*, p. 28.

24 Cf. Ruether in "Feminism and Patriarchal Religion: Principles of Ideological Critique of the Bible," *Journal for the Study of the Old Testament*, Issue 22 (February 1982), pp. 54-66. In this article

Ruether argues that the Bible contains an internal critique ". . . while both testaments undoubtedly contain religious sanctifications of a patriarchal social order, they also contain resources for the critique of both patriarchy and the religious sanctification of patriarchy." (p. 54). See further discussion of Ruether's perspective in Chapter IV.

[25] Mollenkott, *Speech, Silence, Action!*, p. 24.

[26] *Ibid.*, p. 27.

[27] Alexander, "A Conversation . . .", p. 30.

[28] *Ibid.*, pp. 30 and 73.

[29] *Ibid.*, p. 27.

[30] *Ibid.*, p. 28.

[31] Scanzoni and Hardesty, *All We're Meant to Be*, pp. 17 and 18.

[32] *Ibid.*, p. 28.

[33] Jewett, *Man as Male and Female*, p. 94.

[34] *Ibid.*

[35] Mollenkott, *Women, Men and the Bible*, p. 13.

[36] *Ibid.*, p. 20.

[37] Androgyny is "an ancient Greek word—from andro (male) and gyn (female)—defines a condition under which the characteristics of the sexes, and the human impluses expressed by men and women, are not rigidly assigned. Androgyny seeks to liberate the individual from the confines of the appropriate." Carolyn Heilbrun, *Toward a Recognition of Androgyny*, (New York: Harper Colophon Books, 1973), p. x. Here it is used to express the idea that masculine and feminine traits are found in humans regardless of sex and are also found in Jesus.

[38] Leonard Swidler, *Biblical Affirmations of Women* (Philadelphia: The Westminster Press, 1977), p. 281.

[39] *Ibid.*, pp. 282-290.

[40] *Ibid.*, p. 282.

[41] *Ibid.*, p. 283.

[42] *Ibid.*, p. 290. In *The Divine Feminine*, Virginia Mollenkott devotes one chapter to one of the messianic Psalms (Psalm 102) which images the Christ as a female Pelican. She says: Part of that prophecy of Christ's affliction is an image of Christ as a female pelican, for in verse six, the afflicted and suffering speaker moans, "I am like a pelican of the wilderness." Christian tradition has not only understood the speaker to be Christ, but has understood the pelican image to specify a *mother* pelican giving her life to revive her dead

offspring. The analogy is, then, that Christ is to the church as the mother pelican is to her brood. Virginia Ramey Mollenkott, *The Divine Feminine: The Biblical Imagery of God as Female* (New York: Crossroad, 1984), p. 44. Also for a brief discussion of Jesus as Androgynous, see Carolyn G. Heilbrun, *Toward a Recognition of Androgyny*, pp. 17-20.

[43] Swidler, "Jesus Was A Feminist," p. 103.

[44] *Ibid.*, p. 106.

[45] See Kathleen Storrie, "New Yeast in the Dough: Jesus Transforms Authority," *Daughters of Sarah* 10 (January/February 1984). In this article Storrie draws from the work of Elizabeth Fiorenza, *In Memory of Her* (New York: Crossroad, 1983), and Dorothy Soelle, *Beyond Mere Obedience* (Minneapolis: Augsburg Publishing House, 1970). See also Rachel Wahlberg, *Jesus According to a Woman* (New York: Paulist Press, 1975).

[46] Swidler, "Jesus Was A Feminist", p. 103. For practical interpretations of this notion in sermonic form see Rachel Wahlberg, *Jesus According to a Women.*

[47] See the previously cited book, *The Divine Feminine* by Mollenkott.

[48] This line of argument has been criticized by some Jewish feminists. Cf. Judith Plaskow, "Blaming the Jews for the Birth of Patriarchy," in *Nice Jewish Girls*, ed. Evelyn Torton Beck (Watertown, Massacuusetts: Persphone Press Inc., 1982), pp. 250-254. See discussion of this critique below in Chapter VI.

[49] Perhaps with the exception of Paul Jewett, in *The Ordination of Women*. Mollenkott recovers some of the lost tradition in her book, *The Divine Feminine.*

IV

LIBERATION FEMINIST CHRISTOLOGY: JESUS, THE LIBERATOR

Whereas Biblical Feminists are ardent and strong biblically focused thinkers, in the sense that everything is tested against the Bible, liberation feminists, to varying degrees, employ the Bible as merely one of several sources in doing theology. For a Letty Russell who is in the reformed tradition, the Bible is more of a primary source. For a Rosemary Ruether who is in the Catholic tradition, it is an important source which must be critically analyzed.

Letty Russell, believing the central biblical message as one which mandates the liberation of women, accepts the Bible as authority, that is, it is the church's book and a source to which feminists are accountable. Russell's reading of the Bible enables her to make sense of her experience and to bring meaning to her humanity in Jesus Christ. She feels that this can happen in spite of the patriarchal context in which the Bible was written. The various "inconsistencies and mixed messages" in no way reduce the authority of the Bible. Russell writes:

> For me the Bible is Scripture because it is also script. It is an authoritative witness to what God has done and is doing in and through the lives of people and their history. It is authoritative because those who have responded to God's invitation to participate in God's action on behalf of humanity find that it becomes their own lived-out story or script through the power of God's Spirit.[1]

Russell affirms Ruether's position on the Bible as containing a critical and liberative tradition within it.[2] Ruether in a more direct way addresses the matter of feminist use, or more accurately, critique of the Bible. In an article entitled, "Feminism and Patriarchal Religion: Principles of Ideological Critique of the Bible," she analyzes the Bible from a feminist perspective. Her thesis in this article is "that while both testaments undoubtedly contain religious sanctification of a patriarchal social order, they also contain resources for the critique of both patriarchy and the religious sanctification of patriarchy.[3] It is argued that whereas the sanctification of patriarchy is not normative, the critiques of patriarchy are normative. Ruether identifies these two realities as "two religions within the biblical texts."[4]

In the one religion, men are dominant and in a very real sense, they are the only ones who count in biblical–both Hebrew and Greco Roman–societies. Women are generically and generally dependent upon men. There is an understanding of relationship in terms of domination and subjugation . . . the patriarch is forever over the dependents. This relationship exists between king and subject, bishop and priest, priest and laity, husband and wife, father and children, master and servant and God and creature.[5]

In the other religion, which is a critique of patriarchal religion, there are rejections of patriarchal domination. In this religion, there is a focus on such things as justice rather than oppression–economic or political (Isaiah 10:1-2, Amos 8:4-6 and 5:21-24). This critique is climaxed in the work of Jesus (Luke 4:18-19, Matthew 23:25). This second religion represents a prophetic faith. It is one which critiques the first religion–the religion of patriarchy.

Focusing on New Testament hermeneutics, Elizabeth Fiorenza makes a similar argument to Ruether's:

> A feminist theological hermeneutic of the Bible that has as its canon the liberation of women from oppressive sexist texts, structures, institutions, and internalized male values maintains that solely those traditions and texts of the Bible that transcend their patriarchal

culture and time have the theological authority
of revelation if the Bible should not continue to
be a tool for the patriarchal oppression of
women.[6]

For liberation feminists, it is clear that the Bible is a
primary source for doing theology. However, it must be said
with equal fervor that the Bible is to be viewed critically.
Many questions which emerge from women's experience must
be raised.

Pursuing this matter of hermeneutics in relation to
Christology, Ruether, in her book, *To Change the World*,
rejects the notion of objectivity in theological interpretation.
In her argument we see that, not only do liberation feminists
argue that scripture can critique scripture but these feminists
also move on to show the relationship between one's
understanding of the Bible and Christian doctrine, and our
present context. This relationship is described as a
hermeneutical circle:

> . . . this hermeneutical circle between our
> contemporary values, concerns and faith-stance
> and our reading of the Bible is inevitable. Those
> who claim to give us the fully objective and
> finally scientific historical portrait of Jesus only
> illustrate once again the close similarity between
> their Jesus and their own conscious or unconscious
> self-portraits.[7]

The point being made is that the Bible challenges us as we
live and have our being, but at the same time the Bible
viewed out of the context of our experiences can be challenged
as well. In other words, "we must be questioned by but also be
prepared to question scripture."[8]

Some questions are more radical than others. For Russell
the question may be how can Jesus Christ our Lord save
women? But for Ruether it may be can a male saviour help
women? Because of this difference I have divided the

liberation feminists into "right-side" and "left-side" liberation feminists.[9]

A. The Right Side of the Liberation Feminist Perspective

The theology of Letty Russell is one which falls on the right side within the liberation camp. It is characterized in this way for two reasons. One, whereas Russell, along with other liberation feminists takes both the Bible and tradition seriously, Russell seems to be preoccupied with the Bible. Being able to withstand the test of biblical scrutiny is important for Russell. The Bible, although it is not a literal recording of the words of God, is the primary written document from which we do theology. Russell takes pride in taking old biblical symbols and recovering their meaning, making them usable for us today. Russell, then, represents the "scriptural primacy" pole of White feminist liberation theology. Two, as we shall see below, her treatment of tradition, although not extensive, provides a way to deal with old concepts, opening up the possibility for the participation of women in reformed structures.

1. The Context of the Christology of Letty Russell

In her book, *Human Liberation in the Feminist Perspective*, human liberation emerges as the central focus of her method of doing theology. The liberation of women is the starting point of her feminist theology. This theology involves action/reflection on the part of advocates for changes leading toward sexual equality in political, economic and social areas within the Christian context.

According to Russell, since feminist theology comes out of the experience of oppression, its approach must be different from that of traditional theology and philosophy. Whereas traditional theology and philosophy use the "deductive approach"–"deducing conclusions from first principles established out of Christian tradition and philosophy," women prefer to use the inductive method–"drawing out the material for reflection from their life experiences as it relates to the gospel message."[10] The gospel speaks to people only in concrete situations; therefore allowance is made necessarily for variations in situations. This method depends on the "contributions of the many disciplines that help to illuminate the human condition and not just on a particular theological tradition."[11] History, psychology, sociology and political science are significant in portraying the human condition in general and women's condition in particular. These disciplines are analyzed from a feminist point of view. Feminist theology in its earlier formation was genitive theology. That is, it was written by women, about women and for women. As women theologians began to see the need for a more inclusive type of theology, they began to articulate a more universal form of theology. Because oppression tends to dehumanize its victims, women must reconceptualize ideas and images about themselves. But women are not the only victims. An adequate concept of feminist theology would not be that it is genitive but rather that it strives to make women and men become truly human beings.

Therefore feminist theology, according to Russell, "is written out of an experience of oppression in society. It interprets the search for salvation as a journey toward freedom, as a process of self liberation in community with others in the light of hope in God's promise."[12] God's promise is not limited to men or to women.

Women, in liberating themselves, also provide an opportunity for men to become liberated. Women (and men) must be liberated from the tradition (history) which has distorted the experience of women, thereby perpetuating the oppression of women. Russell does not completely reject past history. Her treatment of history or tradition is indeed not hostile, like that of Mary Daly.[13] But she does say of tradition "it is necessary to examine the problem of tradition in relation to a 'usable future' and a 'usable history', as well as a 'usable language' which can help to communicate tradition in present contexts of oppression of groaning."[14] Feminist theology, then, for Russell does not advocate rejecting all of that which has been handed down as tradition. But it is about accepting that portion of that tradition which is relevant or usable for human liberation as conceived in the feminist perspective in contemporary society.

2. The Christology of Russell

a. Tradition as Employed by Russell

In respect to the quest for an adequate Christology, Russell makes use of the same formula of the "usability" of tradition. Envisioning a usable future, in light of the usable past, articulated with the usable language[15] it is possible to arrive at Christology from the feminist perspective. The concepts of "tradition" and "traditioning" are critical in Russell's theology and therefore are quite helpful in illuminating her Christology. She attempts to liberate tradition from the old, static conception of past events. In doing this, she maintains a close connection between Mission and Tradition. See writes:

> In the light of some recent currents in the discussion of Tradition and Mission it is possible to say that Tradition is Mission because its very description is that of God's missionary activity in handing Christ over into the hands of men and women in order that all people may come to the truth (I Timothy 2:4). The Tradition is thus seen as God's handing over of Jesus Christ into the hands of all generations and nations until Christ hands all things back to God. The action of traditioning is seen in God's missionary activity in sending Christ. The object of the activity is Christ himself. The means by which people participate in the traditioning is by sharing in the receiving and passing of Christ. The location of God's concern and actions in sending Christ is

> the world, in order to bring a "new creation."
> When the end and goal of the traditioning is
> completed, Christ will hand himself and all
> things back to God. (Matthew 24:14; I Cor. 15:24-
> 28)[16]

According to this dramatic passage, there are two active and one passive characters in tradition and the traditioning process. It appears that Christ is a passive figure. God acts by way of handing over Christ, while human beings act by receiving Christ. In Paul Tillich's system, this would be called Revelation.[17] Initially Christ is apparently an object in the process, but eventually he becomes a subject. Thus with the activation of Christ which occurs at the emergence of the "new creation," Christ hands all things back to God. Critical to the drama is the fact that Christ is handed over to all generations and nations, inclusive of women and all groupings.[18] Because Jesus has been handed to all of us in order that all people may come to the truth, we all must participate in the traditioning process. What is this truth? The truth has to do with truth about ourselves, particularly as related to God. The search for truth is actually the search for true humanity. The one true representative of the new/true humanity is Jesus Christ who points us to God's liberating action. Again, the seemingly passive Christ takes on an active role, the role of representing.

God through Christ, has entered and changed history (Col. 1:19). God has chosen Christ as representative of true humanity. He exemplified "togetherness with God."[19] Relying on Dorothee Soelle's interpretation in *Christ the Representative*,[20] Russell sees Jesus Christ in the mediational and reconciling functions. Additionally, Jesus opens the "new possibility of a future in which all can become representative of a new personhood" by receiving Christ.[21] As represent-ative, Jesus stood and still stands for us all. Therefore, all, through faith in Jesus, can participate in the new humanity.

b. *Jesus as Male*

Essential to Russell's perspective in the claim of universal participation in the new humanity is Christ as the representative. The maleness of Jesus which has been used against women presents only a minor problem for Russell–a minor problem which can be solved. Russell with G. Kittel affirms the naming of the problem as the "scandal of particularity."[22] Some have chosen to deal with this problem by "looking for further incarnation in the form of a woman."[23] Still, some argue that Jesus was merely a "good person," as found in nineteenth-century liberal tradition.

Others have argued that given the social context which was characterized by patriarchy, Jesus had to have been a man; a woman simply could not have functioned in the society in that time to effect salvation. These proponents argue that because God knew the sin and weaknesses in the culture of the people, God sent a man to do a woman's work. The scandal then rests in the maleness of Jesus: "How is it possible for this male to be the bearer of God's togetherness with women and men when he represents only one half of the human race in this respect"?[24] Russell challenges women to struggle to disconnect Christ's work from his maleness. Rather Christ's work must be connected with his "being the new human." Therefore, the maleness of Jesus is incidental, whereas the humanity of Jesus is paramount.

The idea of "being the new human" is developed more in Russell's second book, *The Future of Partnership*.[25] In articulating her methodology in a more precise way, Russell uses the term "eschatological hermeneutic" to describe it.

Specifically speaking, "eschatological hermeneutic is a process of questioning our actions and our society in the light of the eschatological message of the Bible. We begin with the questions that arise out of our life and out of the experience of those who cry out for deliverance;" . . .[26] The questions are addressed critically to the tradition of the Christian faith and to the Bible as the chief witness to God's promise in Jesus Christ. The Biblical message, in turn, helps us to interpret itself, for a central motif of the Bible is that of "promise on the way to fulfillment." In the light of the moving horizon of Gods promise for New Creation, one interprets the texts, knowing that full eschatological verification of one's interpretation can come only in the "fulfillment of the New Creation."

The eschatological message is that God frees and unites us into true partnership. Thus, the eschatological future which provides the context for our theologizing and our acting out of our understanding of the eschatologized message is the place where the promise of partnership is fulfilled. The traditioning process is appropriate here for it is the handing over of Christ which continues to be the context of the eschatological or the biblical message. We see this in Russell's pursuit of an adequate conception of "partnership", in which she explores what it means to be in partnership with God.[27] Partnership is connected to the idea of God's "New Creation." The drama-like passage discussed above explains that God through Christ brings about the new creation. Here Russell explains this event further. This New Creation is actively introduced by Jesus Christ. In Russell's words, "Jesus as Liberator is the first sign of God's New Creation in which death and suffering are overcome by love so that we are set free for the others even in the midst of our unfreedom and continued existence in Old Creation."[28] Jesus was represented by God. In a sense this was "God's representation" of God's humanity. The New Creation represents the new/true humanity to which we are all called—men and women alike.

In explicating her position that Jesus is the representative for all, Russell draws upon traditional words such as Jesus as Lord (*Kyrios*) and Servant (*diakonos*). Finding no problem with either of these terms, she emphasizes in her discussion that these functions are necessary. Recognizing the possible objection to the use of such metaphors as servant and Lord, Russell is quick to refer to the true meaning of servant, Lord, and Lordship. Servant and Lord are defined not as the titles for oppressed and oppressors or inferior and superior persons, which they have come to mean in our unjust and oppressive church and society, but in the sense of "one divine *oikonomia*." In this sense, she does not only speak of the scandal of particularity as discussed above but also of the scandal involved in using the word servant and Lord together. At this point, the question is not how can the male be God, but how can the servant be Lord? The answer rests in Jesus' proclamation that He came not to be served but to serve (*diakonia*). In the biblical sense, God is both Lord and servant; consequently Jesus is characterized in Lordship and Servanthood:

> . . . neither Lord nor Servant can be removed from our description of God's self-presentation, . . . the key to understanding them is to allow them to remain together in the liberating paradox that witnesses to the story of God's oikonomia. The words cannot be separated if they are to be understood without leading to false dualism and false uses of power. The meaning of God's Lordship in Jesus Christ is clear only in relation to the purpose of that Lordship, which is service. The purpose of God's service and subordination in Jesus Christ is to establish the Lordship of God's love.[29]

Given the accounts of Jesus as recorded in the New Testament, it would appear that Jesus' reward for obedient servanthood was suffering rather than exaltation. What, therefore, is the relationship between servanthood and suffering? In *Becoming Human*,[30] Russell discusses another scandal–that of suffering. How can he who is also Lord suffer? Additionally, if Jesus is Lord and Savior why do humans suffer? There is suffering on the part of the divine as the divine has become human. It is through suffering that justice is established.

> God's power and glory are present in our human
> condition no matter what the dimension of our
> suffering, because in Christ's suffering God has
> chosen to stand with us. Yet when we look to see
> this power and glory in human life, it shines
> through most clearly in those whose lives are
> confronting the suffering by saying *no* [italics
> mine] to its dehumanizing power.[31]

Therefore humans are empowered to reject the dehumanizing
aspects of suffering. Because of the act of caring, we know
that humans are destined not for suffering but for
"partnership with God." Russell adds:

> When God's Spirit breaks into our lives . . ., we
> suddenly discover that we are somebody, but not
> because of anything we have done. . . . We are
> somebody because we have accepted the presence
> in our lives of the One who calls us *partner*.
> It is in this and this only that we can glory, that
> our humanity is more-than human because God
> has chosen to become a nobody and to share
> humanity with us.[32]

As stated earlier, central to her methodology and context is
the idea of traditioning. The traditioning process centralizes
the figure Christ as the connector, the representative. Christ
connects God and humanity and is at the same time
representative of the divine reality which is supreme. That
reality is God. Additionally, Christ is the representative of
the true/new humanity.

The old humanity/old creation in humanity is its fallen
state. Humans were overcome by their own weaknesses and
limitations. This old humanity/old creation is the old order
which is characterized by personal, political and social sins,
all of which have become translated into socio-political
hierarchies for which the primary goal is domination of the
strong over the weak. Consequently, old humanity/old

creation is plagued with suffering, pain and unhappiness of the weak. The strong define humanity in a narrow way which protects their position as human beings while the weak are considered non-humans-non-persons. The weak and helpless are bad and the strong are good. In the old humanity, humanity or the concept of self as human is distorted on the part of both the weak and the strong.

Jesus Christ, the New Being, who came to eradicate this unequal relationship brings about the new humanity. Though both sides began as equals and continue to be essentially equal, Jesus equalizes the distorted unequal relationship and converts it into equal partnership. Jesus, then, functions to free us from the bondage of oppression and the sins of inequality leading to a life of freedom. In other words, for us, Jesus means freedom.[33]

As we can see Jesus Christ is central to Russell's thought. Take away Jesus Christ, and Russell's emerging system has no content.

B. *The Left-Side of the Liberation Feminist Perspective*

In a discussion of her journey in faith, in describing herself in relation to issues of peace and racial justice, Rosemary Ruether says of herself "I seemed instinctively to gravitate to the left."[34] Early in her life, Ruether found herself taking stands against racism, classism, imperialism and then sexism. She developed an activist and rebellious posture reflected in her involvement in the civil rights and Peace Movements which provided the background for her later theological interests in racism and classism. Two other factors contributed greatly to Ruether's development as a feminist theologian. First, after their father's death, Ruether and her sisters grew up with their mother and her circle of women who were feminists of their generation. Other experiences of her life were characterized by women in authority or at least by women "running things." Men in authority were viewed or experienced as intrusions. The second thing which contributed greatly to Ruether's development as a feminist theologian was her experience as a married woman. As a practicing Catholic, being restricted, in fact, controlled, by the Catholic Church did not set well with her. As in the case of many young married women, Ruether found herself being locked-in in her private life as well as public life. Institutionalized sexism in the church restricted her in the area of family planning as well as career development.

Because the Roman Catholic Church condemned family planning and discouraged women in career development, Ruether, having an interest in both of these, responded by using her academic skills to investigate sex oppression and repression in the history of the Church. This reflects her college and graduate training. For as one with training and interest in the "Classics," it seems natural that as a theologian she would focus on historical theology.

1. *The Context of the Christology of Rosemary Reuther*

In her first major publication on institutionalized sexism, *New Woman, New Earth,*[35] Ruether addresses three areas: (1) she examines the social conditioning of women; (2) she shows how this conditioning has functioned to oppress women; and (3) she relates sexism to other forms of oppression.

These three factors are evident as Ruether attempts to explain the origin of sexism by dividing the history of women into four phases: (a) *The Conquest of the Mother.* Ruether traces the development of the roles and functions of women from the ancient tribal or village culture, part of which represents the move from maternal to male dominated mythic system.[36] With its men as hunters and warriors, and women as power holders in the areas of agriculture, economic processing, manufacture, medicine, and marketing, their roles were equalitarian in nature. In this urban culture, "As long as the economy was centered in the family, woman had social bargaining power, despite the development of patriarchal political systems that defined her as dependent and rightless."[37]

This culture gave way to a revolution which created an urban culture which began the negation of women's power. The urban culture "created a new elite group of males whose power was no longer based on the physical prowess of the hunter or warrior, but on the inherited monopoly of political power and knowledge."[38] Women, with few exceptions, were "elevated," or actually relegated, to an "ornamented role" which led to the generally accepted beliefs, later rationalized by ideologies, in the inferiority of women.

In the name of civilization, this urban culture ushered in an industrialized culture "which [diffused] urbanization over more and more of the world and [shifted] economic production increasingly from the family to a work place separated from the home."[39] Along with this culture came the rule and domination of men and the submission and oppression of women. Ruether sees this oppression of women as the core problem which, in the quest for civilization, has led to other oppressions such as imperialism, racism and even oppression of nature-pollution. She writes: "It is perhaps not too much to say that the Achilles' heel of human civilization, which today has reached global genocidal and ecocidal proportions, resides in this false development of maleness through repression of the female."[40] The repression came concurrently with the repression of nature in which

> . . . the mother goddess symbol represents a society directly interacting and dependent on nature for survival, an experience which persisted for peasant peoples even after the urban revolution. The importance of woman in a family-centered economy the centrality of the mother as life-giver of every child, makes woman the symbol of "nature." This symbolic role of women is gradually repressed or subordinated by a male elite, who begin to rationalize an artificial debilitation of women in more

developed social organizations, and who begin to
feel themselves the masters, rather than the
children, of organic nature.[41]

(b) *The Negation of Mother.* This dual role of ruling and
repressing was further institutionalized in the first
millennium BC in Hebrew and Greek cultures. Men positioned
themselves as masters over nature and, therefore, over
women. In so doing, they elevated themselves beyond nature
to the level of the divine.

> This image of transcendent, male, spiritual deity
> is a projection of the ego or consciousness of ruling-
> class males, who envision a reality, beyond the
> physical processes that gave them birth, as the
> true source of their being. Men locate their true
> origins and nature in this transcendent sphere,
> which thereby also gives them power over the
> lower sphere of "female" nature.[42]

Herewith lies the establishment of negative social dualisms.
The higher realm (the divine) is reserved for men, and the
lower realm (nature) is reserved for women. Thus we have
the negation of the power-bargaining female figure.
(c) *The Sublimation of the Mother.* This duality was
continued throughout Catholic and Protestant theological
traditions. Both traditions have affirmed femininity as the
unique and ideal spiritual and moral state of women, and
masculinity as the unique and ideal materialistic state of
men. In the Catholic tradition, this was culminated in the
doctrine of Mariology, a doctrine in which "the Virgin Mary,
was the antetype of spiritual femininity over against 'carnal
femaleness'."[43] In the Protestant tradition, the doctrine of
Mariology was not adopted and accordingly, rather than
idealizing virginity, it elevated marriage. Yet, some
Protestants maintained the idealization of femininity which
kept women in the private sphere and men in the public
sphere.

(d) *The Liberation of Women.* Although some women of the Renaissance and Enlightenment began to challenge the stereotypical dualisms which relegated women to a "woman's sphere" and men to a "man's sphere," it was in the nineteenth century that the move to liberate women made significant headway.[44] In the current movement, women have begun to broaden the areas of struggle to include all aspects of existence. Three constants remain on the agenda of those who are framers of the movement. (1) They must perform the subjective and psychoanalytical tasks of raising the consciousness of women regarding the issues. (2) As consciousnesses are raised women will have to engage in social praxis in order to reconstruct society in an egalitarian way. (3) However, they need to do this and at the same time employ self-criticism to move beyond racial and class narrowness. The self-examination and criticism also must be extended beyond human relationship to our relationship to the environment–that is, ecology.

a. *Tradition as Employed in Ruether's Theology*

As an historical theologian, Ruether would have a special interest in historical developments of Christian theology. This interest is reflected in her examination of the doctrine of Mariology in the tradition of the Church. Mariology has its background in prebiblical religions which held positive images of women. The Great Mother, or the nature goddess, was a symbol not only of "nature" but also of wisdom and law. However, in Old Testament times, the goddess image is for the most part suppressed. The Great Mother is reduced to the bride of the Father God who is created by him.

Further along in Christian Theology, feminine images were created as a continuation of the bride images established in the Old Testament. The church became known as the "bride of God" or the "bride of Christ" or the "mother of the faithful."[45] The feminine aspect of God became expressed through the Hebrew words "ruah" (Spirit) and "Shekinah" (presence), and the Greek word "Psyche" (soul) which means "soul" in relation to God.[46]

These terminologies provide the background for the development of the Mariology doctrine. Early Church Fathers dealt with Mariology only sporadically. The content of this doctrine includes "Mary as the new Eve, her perpetual virginity, her divine maturity, her bodily assumption in heaven, Mary as the Mediatrix of all graces, and her immaculate conception." One of the major considerations of the doctrine took place in the fifth century A.D. Centering upon the controversy on the use of the word "Theotokos" or "Christotokos," the Mariology debate showed what was really at stake, even in Christology. Was Mary "Mother of God" or "Mother of Christ"? The Church declared Theotokos to be appropriate. This line of thought developed in Egypt into the doctrine of the bodily assumption of Mary into Heaven,[47] wherein Mary is present with God and the risen Christ.[48] The significance of the notion is that Mary is the first to participate in the resurrection of the body.

Though rejected by Western orthodoxy this notion was used by some Western thinkers to teach the uniqueness of Mary in another significant way. The development of the immaculate conception was intended to exempt Mary from the usual impurities of original sin. Others provided for the cleansing of Mary by a "special act of divine grace."[49] None-the-less, Mary became the epitome of feminine virtue. Her primary function is the passive act of receiving (divine grace). This passive function, in addition to the great effort to keep Mary subordinate to the Godhead, also serves as a model for women as subordinate to men, the masculine and dominant beings. Because Mariology perpetuates the feminine passive traits for Mary in particular and women in general, it also preserves the social dualisms which are destructive to women. This is true in both dominant and suppressed Mariology, as put forth in Catholicism and Protestantism, respectively, both of which, although in different ways, employed Mariology as a theological doctrine (Catholic) and symbol (Protestant).[50]

Although the doctrine was more significant in Catholic circles, as a symbol in Protestant circles it had the peculiar soteric function of protecting Jesus from sin since his birth. The primary focus, then, was not Mary but Jesus. Mary was merely a passive instrument to effect the soteric efficacy of Jesus. Emphasizing the reverse side of masculinity and the male gods, dominant Mariology of Catholicism protects the virtuous feminine qualities of femaleness, especially those of passive receptivity and submission, and likens Mary unto the Church. Likewise, the suppressed Mariology in Protestantism affirms the same basic theological relationship between the Father God and the male clergy and the virgin Mary and the feminine Church. Thus, women must look elsewhere for a model for the liberation of women. Ruether suggests that perhaps Mary Magdalene would be a better model for women:

> But the Mary whom we should venerate may not be Mother Mary, the woman who represents the patriarchal view that woman's only claim to fame is the capacity to have babies, the relationship which Jesus himself rejected. The Mary who represents the Church, the liberated humanity, may, rather, be the repressed and defamed Mary of the Christian tradition, Mary Magdalene, friend and disciple of Jesus, the first witness of the resurrection, the revealer of the Christian Good News.[51]

As we shall see below, this critique of tradition impacts Ruether's christological proposals. But also impacting Ruether's Christology is her ability to relate sexism to other forms of oppression.

b. *The Web of Oppression*

Ruether was able to relate the oppression of women to other forms of oppression–racism, classism, anti-semitism as well as the oppression of women as witches. Witches, Jews and Blacks were believed to be possessed by some demonic forces. Both witches and Jews were considered heretics and therefore negative attitudes were nurtured and sustained toward them. Attitudes towards witches and Jews were similar in many ways. "The image of the Jew as a demonic alien was similar. . . . The Jew also came to be seen as a sorcerer who defies and blasphemes the faith of the church. The Jew was seen as a devil worshiper. . . . Like the witch, the Jew was believed to steal the Eucharist. . . ."[52]

Interestingly, both witches and Jews have been in some way associated with women. For the most part, witches are thought to be women. When Jews were punished in fifteenth-century Spain, they were "afflicted with menstruation." Often, menstrual blood, along with other hideous things, was used in making "demonic brews." "Jews, like women, were seen as impious, faithless, contumacious, and lusty."[53] Persecution then was the fate of witches and Jews just as it defined the reality of a disproportionate number of women.

Not only is sexism related to witchcraft and anti-Semitism, but it is also related to racism. Ruether's discussion of racism centers on the "undeclared war" between Black theology and feminist theology. She recognizes that the historical social circumstances have kept Black and White women divided, but she challenges women to recover a humanity which is greater than sexist and racist allegiances. The undeclared war between racism and sexism has made it difficult for White women and Black men to claim their own racism and sexism respectively.

The racism of the women's movement was traced back to the earlier nineteenth-century attitudes toward the Negro. The struggle for and between the Negro suffrage and Woman's suffrage revealed beliefs in the ideology of White supremacy within the woman's movement. Public comparisons were made between the literacy of White women and the illiteracy of Black men. In view of the differences in the literacy level of women and Negroes, some women argued that women and not Negroes should be given the vote. Some others, rather than encouching their argument in intellectual differentials, upheld notions of the purity and supremacy of the White race over the Black race based simply on the nature of the races–Anglo Saxons are simply better than Africans.[54]

Essentially both lines of arguments are the same–they advance the notion that Whites are superior to Blacks; the one for educational reasons and the other for national and natural reasons. Later, arguments among radical feminists developed into exclusive sex analysis.

What has happened, even in the contemporary women's movements, is that women, caught up in their own analysis, have neglected class and race analyses. Ruether explains as well as admonishes women against this tendency:

> Women of the elite class and race easily fall into an abstract analysis of women's oppressed status that they believe will unite all women. They ignore their own context of class and race privilege. Their movement fails to connect with women of oppressed groups, and it becomes defined by a demand for "rights" commensurate with the males of the group, oblivious to the racist and class context of these privileges. It may not be wrong to seek such "equality," but it is dangerous to allow the ideology of the women's movement to remain confined to this perspective.[55]

Ruether challenges this line of argument as being inherently racist and classist. "A Monolithic analysis of sexism as the ultimate oppression obscures the way in which sexism is structurally integrated with class and race."[56] This kind of analysis would simply be based on the "experience of a fairly atypical group of White, usually childless women, who belong, racially and socioeconomically, to the ruling class."[57] Consequently, concerns of this movement would be limited primarily to that class. Ruether rather proposes "that the women's movement reach out and include in its struggle the interstructuring of sexism with all other kinds of oppression, and recognize a pluralism of women's movements in the context of different groupings."[58]

Ruether's criticism does not target only the women's movement's single analysis, but it also targets the Black movement's tendency toward single analysis. The Black movement, with its exclusive race analysis, has as its primary interest the liberation of Black men (males). It has refused to address sexism and has been negligent in addressing classism in its community. Although this is recognizably so, many have sought to justify it by pointing out the catastrophic immasculation of Black manhood resulting from socio-economic discriminatory practices. Much of Ruether's discussion centered on the narrow, sexist and somewhat classist ideology of Black nationalism. She observed that Black nationalism took its model from more oppressive ones. Ruether writes in this connection:

> It is unfortunate that the general lack of class analysis in the black left in America has prevented it from incorporating the Marxist feminist tradition which is found in third world liberation movement in China, Vietnam, and Cuba. Instead, the third world model drawn upon by black nationalists has come from an identification with Arab nationalism with its unrevised traditions of total subordination of woman.[59]

The Black Church does not provide any real alternative for Black women. Both the Black nationalist movement and the Black Church are patriarchal in nature. In fact, "the black church has traditionally been highly patriarchal and has served to integrate the black family symbolically into the Western patriarchal family norm."[60] This meant, then, that the role presented for woman would be subservient and private. For Black women, the affirmation of "black pride" meant acceptance of this role. Therefore, rather than serving as a solidifier of the total Black community, both the Black nationalist movement and the Black Church have relegated Black women to the lower level of citizenry.

In addition, the Black church (more than the nationalist movement) has alienated the Black lower class. It has functioned not only to provide the missing father symbol (through the male ministry) of the fatherless Black family, but "the Black church has also been the traditional path toward the embourgeoisement of the Black community."[61] In other words, the primary agenda of the Black church is to produce and maintain a middle-class Black America, thereby ignoring the problems and plight of the masses of Black people. The sexism and classism of the Black church and community have not only caused the alienation of Black women and lower class Black people but White women as well. This alienation has been the source of tension existing between these four groups of oppressed peoples–White men, White women, Black men and Black women. Ruether attributes the source of the tension to the Black middle-class male's agenda of self-affirmation.

> The tension between black churchmen and the women's movement, then, seems to represent the defensive perspective of the black, middle class, patriarchal church. It concentrates on confronting the racism of its counterparts in the white church. But it has not yet opened itself up to the disturbing countertrends in the lower-class black community that not only conflict with bourgeois male and female stereotypes but also are alienated from middle-class values and the Christian identity as well.[62]

This condition is a reflection of the fact that the Black theology emerging from the agenda of these Black churchmen is "Black caucus" theology. That is, to say, it is not a theology of the masses of Black people, but it is a theology which functions "in a confrontational fashion within a white power base. It places demands of conscience on white power and seeks to appropriate its advantages for the training of black leadership."[63] Consequently, Black Theology functions as an instrument for creating a Black elite which feels at home in the main stream of White society. Entrance into the mainstream of society merely means that one participates in the oppressive structures of the American society. In so doing, both humans and non-humans fall victims to their lifestyles and values. One of the interesting and different features of Ruether's theology is her connection of various forms of human oppression with oppression of nature by human beings. The tendency of human beings to pollute the environment is seen as in keeping with these other oppressive tendencies:

> Women must see that there can be no liberation
> for them and no solution to the ecological crisis
> within a society whose fundamental model of
> relationships continues to be one of domination.[64]

The central problem is the domination-submission model of relationship identified earlier. Resolution of the problem involves not only the re-ordering of relationships between human beings but also the re-ordering of relationships with non-human realities. This process requires a total social (socialist) revolution which ranges from the "overhauling of [privatistic, radically polluting] method of transportation" to a globally "planned society."[65]

What is called for is a socialistic type of rule in which relationships and living conditions are communalized. It requires a new way of envisioning our society and world in which previous relationships of power are destroyed and new relationships of balance of power-communalized living— are created. In this context, all relationships of domination between races, sexes, classes, environment and human beings are broken down. What is created is the kind of communal equalitarianism required for a new woman, a new humanity, a new heaven, and a new earth.

2. *The Christology of Ruether*

The general theological concerns of this study are reflected in Ruether's Christological discussion. In her book, *To Change the World: Christology and Cultural Criticism* Ruether examines how past Christological claims have related to classism, racism (including anti Semitism), sexism and the exploitation of nature.[66]

The problem of Christology as it relates to classism has been explored in depth by Latin American liberation theologians. Ruether has been influenced by this perspective. By focusing on the liberating praxis of the historical Jesus, we are able to arrive at the real significance of Christology. With such a focus, we can see that Christ's primary task was one of the liberation of the poor and oppressed and the re-establishing of a just order.

Much of Ruether's work in Christology has been spent on its relationship to anti-Judaism. In clarifying this emphasis, she writes:

> Anti-semitism in Western civilization springs, at its roots, from Christian theological anti-Judaism. It was Christian theology that developed the thesis of the reprobate status of the Jew which fanned the flames of popular hatred.[67]

If the general struggle between Christians and Jews was and is a theological one, the core of this struggle is Christological. In fact, Christology and anti-semitism go hand in hand.

> Theologically, anti-Judaism developed as the left hand of Christology. Anti-Judaism was the negative side of Christian affirmation that Jesus was the Christ.[68]

In order to explain the contradiction created by the Jewish denial of the Christian teaching that Jesus was the fulfillment of the hope, Christians developed an "underside" to their Christology which is fed by three assumptions: 1. Whereas by focusing on the negative side of the prophetic criticism, Christians see God's judgment upon the Jew, while they claim God's promise for themselves. 2. Whereas the religion of Jews is a particular one, the religion of Christians is a universal one (particularism vs. universalism). 3. Whereas Jews were seen as possessors of the law, letter and the Old Adam, Christians superseded the Jews with grace, spirit, and the new Adam, Ruether refers to this as "the supersessionist view of historical relationships."[69]

Because Christology is the core of this problem, it is also the key to the solution of the problem. A two-fold solution is suggested. First, we must abandon our static notion of Jesus Christ as finality and fulfillment and replace it with proleptic and anticipatory notions:

> Jesus should not be said to fulfill all the Jewish hopes for the coming Messiah, which indeed he did not. Rather, he must be seen as one who announced this Messianic hope and who gave signs of its presence, but who also died in that hope, crucified on the cross of unredeemed human history.
>
> In his name we continue to proclaim that hope, and also to begin to experience its presence. But, like Jesus, we also do that under the cross of unresolved human contradictions.[70]

Second, in addition to being dynamic, Christology must be paradigmatic because it is relative to a particular people. To make Jesus relative is to take nothing away from his significance for Christians. "Indeed only when we cease to use Jesus' name to negate other people's experiences of the victory of life over death, can the name of Jesus cease to be a name that creates alienation of Jew from Christian, Christian from non-Christian."[71]

Consistent with her theology in general, Ruether discusses the implications of her Christology upon the non-human world and particularly upon nature. The exploitation of nature is simply another manifestation of the effects of the patriarchal notions of domination. In light of the ecological violations which occur in spite of the various responses–liberal progressive, Marxist revolutionary, and romantic–to scientific and industrial domination, we must begin to move toward a more "ecological-liberation world view," which takes seriously the "inter-connectedness of all parts of the community of creation" wherein we recognize that the destruction of one aspect also minimizes the effectiveness of another.[72] We are, therefore, called to a state of "Shalom" which is achievable by way of the Messianic hope, revised. Reuther suggests that we should

> . . . think of the Messianic hope to which Jesus points us, not as the eschatological end-point of history or as transcendence of death, but rather as the Shalom of God which remains the true connecting point of all our existences, even when we violate and forget it.[73]

The violation of nature is particularly related to the violation of women in patriarchal culture. It is no accident that nature is symbolized as female/feminine. As men have dominated nature, they have dominated women, as they have exploited nature they have raped women. They have been able to do this because of their believed superiority of men over nature and men over women.

> These metaphors of spirit over nature, mind over body, as male over female, master over slave, also sanction the hierarchics of social domination. They are made to appear to be 'natural'; not as social

constructs but as the givers of a necessary and divinely created order of things.[74]

In this so-called "divinely-created order of things," women suffer from the oldest forms of dominations.[75] Because this form of domination is justified christologically in traditional Christian theology, Ruether addresses the topic of feminist Christology in three places: (1) in an article entitled "Feminism and Christology: Can a Male Savior Help Women"?;[76] (2) in this article revised under the title "Feminism and Christology: Can a Male Savior Save Women"?;[77] and (3) in her most recent work *Sexism and God-Talk: Toward A Feminist Theology.*[78]

In the article, Ruether puts the primary critical question in its most simple, yet profound, way. Given the realities of what maleness and femaleness means in the church and in society, the question brings into focus elements of the very basic conflict in contemporary male/female relationships. Traditional understanding of the "nature of man" consisted of a dualism that kept men as "protectors" and women as the "protected."[79] The perimeters of woman's sphere have been limited in order to maintain consistency with this social dualism. Women have begun to challenge the motives of such an arrangement–that is, they have questioned whether men have been protecting women or, in fact, protecting the "sacredness" of their privileged position. A male Christology, developed in the context of a Christian theology which itself perpetuates socio/theological dualisms, is met with the same suspicion by feminists. If the male Christ has like investments in the socio-theological status quo, then he cannot be trusted to help women. Thus, Ruether asked "Can a Male Savior help women"?

When published in her book *To Change the World: Christology and Cultural Criticism,* the question becomes more pointedly theological and specifically soteriological: "Can a Male Savior Save Women"? Salvation in a patriarchal system would be comparable to accepting one's designated place in the "order of Creation." This male Christ figure would merely put its stamp of approval upon the patriarchally-defined place of women. It is here where Ruether prepares the way for her liberation approach to Christology when she poses the question, "Can Christology be liberated from its encapsulation in the structures of patriarchy and really become an expression of liberation of women"?[80] In both essays, Ruether provides a positive response to the question. In the first essay, two concepts are elevated, "service" and "conversion." Service must not be confused with servitude.[81] In her view, "Service implies autonomy and power used in behalf of others."[82] We are all called to service. Our conversion is to accept this call by abandoning previous, inaccurate notions of being called to hierarchical and oppressive leadership and power. The new Christology which is to be developed, then,

> . . . does not exalt a new Lord that can be a role model for new roles of power and domination. Nor does it bring together male and female in sexist patterns of complementarity. Rather it is a Christology of conversion and social transformation. Alienated power is overthrown. Those who presently have and represent power are called to lay this power down in service. The subjugated are lifted up. They will inherit the earth in the new liberated Kingdom of redemption. The despised of the present society lead the way into the Kingdom. Men leaders, even God repent of domination; servants, women, the poor are liberated from servitude. This is a Christology of the process of conversion, the process of creating a new humanity of wholeness in mutuality.[83]

The way to this new humanity of wholeness is to be liberated from the various forms of oppression. Ruether states this explicitly in the second essay:

Jesus as liberator calls for a renunciation and dissolution of the web of status relationships by which societies have defined privilege and unprivilege. He speaks especially to outcast women, not as representatives of the 'feminine', but because they are at the bottom of this network of oppression. His ability to be liberator does not reside in his maleness, but on the contrary, in the fact that he has renounced this system of domination and seeks to embody in his person the new humanity of service and mutual empowerment.[84]

In this section on Christology in *Sexism and God-Talk*, Ruether, affirming the "liberating praxis" emphasis of liberation theologians, says that "a starting point for feminist christological inquiry must be a re-encounter with the Jesus of the synoptic Gospels, not the accumulated doctrine about him but his message and praxis."[85] In so doing, we are able to see the ways in which Jesus challenged the customs and laws of his time regarding women. Ruether stops short of saying that Jesus was a feminist in his time, but she does claim "that the criticism of religious and social hierarchy characteristic of the early portrait of Jesus is a remarkable parallel to feminist criticism."[86] He seems to promote a more egalitarian form of relationship–a lineal rather than vertical–perhaps one of brother/sister. Jesus elevated many who were at the bottom of the social hierarchy to a new level of equality. This trend is especially evident in his relationship to women.

There is a dynamic quality to the redemptive process. This dynamism not only exists between the redeemer and the redeemed community but also within the redeemer itself. For "the redeemer is one who has been redeemed, just as Jesus himself accepted the baptism of John."[87] As Jesus is paradigmatic, we become so when we liberate others as we have been liberated ourselves. Recognition of this dynamism moves us away from the traditional "once-for-all" notion of

Jesus. Because the redemptive process still continues, we cannot only experience the Christ as the historical Jesus, but we can experience "Christ in the form of our sister."[88] This means that neither Christ nor humanity is imaged solely as male.

The historical Jesus was a man, but men do not have a monopoly upon Christ, and Eve was a woman but women do not have a monopoly upon sin. For "Christ is not necessarily male, nor is the redeemed community only women, but new humanity, female and male."[89]

C. *Contributions and Problems of Liberation Feminists*

Liberation feminists have set out to reconstruct Christology from a feminist perspective. They have moved beyond the simple "androgynous Jesus or "Jesus was a feminist" models proposed by biblical feminists. Having taken a look at theology in general and Christology in particular, they have attempted to construct a solid Christology which moves beyond the mere figure Jesus to place Christology in the arena of God's incarnation in human being and not male.

Three significant issues which show the right and left sides of the liberation Christology can be raised: (1) The maleness of Jesus is superseded by the Christness of Jesus. Both Russell and Ruether argue that the redemptive work of Jesus Christ moves us toward that new humanity which is in Christ Jesus. But whereas Russell still holds to the unique Lordship of Jesus, Ruether raises the possibility that this Christ can be conceived in non-traditional ways,–as in sister.

(2) The concept of servant is reaffirmed as the primary characteristic of Jesus. Service (not to be confused with servitude) is the task to which we all are called, since the call of Jesus was for servants. Because the traditional functions of Jesus' call have been associated with leadership, power and domination, then Jesus serves as a power breaker. His call was for servants and not (power) hungry dominating leaders.

(3) Liberationists see the relationship between Christology and the other interconnecting forms of oppression. Ruether, and Russell to a lesser degree, analyze the relationship between Christology and not only sexism but also other forms of oppression, such as racism, classism and Anti-semitism.

Both Russell and Ruether find the reconstructive task of Christology to be primary in the liberation struggle of women within the Christian community. Although Russell hangs onto the traditional notion of the Lordship of Christ (seen in dialectical tension with the servanthood of Christ), Ruether raises the possibility that Jesus may not be uniquely Lord. We must look to the experiences of women to find other possible paradigmatic figures in order that women and men are liberated.

Both Russell and Ruether re-examine the tradition for usable and unusable aspects of it. Whereas Russell tries to make more sense of the tradition by making it possible for us to participate in it (the traditioning process), Ruether focuses more upon recapturing the idiosyncracies and contradictions of Tradition which have held women captives and proposes alternatives to these traditional interpretations. This is seen in her suggestions that perhaps Mary Magdalene is a more adequate model for women than Mary the Virgin mother of Jesus, and that the Christ can be conceived of as sister as well.

This new imagery is possible when women's experience is the primary source for doing theology. This source has enabled White liberationist feminists to forge a new theological agenda. One wonders, however, if even liberationist feminist are able to understand the particularity of non-white women's experience. This is reflected at two points. (1) Whereas Ruether correctly critiques the Black nationalist movement and the Black church for its lack of sex and class analysis, she incorrectly locates the tension between Black churches and the women's movement at the point of the sexism of Black men. One could argue that Black men's responses to the women's movement are due equally to the racism of the women's movement as to the sexism in the Black movement. There is no reason to believe, as Ruether seems to make it appear, that White women are more concerned about Black women and the Black lower classes than are Black men.[90] In fact, evidence shows that this is not the case, as we shall see in Chapter VII. (2) Ruether suggests that perhaps a better model for women would be Mary Magdalene rather than Jesus. As we shall see later, there is little reason to believe that a White woman salvific model would be any more liberating of Black women than a White male model. There is still less reason to believe that Russell's talk of partnership at this historical moment is much more than the zeal for reconciliation without liberation.

Even as resolved by liberationists, the reformatory approaches to the issues are not sufficient in the eyes of some feminist thinkers. Many of the ideas expressed under the liberation umbrella are taken to their most radical formulations in the work of Mary Daly whose thought will be the focus of the next chapter.

NOTES

[1] Letty Russell, *Human Liberation in a Feminist Perspective- A Theology* (Philadelphia: The Westminster Press, 1974), p. 95.

[2] *Ibid.*

[3] Rosemary Ruether, "Feminism and Patriarchal Religion: Principles of Ideological Critique of the Bible," *Journal for the Study of the Old Testament*, Issue 22 (February 1982) p. 54.

[4] *Ibid.*, p. 55.

[5] *Ibid.*, p. 57.

[6] Elizabeth Fiorenza, *Journal for the Study of the Old Testament*, issue 22 (February 1982), p. 43.

[7] Ruether, *To Change the World: Christology and Cultural Criticism* (New York: Crossroads Publishing Co., 1981), pp. 2-3.

[8] *Ibid.*, p. 4.

[9] This is done for the purpose of delineating differences and not to indicate political alliances.

[10] Letty Russell, *Human Liberation*, p. 53.

[11] *Ibid.*, p. 54.

[12] *Ibid.*, p. 21.

[13] See Chapter V for a discussion of Daly's radical perspective.

[14] Russell, *Human Liberation*, p. 73.

[15] Usable future refers to the taking hold of one's life through the traditioning process. Usable history includes the discovery of "history." Usable language involves ridding ourselves/ consciousness of generic nonsense. (See Chapter 3 in *Human Liberation*.)

[16] *Ibid.*, p. 77.

[17] Paul Tillich, *Systematic Theology*, Vol I (Chicago: The University of Chicago Press, 1951), p. 111. Revelation requires a receiving side and a giving side.

[18] *Ibid.*, p. 134.

[19] *Ibid.*, p. 136.

[20] Dorothee Soelle, *Christ the Representative: An Essay in Theology After the Death of God* (Philadelphia: Fortress Press, 1967).

[21] Russell, *Human Liberation*, p. 136.

[22] *Ibid.*, p. 137.

[23] *Ibid.* Mary Daly in her early work takes this course. See discussion in Chapter V. Also see Ruether's discussion below in this chapter.

[24] *Ibid.*, p. 138.

[25] Russell, *The Future of Partnership* (Philadelphia: The Westminster Press, 1979).

[26] *Ibid.*, p. 173. This methodology is an attempt to move beyond the socio-critical hermeneutic of some political and liberation theologians and the historical critical method of Rudolf Bultmann who argues that we have a "preunderstanding" which we bring to the biblical interpretation. Our preunderstanding cannot limit the biblical message and the socio-critical commitment. By employing the concept of partnership in a futuristic way, Russell is able to by-pass the problem of past unequal interpretations of partnership, while invoking the biblical message which, in her view, surpasses previous limitations, be it in terms of political commitment, personal, or social understanding. This appeal to the future, then,

liberates our interpretations from our human limitation. Eschatological hermeneutic functions in this way.

27 Russell says that partnership in general "may be described as a new focus of relationship in which there is continuing commitment and common struggle in interaction with a wider community context" (*Ibid.*, p. 18). Of Christian partnership (or rather Christians who are partners), she says, ". . . partnership of Christians could be described as a new focus of relationship in a common history of Jesus Christ that sets persons free for others." (*Ibid.*, 19).

28 Russell, *Human Liberation.*, p. 33.

29 Russell, *The Future of Partnership*, p. 67.

30 Idem., *Becoming Human* (Philadelphia: The Westminster Press, 1982).

31 *Ibid.*, p. 57.

32 *Ibid.*, p. 58-59.

33 Ernst Kaseman, *Jesus Means Freedom* (Philadelphia: Fortress Press, 1972).

34 Ruether, *Disputed Questions On Being A Christian* (Nashville: Abingdon, 1982), p. 76.

35 Ruether, *New Woman New Earth: Sexist Ideologies and Human Liberation* (New York: The Seabury Press, 1975).

36 *Ibid.*, p. 11.

37 *Ibid.*, p. 7.

38 *Ibid.*

39 *Ibid.*, p. 8.

40 *Ibid.*, p. 11.

41 *Ibid.*

42 *Ibid.*, p. 13-14.

43 *Ibid.*, p. 19.

44 See discussion of women's experience in Chapter 2.

45 Ruether, *New Woman*, p. 42.

46 *Ibid.*, pp. 42-45.

47 *Ibid.*, p. 50.

48 *Ibid.*, p. 51.

49 *Ibid.*, p. 53.

50 Ruether, "Christology and Feminism," *An Occasional Paper* of the Board of Higher Education and Ministry of The United Methodist Church 1 (December 25, 1976).

51 Idem, *New Woman*, p. 59.

[52] *Ibid.*, pp. 105 and 106; cited from Joshua Trachtenberg, *The Devil and the Jews* (New Haven: Yale University, 1943), pp. 196-216.

[53] Ruether, *New Woman*, p. 166.

[54] Ruether cites two pieces of evidence for this. One, at the 1893 National Women's Suffrage Convention the following resolution was passed:

> Resolved: . . . we call attention to the significant facts that in every state there are more women that can read and write than all the negro voters; . . . so that the enfranchisement of such women could settle the vexed question of rule by illiteracy, whether of home-grown or foreign-born production.

Ibid., p. 123, from the NAWSA Proceedings, 1893, p. 84; quoted in Aileen Kraditor, *The Ideas of Woman's Suffrage Movement, 1890-1920* (Garden City, New York: Doubleday, 1965), p. 110. The other was a statement by Belle Kearney of Mississippi at the 1903 convention:

> Some day the North will be compelled to look to the South for redemption from these evils, on account of the purity of its Anglo-Saxon blood, the simplicity of its social and economic structure, . . . the South [will] be compelled to look to its Anglo-Saxon women as the medium through which to retain the supremacy of the White race over the African. . . .

Ruether, *New Woman*, p. 123, from *Woman's Journal*, April 4, 1903, quoted in Aileen Kraditor, *The Ideas of the Woman's Suffrage Movement*, pp. 160-161.

[55] Reuther, "Crisis in Sex and Race: Black Theology vs. Feminist Theology," in *Mission Trends No. 4: Liberation Theologies*, eds. Gerald Anderson and Thomas Stanksky (Grand Rapids, Michigan: William B. Eerdman's Publishing Co., 1979).

[56] Ruether, *New Woman*, p. 125.

[57] *Ibid.*, p. 124.

[58] *Ibid.*, p. 125.

[59] *Ibid.*, p. 131.

[60] *Ibid.*, p. 127.

[61] Idem, "Crisis in Sex and Race," p. 179.

[62] *Ibid.*, pp. 180-181.

[63] *Ibid.*, P. 181.

[64] Idem, *New Woman*, p. 204.

[65] *Ibid.*, 206 ff.

66 Ruether, *To Change the World: Christology and Cultural Criticism* (New York: Crossroads Publishing Co., 1981).

67 *Ibid.*, p. 31.

68 *Ibid.*

69 *Ibid.*, p. 41.

70 *Ibid.*, p. 42.

71 *Ibid.*, p. 43.

72 *Ibid.*, p. 63 ff.

73 *Ibid.*, pp. 69-70.

74 *Ibid.*, p. 61.

75 Ruether, *New Woman*, p. 3.

76 Ruether, "Feminism and Christology: Can a Male Savior Help Women" *Occasional Papers.*

77 Ruether, "Feminism and Christology: Can a Male Savior Save Women"? in *To Change the World*, Chapter IV, pp. 45-56.

78 Ruether, *Sexism and God-Talk: Toward A Feminist Theology* (Boston: Beacon Press, 1983).

79 See discussion of social dualism above in Chapter I.

80 Ruether, *To Change the World*, p. 47.

81 See discussion of Russell's use of "Servant."

82 Ruether, "Feminism and Christology" in *Occasional Papers*, p. 5.

83 *Ibid.*

84 Ruether, *To Change the World*, p. 56.

85 Ruether, *Sexism and God-Talk*, p. 135.

86 *Ibid.*

87 *Ibid.*, p. 138.

88 *Ibid.*

89 *Ibid.*

90 Barbara Andolsen also appears to naively parallel the sexism of Black men with the racism of White women, see *Daughters of Jefferson, Daughters of Boot Blacks* Racism and American Feminism, Macon: Mercer University Press, 1986, see especially p. 107.

V

THE REJECTIONIST FEMINIST PERSPECTIVE IN CHRISTOLOGY: BEYOND CHRISTOLATRY

Mary Daly represents the most radical perspective in feminist theology and Christology. One can see in Daly's works a theological evolution from reformist to radical and then to rejectionist, at which point she breaks with all positive christological claims. In this chapter, I will trace this development in Daly's thought. Concurrently, the movement in her general theology as well as Christology will be seen.

A. *The Context of the Christology of Daly*

Daly the reformist emerged in her first publication, *The Church and the Second Sex.*[1] She develops her case against the church by relying on Simone de Beauvoir's analysis of the condition of women in *The Second Sex.*[2] They both attribute the oppression of women largely to religion, Christianity, and the church. These institutions have conspired to make women passive and subordinate in both the church and the society. Women's passivity and subordination are kept intact by the patriarchalism which characterizes both areas of life. Recognizing that there are other factors which contribute to the sustained oppression of women, Daly writes of religion:

> It is seen as one factor in the complex context of patriarchal structures, of which it is both product and perpetuator. Rather than being the cause of woman's unfortunate condition, religion appears rather as a superstructure, as an instrument of oppression and deception appropriate to a culture with given thought-patterns.[3]

Daly takes Simone de Beauvoir's analysis and gives further content to the argument that Christianity is largely responsible for the oppressed condition of women. The question is posed, "to what extent is this interpretation of Christianity's role in the oppression of women in accord with the data of experience, that is, with historical fact"?[4] In response to this question, Daly examines Christian sources–the Bible, Christian tradition and experience.

The reformism of Daly emerges as she attempts to elevate positive interpretations of critical biblical passages, even though in much of the Bible, women are portrayed as "subjugated and inferior beings." She analyzes the two creation stories, Jesus' treatment of women; as well as Paul's instructions regarding women. Her analysis leads her to the conclusion that "[t]he equal dignity and rights of all human beings as persons is of the essence of the Christian message."[5] Continuing along the reform track, Daly looks at the mysogyny found in the writings of the Church Fathers from the Patristic period onward.[6] Except for a few brief references to persons such as Teressa, who, like Catherine of Siena, was able to transcend the theology of her times, Christian tradition through the work of some well-known figures, as well as some lesser-known theologians, kept the lid on women's place in the church and society. "Winds of Change"[7] began to blow with the reign of Pope John XXIII and Vatican II. These two events represented the liberalizing of the "official" view regarding the progress of women in the Catholic Church.

Perhaps the most radical point to be made in this book is Daly's identification of sexual prejudice as a demon which needs to be exorcised. It is a demon because it skews the existence of humanity by denigrating the reality of women and elevating that of men. The process of exorcism can begin with the development of a new theological anthropology. This theological Anthropology

> . . . will study the dynamics of human personality and social relationship from a radically evolutionary point of view. Within this context there

needs to be developed a theology of the man-woman relationship which rejects as alienating to both sexes the idea of a sexual hierarchy founded upon 'nature' and defined once and for all.[8]

There is a dynamic quality here. "The static world view" resulting from traditional ways of doing theology must be combatted because it has led to static notions about how men and women should relate to each other. However, a dynamic world view would alter our theology as well as our conceptions of relationships.

This much needed theology will recognize that the relationship between the sexes evolves, that its forms must change according to the conditions of diverse historical epochs and according to individual differences. It will reject any conception of 'the common good' which would diminish the potential of one sex for the sake of the other. It will place value in personal liberty and growth, which must be seen not as opposed to, but as essential to, love and commitment. Rejecting the old obsession with sex roles, it will be concerned with the problems of persons in relation to others. It will be honest enough to admit the ambiguity of concrete reality, which the theologian's abstractions cannot fully clarify or encompass.[9]

Obviously, Daly is moving toward an idea of partnership which radically changes the roles of both men and women. This idea of partnership is actualized through the equalizing of women and men as far as the structuring of church and society is concerned. At this point in her development, Daly is in line with the goals and objectives of the women and men discussed in chapters 3 and 4. Daly states that her goal is as follows:

Men and women, using their best talents, forgetful of self and intent upon the work, will with God's help mount together toward a higher order of consciousness and being, in which the alienating projections will have been defeated and whole-ness, psychic integrity, achieved.[10]

Both biblical feminists and liberation feminists share their vision toward wholeness. This is an ecclesiastical vision. That is, it represents the hopes and aspiration of women still in the Church with designs on reforming present oppressive church structures.

1. *Daly in Transition*

It is interesting that this very modest book which con-tains such reasonable and reformist suggestions would have met with the kind of hostility from the Catholic community as it did.[11] The reaction of the Church forced Daly to a more radicalized position–thus, the end of Daly the reformist. The period between 1968 and 1975 was one of growth during which time she evolved from a reformist to a radical. Beginning in 1971, a series of articles was published in which we see progress from Daly the reformist to Daly the radical.[12] In a critical review of *The Church and the Second Sex* entitled, "Feminist Post-Christian Introduction" (1975), Daly the radical parted with Daly the reformist.[13] At the point of *Beyond God the Father*[14] there are two significant changes in Daly's perspective. Changes occur (1) in language/symbolism; and (2) in intellectual location. Daly the radical, views Daly the reformist, as naive and unrealistically hopeful that equality could even exist in the church. Inequality, in fact, was in the structure of things. In the Post-Christian Introduction, Daly the radical differentiated between Daly the reformist and Daly the radical. The reformist used terms such as "discrimination" and "misogynism" in describing the condition of women. The radical preferred stronger terms such as "sexism" and "rapism."[15] Whereas the reformist felt that the Church could eliminate the discrimination and misogynism against women, the radical was able to perceive that sexism was inherent in Christian religion. Daly the radical said of Daly the reformer that the latter was so blinded by her optimism that she "was unable to perceive that sexism was inherent in the symbol system of Christianity itself and that a primary function of Christianity in Western culture has been to legitimize sexism."[16] With this different view of the primary problem itself, Daly the radical emerges as a "deeper thinker" and develops an analysis of the primary problem—an analysis which she describes as "stunning."

This is how Daly described herself in the Post-Christian Introduction in 1975. However two years prior to this we see this radical Daly in full bloom in her second book, *Beyond God the Father (1973)*. In this book, she articulates her own methodology which is one of liberation which "involves a castrating of language and images that reflect and perpetuate the structure of a sexist world."[17] Daly calls the traditional use of method a "god" (Methodolatry) which necessarily precludes women's questions. The "phallocentric value system," the demon which produces the language and images, must be exorcised. The method in fact is a three-fold process: "liberation, castration, exorcism."[18]

2. *Critical Doctrinal Critique*

Doctrines or issues are examined, making use of this three-fold method. Daly's analysis of the doctrines of God, the Fall and Humanity set the context for her treatment of Christology.

a. *God—From the Static to the Dynamic*

Liberation begins with the destruction of the traditional oppressive structures, language and images. This is done by way of castration and exorcism. "God the Father" is the prime target for which this process is intended. The God of patriarchy is a static Being. The idea is reflected in the fact that "God" is a noun. Daly proposes that God is a verb–"the Verb of verbs."[19] God is an intransitive verb, that is, a verb without any (limiting) object. A verb is active, therefore dynamic. This dynamism allows women to participate in "being" rather than being dictated to by a static noun, "God." In participating in being, women are helping to create "a new experiential context" out of which a new language about "a developing God" will emerge.[20]

In addition to a new language, our concept of God changes. God is no longer viewed as a power over against creation in Daly's system. Creation has "no power over the ultimately real"; rather our power is "derived from participation in ultimate reality."[21] This participatory process eliminates our traditional fixation upon a static God who is limited by our imaging of "Him." Our images of God have in fact been idolatrous. We have made idols of the images of ourselves which we project upon God. In de-idolizing our concepts of God, we must re-image God. And in re-imaging of God, we must reconsider the nature of human beings,–both men and women. We can no longer hold to such a phallocentric notion that men are associated with good (God) and women with evil (Eve). God must be re-imaged so as to really represent ultimate reality rather than the figment of man's imagination.

b. *The Fall–Eve for Evil*

The traditional way of talking about alienation from this reality which is God is through the Doctrine of the Fall. Theologians have attempted to explain the contradiction between a good, just and perfect God, and the existence of evil in our society. The doctrine (Myth) has in fact been the basis for the believed subordination of women. Certainly, it has been used primarily against women. In other words, since women were responsible for the "original sin," they have carried the primary burden of the "blame" for the fall of "mankind." Daly summarizes this idea when she observes the tendency of theologians and scholars to ignore the fact that the "medium is the message" in the case of the Fall. Daly looks again at the myth and continues:

> In a real sense the projection of guilt upon women is patriarchy's FALL, the primordial lie. . . The message that it un-intentionally conveys . . . is that in patriarchy, with the aid of religion, women have been the primordial scapegoats.[22]

In making women scapegoats of patriarchy's sin, the society has imposed many restrictive and debilitating conditions upon women. Daly describes them as "side effects of original sin." Four of the side effects are psychological paralysis, feminine anti-feminism, false 'humility', and emotional dependence. From the paralysis characterized by "hopelessness, guilt, and anxiety over social disapproval," we get the intracommunal conflicts emerging from the feminine distrust of the feminine (the power-structure-identified-women, versus the non-powerstructure-identified-women). Low feminine esteem and aspiration levels as well as emotional dependency are by-products of the embracing of masculine standards for the feminine. Masculine standards for the feminine are based on the myth of the Old Eve, which was never really eradicated or redeemed by the New Mary. Consequently, women must start from the ground and shirk off the imposed burden of the responsibility of the Fall. In doing so, women are rejecting the oppressive structure which places the guilt and blame of the fall of humanity primarily upon them.

c. *Humanity: Women's Experience as Sisterhood*

In shirking the burden of the blame, women must begin to affirm themselves as sisters in a community of sisterhood. Because this affirmation requires that the teachings of Christianity–the church–be rejected, sisterhood implies a rejection of the church as we know it as well as its doctrines which tend to work out, in detail the meaning of patriarchy.

Sisterhood does not mean brotherhood's sister. A requirement for sisterhood is "strategic polarization." Essentially, this means separation for specific purposes. This is needed for two reasons: (1) "Polarization for the sake of women's internal wholeness or oneness–because, like all oppressed groups, women suffer from a duality of consciousness in their innermost being"; and (2) "Polarization for the sake of political oneness for the sake of achieving liberation in society."[23] In other words, women must reconcile themselves with themselves and with each other. In being reconciled with each other, women will find it necessary to become "friends." Quoting J. Glenn Gray, Daly points out that male comradeship and friendship are not the same things and are not necessarily inclusive of each other. Unlike brotherhood, sisterhood includes friendship: "Since sisterhood is deeply like female friendship, rather than being its opposite . . . it is radically self-affirming. In this respect it is totally different from male comradeship/brotherhood, in which individuals seek to lose their identity."[24] In sum, sisterhood (humanity) is an alternative to the phallocentric society which serves as the context for the creation of oppressive doctrines. It is within this context that Daly forged her move out of Christianity. Feminist thinkers must now do philosophy and theology within this strong affirmation of solidarity with other women, and the idea that the mutual religion of friendship is the God-bearing one.

B. *Daly's Critique and Reconstruction: Christology as Christolatry*

It is against the background of the analysis of the doctrine of God and the Fall and out of the experiences of women that Daly offers her Christology. Both ends of the spectrum must be examined again. God, the being to whom total allegiance is given, and women, the most oppressed of the oppressed, must both be re-imaged. Neither the masculine patriarchal God nor the evil, sinful feminine woman is a liberating image for women. Christology has played its part in keeping these two images intact. Obviously, in light of Daly's criticism of theology in general, and her criticism of God and Evil, her Christology would take radical form. For indeed, it was the blame and responsibility placed on Eve which brought about the need for a Christology. The blame placed upon Eve meant perpetual women's oppression and subjugation. The rejection of the burden of the blame is a primary step in the liberation of women. In other words, "a logical consequence of the liberation of women will be a loss of plausibility of christological formulas which reflect and encourage idolatry in relation to the person of Jesus."[25]

Most theologies have focussed on the person, Jesus of Nazareth, because all of Christendom, it is felt, viewed its beginnings in the birth of Jesus. Therefore, it continues to centralize the person Jesus in its theology. Daly in particular, challenges this reality in Christian Theology and quotes Ralph W. Emerson on the point: "Historical Christianity has fallen into the error that corrupts all attempts to communicate religion . . . it has dwelt, it dwells with noxious exaggeration about the person of Jesus."[26] For many Christians, the person Jesus has become Alpha and Omega. He has become the answer, even to unasked questions.

The radical/revolutionary perspective of Mary Daly represents an attempt to move totally beyond these limitations of Christology. She seeks to break the idolatrous relationship Christians and Christian scholars have with Jesus.

> It is still not unusual for Christian priests and ministers, when confronted with the issue of women's liberation, to assert that God (became) uniquely as a male and then to draw arguments for male supremacy from this. Indeed the Christological tradition itself tends to justify such conclusions. The underlying–and often explicit–assumption in the minds of theologians down through the centuries has been that the divinity could not have deigned to "become incarnate" in the "inferior" sex, and the "fact" that

"he" did not do so of course confirms male superiority. The erosion of consent to male dominance on
the part of women is undermining such assumptions of the tradition.[27]

The Christian fixation upon the person of Jesus represents
pure idolatry. Daly proposes that this "Christian idolatry
concerning the person of Jesus is not likely to be overcome except through the revolution that is going on in women's consciousness."[28] It is this revolution of the new women's consciousness which will destroy the structures, even the
christological ones, which oppress women.

1. *Jesus as Male the Male as Jesus*

Daly's central argument is that because the person Jesus is
male, the male is lauded as the superior being. There is simply a direct correlation between the two.[29] Because male
domination is the very content of patriarchy, it is the male
who is exalted to the superior status in the church and the society, both of which are characterized by patriarchy.
Feuerbach's critique of theology is apropos here. It is the
male who has the power of self-objectification, so that his
nature is projected as God's nature and vice-versa. Therefore,
to conceive of the person of Jesus as the "unique male savior
may be seen as one more legitimation of male superiority."[30]
Incarnational theology verifies this. "'The Second Person of
the Divine Trinity who became incarnate'," symbolically
emphasizes God-the-Son. Daly observes:

Dogmatically speaking, "the word became
Flesh." Thus in Christian doctrine, the "fact"
that god-the-son became man (male) assuming a
human–that is, male-body, enabled males to become gods. It prepared the way for the
Brotherhood representing, replacing Yahweh
and Son.[31]

On the one hand there is Eve, the woman, who bears the blame for humankind's destruction, and on the other hand, Jesus, the man who bears the glory for humankind's salvation. The one represents sin; the other salvation. The one is negative, while the other is positive. Because the positive is generally preferable, it is easier to ascribe superiority to it and inferiority to the negative which is the "notgood" (evil). The sin-salvation dichotomy invokes an inferior-superior concept in male-female relationship, as the female represents sin and the male represents salvation.

This dichotomy serves the interests of the Christian patriarchal power structure. It is fundamental to the very structure of Christianity. If there were no Fall, there certainly would not have been a Christian faith. Daly affirms Elizabeth Cady Stanton's belief that without Eve (The Woman) there would be no need for Jesus (The Savior).[32] In other words, for Daly the other side of the Christology coin is not necessarily anti-semitism, as for Ruether, but it is most directly sexism. The man Jesus is a reminder of what the woman Eve has done to humanity. Through Christology man is able to overcome the Fall which was caused by evil (Eve) in the World. This is the reason that the "EVE MYTH" must be seen in relation to its function in the Christian patriarchal power structure. It provides the rationale for the dichotomous/dualistic way in which the church and society are structured.[33] Therefore, Daly argues that the problem of the oppression of women is basic to Christianity. ". . . Christianity itself should be castrated by cutting away the products of super-male arrogance: the myths of sin and salvation that are simply two diverse symptoms of the same disease."[34] Nothing less than a complete healing of the disease itself will do. This is done only by cutting away the sick or cancerous parts in order to stop the spread of the illness. Put pointedly, in order for women to be liberated, Christianity, God and Jesus must be "castrated."

2. *Meaningless Theology and Christology*

In her transition from reformist to extreme radical, Daly addressed the various criticisms feminists faced as they forge an analysis which is anti-sexist. Critics of feminist theology and Christology tend to use four methods to avoid dealing with the issues themselves: (1) universalization, (2) particularization, (3) spiritualization, and (4) trivialization.[35] The method of universalization involves rejecting the idea of conceiving Jesus as woman, black, brown or yellow. The fact is that since Jesus came for all to be saved, He was none of these. Daly calls attention to the fact that the particularity of Jesus as Jewish and young does not present the same kind of problem as the particularity of Jesus' maleness. No one would argue that only Jews or young people could be identified with the divine nature of Jesus. Even though he was Jewish and a youth, it is fruitless to argue that Jews or young people were superior to others because of Jesus' particularity.[36] Additionally no one would argue against the ordination of the non-Jew or the "unyoung" because Jesus was a Jew and young.[37] However, the particularity of Jesus as male has functioned differently in the history of Christianity. According to Daly, "the problem lies in the exclusive identification of this person with God, in such a manner that Christian conceptions of divinity and of the 'image of God' are all objectified in Jesus."[38] Because the divinity came in the form of male, the male has been divinized. Consequently, to argue that Jesus is universally for all is to ignore the fact that it is because of Jesus' maleness that women are "universally" excluded from the hierarchy of the church (particularly mainline denominations). It is this very "maleness," inspite of arguments for universalism, which has been problematic for women.

By particularization, Daly refers to the tendency to argue that the problem–the suppression and oppression of women–lies in a particular time, place or institution. It is not a problem universally. Some Protestants, then, would say that the problem is a Catholic problem. Even some Catholics would maintain that it is a problem peculiar to some of the Pentecostal traditions, while Pentecostals argue that women are free in the church to do anything a man can do but they cannot be ordained. Based on these various self-exemptions, therefore, many feel that the problem is not the universal oppression of women. There are proponents would even argue that there *is* no problem–women are just restricted in certain geographical, temporal and denominational areas. Daly challenges this position by arguing that sexual oppression is a part of the basic core of Christianity. Therefore, it is more than a problem in a particular Christian community, but one in the general community.

Spiritualization is operative when critics quote Galatians 3:28 in response to the raising of the problem. They ignore the fact that in reality, there is male and female and that the functional discrepancy between the roles each is expected to play results in the subordination of women. To eschatologize role differentiation does not alter present reality. If Christ cannot do anything for women now, then women do not need Christ in the eschaton.

The commonly-heard phrase, "Now let's get on to the serious matters," reflects the response of critics who tend to trivialize women issues. Trivialization is a method by which women's issues are reduced to a level of subordination, just as women themselves continue to be. These issues are insignificant and parochial as compared with men's issues which are important and universal. Consequently, they are (treated as) non-issues.

There are two points to be made here. First, if women's issues are trivial and too particular to be appropriate subject matter for theological and specifically Christological formulations, then women must seriously consider the possibility that theology and Christology are irrelevant to women. Second is the idea that if the only hope for the liberation of women is for women to accept their functional subordination here on earth while pressing forward to the state of heavenly bliss where there shall be neither male nor female in Christ, then this functionally-impotent Christ must be discarded.

This line of argument is developed further in her third book, *Gynecology: The Metaethics of Radical Feminism*,[39] in which Daly's rejectionist stance reaches fruition. Following her tradition set forth in the 1975 postscript to *The Church and The Second Sex*, Daly critiques her previous position held in *Beyond God the Father*. In *Gynecology*, her "beyond Christianity" state is reflected particularly in her use of language. She drops the word "God," among other words, and speaks of God gynomorphically (Goddess) rather than anthropomorphically, explaining, "I do so because God represents the necrophilia of patriarchy, whereas Goddess affirms the life-loving being of women and nature."[40]

Even so, Daly continues her radical attack on Christology and its destruction of women. She sees a direct relationship between violence against women and christologies. The evidence which Daly provides for this claim ranges from the sado-masochistic fantasies of male theologians who "have always fantasized a female hanging on the cross"[41] to European witchburnings which have been viewed as acts "purifying the Body of Christ."[42] The purification process was necessary for the protection of the larger community. Daly therefore sees the real function and purpose in this way:

> The purification of society was legitimated as a cleansing not only of the "body politic," but more specifically, of the Mystical Body of Christ. Since Christ was believed to possess not only his own body but also a Mystical Body–extended Body had to be kept pure enough to perform the functions required by its divine Head. This extended Body symbolism had commonly been invoked by fathers and doctors of the church when confronted with the problem of heretics. The latter–like diseased members–had to be cut off (killed) for the good of the whole organism.

This tradition provided a ready-made solution for the problem presented by the witches.
Moreover, while the argument had frequently
functioned to legitimate the "amputation" of
heretical male members, it was particularly appropriate in the case of deviant women, for there
is something basically incongruous in trying to see
women with any sense of Self as incorporated into
The Male Mystical Body. This incongruity was
partially and convolutedly expressed by Kramer
and Sprenger when they declared that males
were protected from so Horrible a crime as
witchcraft because Jesus was a man.[43]

The mystical Body of Christ here is associated only with
males. It is the continued affirmation of the male and the
negating of the female, so that the torture for witchcraft is
done primarily by males and primarily on females. The
witch craze of earlier centuries represents a threat to
Christian deity. Women, especially independent women,
threatened the "majesty" of the Christian God.[44] ". . . The interest in the punishment of witches was to break down and
destroy strong women, to dismember and kill the Goddess, the
divine spark of being in women."[45]
Because this view is tied to the maleness of Christ and
the Mystical Body of Christ, rather than being redemptive
for women, Christ is, in fact, destructive of women. Therefore,
in traditional Christology, redemption as related to women
could only mean violence, subjugation and acceptance of second-class citizenship.

3. "Be-Friending" as Redemption: From Sisterhood to Be-
Friending

In her fourth book *Pure Lust: Elemental Feminist
Philosophy*,[46] Daly continues her journey out of patriarchy
into a new world of women in the process of be-friending. In
order for this be-friending to take place women must rid

themselves not only of (oppressive) Christolatry but also of the sado-sublimation as expressed in the Catholic Church's teaching about Mary which served to protect the Christ figure. Inherent in traditional Christology is the oppression of women, re-enforced by such subsidiary doctrines as these surrounding the Virgin Mary.

Daly argues that Mary, the Arch-Image, has been tokenized by Catholics and killed by Protestants. In either case she has been used to keep women in their place. For example she says that "although belief in the 'immaculate conception' of Mary was part of popular piety for centuries, it was not made an official dogma of Catholic faith until 1854." This fact makes it possible for Daly to suggest that this official act was intended to undercut the rise of the first wave of the feminist movement.[47] The church gave women a token model/goddess that they might be appeased.

> According to this inconceivable doctrine [the immaculate conception], Mary was "preserved" from original sin by the grace of her son immediately at the moment of her conception–not only in advance of his birth, but also in advance of her own. Nor was she merely "purified" as an embryo in the womb of her mother. Indeed, according to this astonishing doctrine, Mary never had a moment of life, even of embryonic life, without being "full" of the "grace" merited by her son through his death on the cross. Thus she was purified of autonomous being before ever experiencing even an instant of this.[48]

Essentially, Mary was "de-natured" in order to serve the purposes of the "god-son." To put it another way, she was raped of her self. Mary (as all women), has been denied her female "Elemental be-ing."[49] In presenting her as a token the male interest is served. Four effects of such tokenism are pointed out. Women are given (1) an *illusion of progress* and (2) the *delusion of exceptionalism* (because she is full of grace or male identification); (3) Because of this identification, she is in *a role of partnership with a male sponsor/savior;* and (4) as immaculately conceived she is *emptied of autonomous intellect and will* (meaning actually she is *deceived*). What Daly is suggesting then is "that the mythic paradigm of the immaculate conception carries the war against female Elemental Being beyond earlier stages."[50]

This violence perpetrated against Mary and subsequently women in general was validated by the Christolatry which functions as its flip side. Women, therefore, can look to neither Mary nor Jesus Christ for redemption. Daly argues that women must look to other women in the process of Be-Friending in order to develop a meta-patriarchal consciousness. At this level women become deviant/defiant taboo breaking, rejecting sadomasochiastic existence and lusting for happiness. This requires a radical feminist separatism which "is a communal process, affirming the flow of connectedness within each woman–her Presence of Presence."[51] This separatism makes possible Be-Friending which "is the creation of a context/atmosphere in which acts/leaps of Metamorphosis can take place."[52] Distinguishing between Be-Friending and friendship, Daly recognizes that all feminists will not be friends.[53]

> Although friendship is not possible among all feminists, the work of Be-Friending can be shared by all, and all can benefit from this Metamorphospheric activity. Be-Friending involves Weaving a context in which women can Realize our Self-transforming, meta-patterning participation in Be-ing. Therefore it implies the creation of an atmosphere in which women are enabled to be friends. Every woman who contributes to the creation of this atmosphere functions as a catalyst for the evolution of other women and for the forming and unfolding of genuine friendships.[54]

Be-Friending simply means being in relationship with women who are *for women*. The more specific level however– to identify within this group those women with whom elemental friendship is possible.

> Within this context, women can hope to re-alize our potential for finding and developing deep, Self-transforming friendships. Such friend-ships imply communication of Happiness. For Hags, this means sharing, on many levels, ac-tivities of our Metamorphic being, risking to-gether our metapatterning living, our creativity. It means diving together into the wonderful depths of Metamemory. It means voyaging to-gether beyond civilization, always/all ways fur-ther and deeper into Metamorphospheres. This Realizing of the Lust to share Happiness, to respond with Others to the Wild calls of Be-Longing, implies waking Weird Powers of Be-Witching.[55]

If there is any redemption in Daly's thought this is it.[56]

C. *Contribution and Problems of Rejectionist Feminists*

Daly "progresses" from her stance as a reformist in her first book to a radical in her second book, and to a rejectionist in her third. As a reformist, Daly saw hope in reinterpreting the doctrine of Jesus Christ. Attempts to give evidence of this hope included appeals to the work of other reformists as well as the documents of the church and a critique of the writings of theologians. As a radical, Daly no longer uses Jesus as a model. Even though she recognizes the attempt of reformists to reinterpret Jesus as a feminist, she responds: "Jesus was a feminist, but so what"? "Even if he wasn't, I am."[57] Jesus be-comes a good person, merely a model breaker, if anything of significance at all. As an extreme radical, Daly claims that there is no salvific efficacy of Jesus (or Christology) for women. Christology becomes synonymous with the destruction of (strong, independent) women. Consequently, salvation for women rests within the context of women's experience itself.

As a radical, Daly has more concisely and precisely focussed the problem of women on patriarchy. Patriarchy, the keepsake of man, is pervasive as a political, psychological and religious imprisonment for women. Of patriarchy, Daly says:

> Patriarchy is designed not only to possess women, but to prepossess/preoccupy us, that is, to inspire women with false selves which anesthetize the Self, breaking the process of be-ing on the wheel of processions. This condensing and freezing of be-ing into fragmented being is the necessary condition for maintaining the State of Possession.[58]

Because it is unrealistic to believe that men will abnegate their priviledged status in society–to give up possession–in order that women might be free, women must "take" control of their lives even if taking control means total separation. For Daly, this total separation–physical, psychological, spiritual–is necessary.

Men cannot define women. Women must "escape" the tyrannical definition of men; "unweave" the ghostly false images of themselves; "uncreate" the created fixtures of patriarchy; "expell" the patriarchal past and future; and "unpaint" themselves and polish their natural armor. Then women must be about the constructive task of "inspiriting" themselves to becoming their genuine selves. Put simply, women must uncreate; women must create.[59]

Here Daly impresses upon women theologians the critical and constructive tasks of theology and Christology. Not only must women destroy the fixation upon Jesus as the Christ, but women must construct/create out of women's experiences their models of liberation/ salvation.

The primary contribution of Daly is that she calls attention to the fact that aspects of reality cannot totally escape the general characteristics of reality as a whole. Jesus, as an entity of patriarchal religious traditions has not escaped the demonism of that reality. Daly challenges reformist Christians to examine the context within which they have chosen to function, for it may well be that the context as well as the content are enslaving for women. That is to say the religion of Christianity itself may be as enslaving as its patriarchal context. If Daly's analysis is taken seriously, one is forced to ask fundamental questions, such as, does it make sense for women to adhere to a religious tradition which enslaves women?

Because Daly is an exclusionary feminist most of her energies are spent addressing sexism, the oppression of women as the problem of theology. Racism becomes an issue only tangentially important because some who are black experience it. However just as Black women do not have lives of their own, racism does not have a life of its own; it is merely a subsidiary of sexism. Racism and slavery are described as patriarchal institutions as is marriage.[60] Daly makes the comparison based upon two slave incidents which she cites. The one story was told by Sarah Grimke. It is of the slave woman in South Carolina who bore scars upon her body from the horrors of slavery and a Bible reading mistress who seemed not to be disturbed. The other story told by Solomon Northup concerned a slave woman, Patsey, who suffered the rape of her inhumane and vicious master only to be harassed and ordered beaten by her jealous and likewise inhumane and vicious mistress.[61] Daly then proceeds to suggest that the victimization of the "bible reading mistress" and the "vicious mistress" and the victimization of the two tortured slave women have the same origin–patriarchal religion. "None of these institutions, she argues, "were invented by women or have ever been under the control of women."[62] Even if this were true, ownership of racism and slavery has been claimed by White women along with white men. The apparent equation of these two experiences slavery/racism and marriage–is only possible if racism is treated as a non-entity and not an independent reality which would exist with or without patriarchy. What about other forms of oppression? Recognizing them only as expressions of patriarchy, they become secondary to the real pervasive problem in the world which is sexism. Therefore Daly warns: "Women can easily fall (or be pushed) into forgetting that racial and ethnic oppression, like sexual oppression which is the primary and universal model of such victimization, is a male invention."[63]

Because Daly refuses to recognize that White women are racist, and subsumes racism under sexism, she proposes that Black women could participate in the Be-Friending process. Audre Lorde reveals further how Daly's racism makes her proposal unacceptable to Black women. The proposal that women return to goddess spirituality in *Gynecology* is a case in point. Daly, she charges, uses only European goddesses as her images. The combination of using only a negative example from the African experience[64] and the complete ignoring of Black/African goddesses causes Black radical feminists to question Daly's perspective. Lorde asks:

> . . . why doesn't Mary deal with Afrekete as an example? Why are her goddess images only white, western european, judeo-christian? Where was Afrekete, Yemanje, Oyo, and Mawulisa? Where were the warrior goddesses of the Vodun, the Dahomeian Amazons and the warrior–women of Dan?[65]

By ignoring these and other non-European goddesses Daly is essentially ignoring the heritage of non-White women. Having done this the proposal that non-White women can participate in Sisterhood/Be-Friending is to further ignore the experiences of non-White women. Lorde continues:

> To imply . . . that all women suffer the same oppression simply because we are women is to lose sight of the many varied tools of patriarchy. It is

to ignore how those tools are used by women without awareness against each other.[66]

If Daly's exclusionary approach to feminist thought precludes racism and classism as independent realities how are non-White women to participate in her *Be-Friending* system which I believe for Daly is the equivalent of redemption? I would suggest that in view of Daly's definition, Black women may be participants in the Be-Friending process as women but they are excluded as Blacks. Therefore, defined merely as a function of patriarchy it is impossible to grasp the true experiences of racism. Consequently, because Daly structures racism as a part of patriarchy (sexism) it is impossible to give Black and other third world women equal participation in her system. *Salvation* for Black women and other non-White women means giving up racial identity (or at least de-prioritizing it) in order to participate fully in the redemptive community–Sisterhood/Be-Friending. Be-Friending for Black women could mean only bifurcated existence–ignoring the real substance of racial existence while *spinning and sparking* with White women occasionally *re-membering* that racism is also a son of patriarchy.

NOTES

[1] Mary Daly, *The Church and the Second Sex* (New York: Harper and Row, Publishers, 1975).

[2] Simone de Beauvoir, *The Second Sex* (New York: Vintage Books, 1982).

[3] Daly, *The Church and the Second Sex*, p. 69.

[4] *Ibid.*, p. 72.

[5] *Ibid.*, p. 83.

[6] *Ibid.* For example: Jerome said, ". . . When the woman wishes to serve Christ more than the world, then she will cease to be a woman and will be called man vir." (p. 85; taken from PL 26, 567 comm. in epist. ed. Ephes, III 5). Tertullian said ". . . You are the devil's gateway. . ." (87; taken from PL I, 1418b-19a. De cultu feminarum, libri duo I,1.) Besides teaching that woman was the "misbegotten male,"

Thomas Aquinas felt that ". . . the father is principle (in natural order) in a more excellent way than the mother, because he is the active principle, while the mother is a passive and material principle."
(p. 91; *Summa Theologiae*, I, 92, I c).

7 Daly, *The Church and the Second Sex*, chapter 3, passim.

8 *Ibid.*, pp. 189-190.

9 *Ibid.*, p. 190.

10 *Ibid.*, p. 223.

11 After the publication of *The Church and the Second Sex*, Daly
found herself in middle of a fight for her job at Boston College, after
a long struggle she was re-instated with promotion and tenure (pp.
11-13).

12 Among them were "The Courage to See: Religious implications of The New Sisterhood," *The Christian Century* 88 (Sept. 22,
1971), pp. 1108-11. "The Spiritual Revolution: Women's Liberation as
Theological Re-education," *Andover Newton Quarterly* 12 (March
1972), pp. 163-176. "The Women's Movement: An Exodus Community," *Religious Education* 67 (Sept.-Oct. 1972), pp. 327-35.

13 Daly, *The Church and the Second Sex*, pp. 15-51.

14 Idem, *Beyond God the Father* (Boston: Beacon Press, 1973).

15 Idem, *The Church and the Second Sex*, p. 15.

16 *Ibid.*, p. 17.

17 Idem, *Beyond God the Father*, p. 9.

18 *Ibid.*, p. 10.

19 *Ibid.*, pp. 33-34.

20 *Ibid*. Note that Daly distinguishes what she is proposing from
similar concepts in modern philosophy through the work of White-
head, Hartshorne and others (pp. 36-37). Rather than adopting their
categories, she prefers to listen to women's experiences "to discover
the spiritual dynamics of this revolution and to speak these dynamics in our own lives and words" (p. 37).

21 *Ibid.*, pp. 28 and 29.

22 *Ibid.*, p. 47.

23 Daly, "The Courage to See," pp. 1108-9.

24 Idem, *Gynecology: The Metaethics of Radical Feminism*
(Boston: Beacon Press, 1978), pp. 369-70. Partially cited from J. Glenn
Gray, *The Warriors: Reflections on Men in Battle* (New York: Ran-
dom House, 1969), p. 90.

25 Daly, *Beyond God the Father*, p. 69.

[26] *Ibid.*

[27] *Ibid.,* p. 70.

[28] *Ibid.,* p. 71.

[29] As argued in the current debates surrounding the ordination of women, only the male can represent Jesus Christ. Cf. in *The Ordination of Women; Pro and Con,* and the Vatican statement of October 15, 1976. See earlier discussion in Chapter I.

[30] Daly, *Beyond God the Father,* p. 71.

[31] Idem, *Gynecology,* p. 187.

[32] Idem, *Beyond God the Father,* p. 69.

[33] Cf. Ruether's discussion of dualism in Chapter 4.

[34] Daly, *Beyond God the Father,* pp. 71-72.

[35] This is discussed in the article cited above, "The Courage to See."

[36] Daly, *Gynecology,* pp. 369-70.

[37] See discussion of Christology in relation to ordination in Chapter I.

[38] Daly, *Beyond God the Father,* p. 79.

[39] See footnote #24 for complete citation. This rejectionist stance is taken by other feminists as well who have left patriarchal religions. Representatives of this group include: Naomi Goldenberg, *Changing of the Gods: Feminism and the End of Traditional Religions* (Boston: Beacon Press, 1979); Carol Christ, ed., *Womanspirit Rising* (New York: Harper and Row, 1979) and *Diving Deep and Surfacing: Women Writers on Spiritual Quest* (Boston: Beacon Press, 1980); Charlene Spretnak, ed., *The Politics of Women's Spirituality: Essays on the Rise of Spiritual Power Within the Feminist Movement* (Garden City, New York: Anchor Books, 1982). For a critique of this school see Rosemary Ruether "A Religion for Women: Sources and Strategies," in *Christianity and Crisis* (December 10, 1979), pp. 307-311, and "Goddesses and Witches: Liberation and Countercultural Feminism," *The Christian Century* (September 10-17, 1980).

[40] Daly, *Gynecology,* p. xi.

[41] *Ibid.,* p. 94.

[42] *Ibid.,* Chapter 6, pissim.

[43] *Ibid.,* pp. 186-187. Cf. Heinrich Kramer and James Sprenger, *The Malleus Maleficarum,* trans. by Rev. Montague Summers (New York: Dover, 1971). Part I, Question 6, p. 47.

44 Daly, *Gynecology*, p. 182.

45 *Ibid.*, p. 183.

46 Mary Daly, *Pure Lust: Elemental Feminist Philosophy* (Boston: Beacon Press, 1984).

47 *Ibid.*, p. 102. Daly acknowledges that this may not have been the intended purposes of the doctrine, but argues that it functioned in that way.

48 *Ibid.*, pp. 103-104.

49 Daly uses "be-ing" in this hyphenated form to signify that this is intended not as a noun but as a verb, meaning participation in the Ultimate/Intimate Reality: Being, the Verb. (p. 2) " Elemental" has to do with simplicity, naturalness or unrestrained, fundamental; or first principle, or spirit. "Elemental women experience our Selves, and therefore, our philosophy, as rooted in love for the earth and for things that naturally are on earth." (p. 8).

50 *Ibid.*, p. 111.

51 *Ibid.*, p. 372.

52 *Ibid.*, p. 373.

53 This is a point she did not seem to fully recognize in the earlier discussion of sisterhood.

54 *Ibid.*, p. 374.

55 *Ibid.*, p. 386.

56 Others have also argued that not only should women's experience be the source of feminist theology but it is the only context in which wholeness can be achieved. See sources in footnote #39. Note especially chapter 8 in Christ, *Diving Deep and Surfacing*.

57 Daly, *Beyond God the Father*, p. 73.

58 Idem, *Gynecology*, p. 322.

59 *Ibid.*, The Third Passage, passim.

60 Daly, *Pure Lust*, p. 378.

61 *Ibid.*, pp. 376-377. Quoted from Gerda Lerner, ed., *Black Women in White America: A Documentary History* (New York: Random House, Vintage Books, 1972), pp. 18-19 and 50-51.

62 *Ibid.*, p. 378.

63 *Ibid.*, p. 381.

64 In *Gynecology*, Daly used non-European materials as negative examples. For example she discusses the African genital mutilation.

[65] Audre Lorde, *Sister Outsider: Essays and Speeches* (New York: The Crossing Press, 1984), p. 67.

[66] *Ibid*.

VI

AN ANALYSIS OF FEMINIST CHRISTOLOGY

The discussion in the preceding chapters elucidated the three categories of feminists doing theology and Christology. As the context for doing feminist Christology and as its primary source, women's experience in general and sexism in particular represent the point of departure for feminist theologizing. The Bible–the basic authoritative book of the church–as a source, generates both positive and negative responses. The authority placed in either or both of these sources accounts for the variations in the three perspectives:

(1) For Biblical feminists, the Bible is more authoritative than women's experience so the Bible critiques women's experience. Though the Bible is read in the light of women's experience, it (the Bible) holds primary authority.

(2) For Liberation feminists, two trends emerged. For the one, the Bible is read in light of women's experiences, however the Bible is primary therefore it critiques women's experience. For the other, the Bible is read out of women's experience, and women's experience critiques the Bible in the sense that it is possible to elevate the internal critique present in the Bible itself using women's experience as authoritative (normative).

(3) For Rejectionist feminists, women's experience critiques the Bible, therefore women's experience and not the Bible is solely authoritative. Because the Bible has been used primarily against women, it is used as a negative source by rejectionists.

We have seen that these perspectives have resulted in different Christological positions. Their commonalities and differences are reflected in their views on various themes. In this Chapter White Christian feminists will be engaged in dialogue on four christological themes. This dialogue focuses upon the different ways in which feminists resolve the Christological dilemma for women seeking liberation from oppression.

A. *On Redeeming Jesus*

Liberationists have argued that the problem of women is not Jesus but the historical distortions of who Jesus was and what he did for and with women. Therefore, Christological formulations based upon these historical distortions have been detrimental to women. However the extreme method/action of castration, used by rejectionists is not necessary to correct the problem. The strictly reformist view of liberationists would be to correct the historical distortions of the figure Jesus. However, as we have seen, there is a radical dimension represented by Ruether who proposed that Christology move beyond the figure of Jesus. Daly holds that this corrective task would be complicated and endless, if not in fact impossible. Additionally, it does not get at the basic question, what is wrong with the symbol itself? Those taking a more or less reformist position argue that nothing is wrong with the symbol, but much is wrong with the use of the symbol. That is to say Jesus did not oppress women but he has been used in such a fashion. This view is unacceptable from Daly's perspective. Consequently she pushes the basic question, "If the symbol can be 'used' that way and in fact has a long history of being 'used' that way, isn't this an indication of some inherent deficiency in the symbol itself?[1] Implied in this question is the belief that embedded deep within the nature of Jesus (the male) and the context (Christianity) which produced this figure, is the essential problem. Castrating Christianity, therefore, involves cutting away the fixation upon the male Jesus.

Daly's answer to Ruether's question, "Can a male savior help women"?[2] would be an emphatic, "NO." The only thing a male savior can do is what the male savior, Jesus, has done, and that is to legitimize the oppression of women through the perpetuation of the "myth of sin and salvation." This male savior is not capable of helping women. Women must look for the New Being. The bearer of the New Being is not one male in a patriarchal society, but there are heavens of this New Being. These bearers of the New Being are women. They are "those who live precariously on the boundary of patriarchal space–the primordial aliens."[3] Women must look to themselves and to their own experiences for the New Being which will be capable of correcting the mistakes of the "old inadequate male Being."[4]

Jesus does represent a positive notion from Daly's perspective. Jesus did not project himself as the ultimate power requiring strict imitation. But Jesus did advance the ideas of freedom and participation in the power of being and engaged others to incorporate these ideas in their lives. In this sense, Jesus was no different from any other "liberated person," a "model breaker" if any thing of note. He, as other liberated persons have done, pointed beyond himself "to the potential for full liberation."[5]

In light of this reality Daly's analysis of the problem and her proposal for the solution are very significant. If one is to accept the proposition that the problem is endemic to Christianity, then it becomes rather difficult to take a stance other than a rejectionist one if one is seriously committed to eliminating the problem of women's oppression. Yet the question remains, "Is it necessary to throw out the baby with the bath"? In other words, "Is patriarchalism endemic to Christianity"? Is it necessary to throw out Christianity with patriarchalism? Can Jesus be separated from the historic oppressive interpretations?

Daly sees no redemptive quality in Jesus as far as women are concerned. She proposes instead that women must look not to past patriarchal history, but rather to women's experiences–Be-Friending. Jewish feminist thinker, Naomi Goldenberg, is in line with Daly as she argues that "Jesus Christ cannot symbolize the liberation of women. A culture that maintains a masculine image for its highest divinity cannot allow its women to experience themselves as the equals of its men."[6] Women need neither Jesus, nor history to legitimize their experience. "Women have the option of giving priority to what we find valid in our own experience without needing to look to the past for justification.[7] It appears that women's experience becomes the norm and the content. For this reason, most women reject Daly's rejectionist stance. Nevertheless, Daly's point is well made. Since women's experience has been negated, the primary task of feminist scholars is one of affirmation of women. Affirming women necessarily implies negating previous patriarchal views of women. The significance of Daly lies in the fact that she shakes the foundation upon which patriarchalism is based. In shaking that foundation, she proposes other structures which take their content totally from women's experience.

In light of this discussion two questions are critical: Can women redeem Jesus? and can Jesus redeem women?[8]

In an article entitled "The Feminist Redemption of Christ," Rita N. Brock appears to be addressing both questions simultaneously. Regarding the redemption of Christ by women, Brock says:

> If Christology is to be reclaimed in feminist visions, the image of an exclusive divine presence in a "perfect" man called Jesus who came to be called the Christ is disallowed. The doctrine that only a perfect male form can incarnate God fully and be salvific makes our individual lives in female bodies a prison against God and denies our actual, sensual, changing selves as the lover of divine activity.[9]

For Brock redeeming Jesus means putting him into proper historical and especially theological perspective. Redeeming Jesus means decentralizing Jesus in Christian community. At the same time, it means centralizing women's experiences. In so doing, the damage perpetrated against

women must be repaired, the brokenness created among
women must be overcome and the wounds inflicted upon them
must be healed. However, in spite of what mainstream
Christian theology teaches, the required "healed wholeness
is not Christ," but "it is ourselves" (women).[10] In the process
of redeeming women, the empowerment which emerges out of
community in general and relationship(s) in particular causes
a relocation of women's experience to the center of feminist
Christian faith.

> Removing the exclusive, perfect god-man Jesus
> Christ from the center of our Christian
> commitment allows us to claim ourselves and,
> then, to reclaim the historical Jesus and Jesus
> Christ.[11]

Theologically, however, this is not the same Jesus Christ as
given in mainstream orthodox Christology. For this Jesus of
Brock's thought is merely "a remarkable man for his time."
Therefore we must "dedivinize" him in order that we may
"appreciate" his remarkability with his humanity or
theology being the measuring rod for our existence."[12] With
such emphasis upon challenging the divinity of Jesus, Brock
then falls somewhere between the rejectionist and liberationist perspectives.[13]

Whereas rejectionist feminists respond no to both
questions—can women redeem Jesus and can Jesus redeem
women?—biblical feminists and liberation feminists answer
yes on both accounts and as seen with Brock, some feminists
would respond yes and no.[14] However, with reference to the
liberation perspective, characteristically, whereas
proponents of the one side of the liberation perspective say
yes women can redeem Jesus and only Jesus (the Lord) can
redeem women, the proponents of the other side say that
women can redeem Jesus, but Jesus as we have understood him
is not the only redeemer of women. In other words, Jesus is not
uniquely the Christ.

182   White Women's Christ and Black Women's Jesus

B. *Jesus the Feminist: Reconsidered*

Biblical feminists have vested considerable energies in providing evidences for the feminist orientation of Jesus. In effect, they have said that women must redeem Jesus from historical distortions. The evidences unearthed by these feminists have given hope to many women, who previously were disillusioned with the apparent hopelessness of Christianity in general and Christology in particular, in terms of their salvific efficacy for women. Even before the on-slaught of biblical feminist liberation some women had already begun to re-interpret Jesus' relationship with women. Rachel Wahlberg, for example, was encouraged by the article "Jesus Was a Feminist," and the work of other women in religion. Her work had already begun under the title "Jesus Was a Woman's Liberationist."[15] In her book of nine sermons which resulted, Wahlberg offers feminist interpretations of passages in which Jesus is relating to women. She obviously sees Jesus as a feminist and verifies it through her reading of the gospels through feminist spectacles.

This reading through feminist spectacles reveals a non-conformist Jesus who preaches mutuality in relationship rather than domination and submission and who is comfortable imaging God in both feminine and masculine ways. However, Jesus does not stop there, he openly violated sexist/patriarchal custom regarding the treatment of women.[16]

Some women, however, have challenged the notion that Jesus was a feminist. Daly does not debate the issue. She argues instead that the question, of whether or not Jesus was a feminist, is irrelevant and immaterial. This sudden discovery does not erase the centuries of using the figure of Jesus as a tool for the oppression of women. Even the scrutinous tools of scientific biblical criticism have not been able to unearth this feminist orientation of Jesus before now. Judith Ochshorn, a Jewish feminist, however chooses to argue the point. According to her, if Jesus were a feminist, he would not only have defended Mary's right to sit at his feet in intellectual pursuit, but he would have advocated the right of all women to share in intellectual and spiritual pursuits and in domestic duties. Ochshorn writes: "The notion of 'service' exemplified in the life of Jesus is nowhere extended by him in admonitions to his male followers to share more fully in the material labor of cooking, spinning, and child care so that women might share more fully in the life of the spirit."[17] That is, if women are encouraged to cultivate the intellectual and spiritual, men should be encouraged also to cultivate the domestic areas of life. Jesus did set a personal example as he related to individual women in particular situations. However, He did not actively or directly teach the equality of women. In other words "He does not insist that every one else must act in a like manner in order to follow him."[18]

To further explicate her point, she examines the significance of the life of the Spirit. Jesus spoke often of the spiritual world (John 6:63, Luke 12:15, Luke 12:22-24, Luke 12:32-34), and de-emphasized the material world (Matthew 19:29, Mark 10:29-30, Luke 9:61-62, Luke 14:26, John 6:41).

> And this emphasis on the *spiritual*, affects women as a group more than men, because they are the ones who literally baked the bread and bore the children; very young children require material as well as spiritual nourishment and care; and nursing an infant and disposing of its bodily wastes are very *material* work.[19]

In other words, because of the pre-delegated responsibilities of women, they were unable to be spiritual. If Jesus were really a feminist he would have addressed directly this glaring contradiction. Ochshorn hastens to add, however, that, based on his personal relationship with women, Jesus also was not a misogynist. The simple fact is that he was concerned about other things, primarily matters of the spirit.

> Indeed, it is not that Jesus viewed women with ambivalence, but his emphasis on the superior value of the spiritual may have placed women more than men in an ambivalent relationship to the divine.[20]

Ochshorn, in spite of her radical tendencies, seems to have accepted conservative interpretations of the life and work of Jesus. Perhaps the only way she could offset the use of Jesus as a political tool of oppression is to spiritualize him, thus removing him from the realm of political realities. Some other Jewish feminists, rather than dichotomizing Jesus' interests, have simply challenged in its entirety the "Jesus was a feminist" *myth* [italics mine] of Christian feminists. They view this line of argument as an anti-Judaic movement. Judith Plaskow challenges these Christian feminists on three grounds: (1) In using the Talmud, they mistakenly use materials which may be sixth century materials rather than those which were contemporary with Jesus; (2) They deceptively speak of all rabbinic opinions and customs as monolithic; and (3) They mistakenly compare the words and attitude of an itinerant preacher with the thoughts of Rabbis in academics. For these reasons, the Christian feminists are at best anti-semitic and at worst "sloppy scholars."[21]

Notwithstanding the criticism, the discovery that Jesus was a feminist or at least had feminist leanings is a significant one.[22] If we argue that the context of biblical recording and exegesis was patriarchal, then why is it difficult to understand that the figure Jesus is distorted in the interest of those structures? Given this distortion, the critical agenda item for women should be its elimination through re-interpretation of biblical texts. Most women would hold that it is not necessary to throw out the baby with the bath as Daly seems to suggest. Likewise, it is not necessary to settle for overspiritualized interpretations of Jesus, as Ochshorn appears to do in explaining Jesus' actions (or non-actions) with respect to women.

In rejecting both the elimination of Jesus and the overspiritualization of Jesus, one must nonetheless take seriously some explicit and implicit questions. If Jesus was more than human–that is, also divine, why did he not miraculously or directly overthrow the evil powers which keep women in oppression? It is true that feminists do have much explaining to do when it comes to the feminism of Jesus. Pains must be taken to explain the context of patriarachy and the departure of Jesus from normal patriarchal actions, therefore noting the significance of his actions. In light of this, one must still ask, Why did Jesus have to play patriarchal games? Why did he not directly attack the status quo rather than merely breaking a few norms here and there? If Jesus is divine incarnation, then why were his divine powers subsumed by human principalities and powers These questions beg the ultimate question, Was Jesus really divine?

C. *Jesus as Human or Divine*

If Jesus is human, how is he human? At the Council of Chalcedon, the church fathers set about the task of deciding how Jesus was God, and they determined that Jesus was simultaneously God and Human, perfect God and perfect human. Affirming the tradition set forth at Nicea it was believed that Jesus was human, sin only excepting. As already indicated this dual affirmation was necessary in order to avoid the pit-falls of the various heresies of the fourth and fifth centuries. Though it is clear that the church fathers intended that Chalcedon would clarify matters regarding who Jesus was/is, it was not always clear how Jesus lived up to their expectations. How was it possible that the Almighty God could be incarnate in a mere *male-man*?[23] Was Jesus merely a man of Nazareth? Or was it that the incarnation was made manifest in a broader *hu-man* who happened to be male but representing all humanity.

In attempting to explain the special or exceptional character of Jesus as human some scholars, as Swidler, have portrayed the human nature of Jesus as androgynous. Jesus was characterized by both masculine and feminine traits. As the more radical statement that Jesus was a feminist, invoked many critical responses, so did his view of androgyny.

For example, Ruether challenges the notion of femininity. Implied in her critique is the suggestion that femininity distorts and limits the female reality. The complementarity model of male/female relationship embraces this notion of femininity which goes hand in hand with masculinity. Femininity and masculinity in fact are thought to be creations of male ideology. Not only is femininity oppressive of women as already argued but masculinity is oppressive of men, as each is oppressive of the other, because they are locked into narrow spheres of existence. Just as the application of these terms to women and men is delimiting to them, these terms are also delimiting when applied to Jesus Christ. Bringing them together in the person of an androgynous Jesus is like gluing together two separate and oppressive realities.

> The very concept of Androgyny presupposes a psychic dualism that identifies maleness with one half of human capacities and female-ness with the other. As long as Christ is still presumed to be, normatively, a male person, androgynous Christologies will carry an andro-centric bias. Men gain their "feminine" side, but women contribute to the whole by specializing in the representation of the "feminine," which means exclusion from the exercise of the roles of power and leadership associated with masculinity.[24]

Consequently, an androgynous Jesus is not an adequate liberation model for women. At best women could only hope to identify their feminine psychological traits in the person Jesus.

Perhaps as Mary Daly says, the best that can be said of such a human being is that he is a model breaker. As a model-breaker, Jesus enables us to break our idolatrous relationships not only with him, but with other Christian symbols as well. Some Liberationists such as Ruether, have moved beyond others like Russell, by suggesting that Jesus can be considered as sister. Paralleling the Jesus–the sister concept, is Jesus–the brother. In arguing the latter, Carter Heyward rejects the proclamation of Jesus as Lord.

> . . . I do not find it helpful to think of Jesus as Lord. I may call him "Christ", but it is not because he was divine, different from us, in any superhuman or supernatural way, but rather because he was exactly human, like us.[25]

Ruether stops short of saying that Jesus Christ is only human. What she does suggest is that the redemptive process did not stop with the historical figure Jesus. Heyward seems to say, however, that Jesus as brother was only human. The lauding of Jesus is simply misplaced praise. She explains:

> Jesus is to be remembered, not revered. Remembering Jesus does not warrant Jesusolatry or Christolatry, the idolatry of a male God. Remembering Jesus does not warrant the worshipping of Jesus, but rather must compel us to look prayerfully to the God of Jesus. The one whom Jesus called "Abba": Daddy. Moreover, to remember Jesus does not mean that we "imitate" Jesus, but rather that, like him, we seek to act with God in our own time, under the political, social, psychological, physical, and institutional conditions of our own place. Jesus' "Daddy" may be our Mama, or "sister," or "friend," or "lover," or simply the "Holy Spirit," which Christians have always believed is the active power of God in our own time.[26]

Feminists have viewed the humanity of Jesus in different ways. They range from the reformist view of meaning the embodiment of femininity and masculinity of Jesus to the view that Jesus is (as) brother/sister. Do these character-istics totally encompass the reality of Jesus? or was he more? This brings us to the other major consideration which is already implied above, "Is Jesus divine and how is he divine?"

Without a doubt biblical feminist and right-sided liberationists affirm the two natures of Jesus Christ. Jesus is human and also divine. Mollenkott and Russell both hold to the Lordship of Christ. At least Christ uniquely functions as Lord in their lives. Christ is that unique person who in his lordship, represented the real and ultimate meaning of servanthood. Even more, Jesus was that "once-for-all" Christ whose "raison d' etre" was salvation for us.

On the left-side of the liberationist camp, Ruether takes exception to this "once-for-all" view of the historical Jesus as the Christ. But the Christ event actually continues and may appear in the form of other human beings. "As vine and branches Christic personhood continues in our sisters and brothers."[27] The divinity which Jesus experienced then was not peculiar to him. This is contrary to the traditional exclusionary views regarding Jesus as reflected in Chapter II. Ruether, and feminists to the left of her, challenge either the notion of the exclusivity of the divinity in Jesus or the no-tion of any divinity in Jesus at all. In some of the sermons in *Jesus, According to A Woman*, Wahlberg really emphasizes the humanness of Jesus. In his relationship with Mary and Martha, He acts in a particularly human way. Wahlberg does not explicitly say that Jesus is not divine, but she certainly de-emphasizes the divine and stresses the human in this particular sermon.[28] Other, more radical, feminists have not hesitated even to reject the notion that Jesus is divine. For example, as indicated earlier Carter Heyward suggests that Jesus is brother rather than Lord. In her book, *The Redemption of God*, she reiterates this purely human understanding of Jesus. She says first of all, that "The God of whom I speak, . . . is in flesh (Sarx), alive in human beings, active in human life, on earth, in history."[29] Recognizing the traditional tendency of Christians to believe that God became human in Jesus, yet down playing the human role, Heyward proposes something radically different. She says:

> The centrality of Jesus' place in Christianity has resulted from a mis-conception of Jesus as a divine person rather than as a human being who knew and loved God.[30]

This mis-conception affirmed by classical Christology and held to by most Christians has distorted our image of Jesus. What is required is a re-imaging of Jesus. Heyward provides such re-imaging of Jesus by re-interpreting many passages, which have heretofore elevated Jesus' divine powers, to reflect the mutual power of him and those surrounding him. Her focus is on the participatory nature of existence. As Jesus acted in this time, so do we act in our own existential situation. Heyward takes liberties with Scripture and tradition in order to get to her fundamental interest–that is, "to comprehend our own existence."[31]

In her attempts at "de-idolatrizing Jesus and de-centralizing salvation," Heyward interprets some of the so-called miracles of Jesus as the community (or individual) participating in its own healing through the inner capacities of faith, rather than faith in Jesus. For example, the woman with the flow of blood is not healed by Jesus; rather "her faith heals her."[32] Jesus then is not the exclusive miracle worker, but if women allow themselves to claim the divine within, they have the capacity to effect some such miracles as healing.

On the question of the two natures of Jesus Christ, whereas for some feminists Jesus is divine in the traditional sense of being God, but a God/Divine reality which does not oppress women, for others Jesus' divinity is one point in a continuum.

All of the feminist theologians use as their source women's experience, which is also the context in which the Bible as a source is interpreted. In so doing biblical feminists have been led to see Jesus as a feminist on the side of women— affirming the personhood/womanhood of women. They see Jesus and consequently God as having the manifestations of both masculine and feminine traits thus reaffirming women as being as important as men. Because there is no inequality in the Deity which is masculine and feminine, there is also no inequality in human beings who are masculine and feminine. Consequently the experience of women as a part of the divine reality is affirmed. Because the feminine and masculine are in partnership in the divine, the feminine and the masculine should be in partnership in humanity.

Biblical feminists have developed a single analysis perspective which does not do justice to other forms of oppression. They do occasionally mention racism as an alienating force in the world. However, what is proposed by biblical feminists is not entirely helpful for Black women. For example, a careful examination of Black women's experience reveals that because they are triply oppressed an adrogynous model for reality may not be adequate. Black women's role in the society has been neither feminine nor masculine. That is to say, in the same way that Black men were denied masculinity, Black women were robbed of femininity. Conditions made the question of Jesus' androgynous or even his male existence irrelevant. However, the critical questions are, was Jesus just, and did he intend for Black people to be slaves and servants of White people? Another question is a variation of William Jones' question, is Jesus a White racist?[33] At various historical moments a few Black women have asked was Jesus a White racist and a male sexist?[34] Consequently, Black women's attempt at redeeming Jesus from racist, sexist, classist America has its origins in slavery as they claimed and proclaimed Jesus as redeemer.

Liberation feminists have taken seriously the interstructuring of racism, sexism and classism. However, interstructuring of these forms of oppression does not dismiss the reality of conflict. Though there are points of commonality between all forms of oppression there are points of tensions.

The quest for partnership as advanced by both biblical and liberation feminists does not address the fact that partnerships are neither necessarily equal nor necessarily healthy. As already seen in some feminists critique of androgyny, partnership between traditional masculine and feminine roles does not bring about equality–it is simply complementarity. Partnership implies "vested interests" but the interests are not always equal.[35] Partnership as discussed by biblical feminists refers primarily to the relationship between women and men. For liberationists the vision of partnership is cross-sexual and cross-racial. That is, it is a bond which connected all parts of humanity.

It would seem to me that the language of partnership lends itself easily to White women who, for the most part, have been a part of the oppressing class and additionally who are victimized primarily by one form of oppression.[36] Since White women and men share the same racial identity, Black women perceive White women as being more oppressors than victims. From a Black woman's vantage point then, the language of partnership is merely a rewording of the language of "reconciliation,"[37] which proves to be empty rhetoric unless it is preceded by liberation.

Partnership/reconciliation implies three things: (1) a basis for bonding, (2) a relationship of trust, and (3) more commonalities than differences. Given the absence of any of the three, perhaps the best that one can hope for would be coalition. Coalition is temporary alliance for some specific purpose.[38]

The reasons for these reservations about feminist language will become clear in the next chapter as I articulate the differences between the experiences of Black women and White women which will provide some insight into the christological beliefs of Black women and how they differ from biblical, liberationist and rejectionist feminists.

NOTES

[1] Daly, *Beyond God the Father*, p. 72.

[2] See discussion in Chapter IV.

[3] Daly, *Beyond God the Father*, p. 72

[4] As we have seen by the time of Daly's fourth book, *Pure Lust*, she was referring to this community as Be-Friending community/process.

[5] *Ibid.*, p. 75.

[6] Naomi Goldenberg, *The Changing of the Gods*, p. 4.

[7] Daly, *Beyond God the Father*, p. 74.

[8] With respect to the first question "can women redeem Jesus?" what is meant here is: can women save Jesus from the historical and theological distortions which have enabled many to use Jesus and Christology to oppress women?

[9] Rita Brock "The Feminist Redemption of Christ," in Judith Weidman *Christian Feminism: Visions of a New Humanity* (New York: Harper and Row, 1984), p. 68.

[10] *Ibid.*, p. 69.

[11] *Ibid.*

[12] *Ibid.*, p. 68. In Chapter VII, I make just the opposite argument that the divinity of Christ allows us to appreciate the humanity of Jesus rather than the maleness, for God cannot be exhausted in male-ness. In other words, when the divinity encounters the individual, true humanity bursts forth.

[13] Brock (a woman of Asian and Latin descent) falls somewhere between Ruether and Daly's perspective. She agrees with Daly that Jesus Christ has been an idol in Christian thought. "The idolatry of Jesus Christ must cease to hold us and oppress all who do not pledge allegiance to the heart of the idolatry." Ruether argues that Jesus is not uniquely or exclusively the Christ. Christ (the Christic personhood in our sisters and brothers) remains at the center of the Christian community. For Brock it appears that the event is (in women's experience) in relationships. The significant difference between Brock and Daly is that Brock retains the "Christic" language, though locating the Christ event in women's experience. Daly, however, drops the Christic language.

[14] Interestingly, though Brock responds yes to both questions, they are both a qualified yes. Women can redeem Jesus, however

this Jesus becomes not the unique, exclusive Christ but a "reasonable man." By the same token Jesus can redeem women, but not as an all inclusive, once-for-all-saviour, but as a healer of the patriarchal wounds and sufferings of women. However it is critical to note that Jesus is not the only healer for "healing can have an authority outside the realm of Jesus' powers." Even the Bible records others as healers–Mark 9:38ff, Luke 9:1ff, Acts 3:1ff–having been empowered by/through Jesus Christ. Others such as in Luke 9:49-50 are a part of God's salvific work. Because she sees Christ "in an image of shared power" then, healing may come even from shared relationships.

[15] "Jesus was a Woman's Liberationist" was an earlier unpublished version of the small book, *Jesus According to a Woman*.

[16] See discussion in Chapter III.

[17] Judith Ochshorn, *The Female Experience and the Nature of the Divine* (Bloomington, Indiana: Indiana University Press, 1981), p. 169.

[18] *Ibid.*, p. 170.

[19] *Ibid.*, p. 171.

[20] *Ibid.*, p. 173.

[21] Judith Plaskow, "Blaming the Jesus for the Birth of Patriarchy," passim.

[22] Plaskow offers little evidence that the basic argument which biblical feminists employ is erroneous. Her major objection seems to be that the tendency to present Jesus as an exceptional Jew implies a categorical condemnation of all Jews who do not accept Jesus as Messiah. Her contention is that this undergirds anti-semitism.

[23] See discussion on the scandal of particularity in Chapter IV.

[24] Ruether, *Sexism and God-Talk*, p. 130.

[25] Carter Heyward, "Jesus Lord and Brother," unpublished sermon, p. 8.

[26] *Ibid.*, p. 9.

[27] Ruether, *Sexism and God-Talk*, p. 138.

[28] Wahlberg, "Jesus and the Critical Sisters," *Jesus*, pp. 75-88. See also "Jesus and the Uppity Woman," pp. 9-14.

[29] Carter Heyward, *The Redemption of God: A Theology of Mutual Relation* (Washington, D.C.: University Press of America, 1982), p. 32.

[30] *Ibid.* Heyward actually progresses to a relational Christology in which redemption is found in (human) relationships. Total responsibility for what happens in relationships rests with human beings. Thus, Heyward joins Tom Driver in a paradigm shift from the fixed, exclusive Christ who stands at the center of history to an inclusive Christ which resides within humanity. See Heyward, *The Redemption of God* and Tom Driver, *Christ in a Changing World* (New York: Crossroad, 1981). For a discussion of these two perspectives see Susan Brooks Thistlethwaite, *Metaphors for the Contemporary Church* (New York: The Pilgrim Press, 1983), chapter 3.

[31] *Ibid.*, p. 30.

[32] *bid*, p. 46. See earlier discussion of Rita Brock's perspective. For her the christological impact of Jesus is to be the healer; but he is not the only healer and not the only Christ. I would characterize Brock as a liberationist moving toward radical.

[33] William Jones, *Is God a White Racist?* (Garden City, New York: Anchor Press/Doubleday, 1973).

[34] This question will be explored in Chapter VII as we will see it emerge in Black women's struggle for recognition (and ordination) in the Black church.

[35] See Webster's New Twentieth Century Dictionary Unabridged, second edition.

[36] Ruether, *New Woman*, passim.

[37] Reconciliation is a favorite topic of oppressors which has the effect of reducing the emphasis on liberation. See James Cone, *Black Theology and Black Power* and *A Black Theology Liberation*.

[38] Webster's New Twentieth Century Dictionary.

VII

WOMEN'S EXPERIENCE REVISITED: THE CHALLENGE OF THE DARKER SISTER

Although feminist theology has made an important critique of the sexist limitations of the dominant theologies of Europe and North America, it is not without serious limitations, especially when evaluated in the light of Black women's experience. What are these limitations and how serious are they, especially as they are related to Christology? In this chapter, I will discuss these limitations and, in my concluding remarks, point the way towards a theology that is grounded in Black women's experiences.

A. *Limitations of Feminist Theology*

Feminist theology is inadequate for two reasons: it is *White* and *racist*.

1. *Feminist Theology as White Theology*

Feminist theologians are white in terms of their race and in terms of the *nature of the sources* they use for the development of their theological perspectives. Although there are sharp differences among feminist theologians, as we have seen, they are *all* of the *same* race and the influence of their race has led them to similar sources for the definition of their perspectives on the faith. Of course, chief among the sources is women's experience. However, what is often unmentioned is that feminist theologians' sources for women's experience refer almost exclusively to White women's experience. White women's experience and Black women's experience are not the same. Indeed all experiences are unique to some degree. But in this case the difference is so radical that it may be said that White women and Black women are in completely different realms. Slavery and segregation have created such a gulf between these women, that White feminists' common assumption that all women are in the same situation with respect to sexism is difficult to understand when history so clearly tells us a different story.

a. *Black Women's Experience Compared to White Women's Experience During Slavery*

The first two and a half centuries of Black presence in the United States was characterized by servitude and slavery.[1] African men, women and children were ruled by their captors, and even owned as property, subject to be sold at the owner's will. Slavery in the United States has been described as one of the most abominable systems in history.[2]

Because Black women were not considered the sisters of White women during slavery, they were not exempt from the tyranny of this system. In fact when we read narratives of slaves and ex-slaves, current "sisterhood" rhetoric appears simply as one of two possibilities: (1) a crude joke, or (2) the conciliatory rhetoric of an advantaged class and race. The life and times of Black women gives evidence of the fact that Black women and White women lived in two very different worlds. The biographies, autobiographies, and narratives reveal many of the stories of how Black women (and men) withstood the physical and psychological violence of slave existence.[3] They also reveal how Black women experienced White women. White women in slave and ex-slave narratives are always identified as members of the oppressor race. The terms "misus" and "mistress" implied for White women a status which Black women did not have.

Black women, as a part of the servicing class, were not awarded the protection of White patriarchy. Apparently from the point of view of the mistresses, Black women's purpose in life was to serve their domestic needs.[4] No special and very little different treatment was accorded slave women because they were women. The Victorian concept of ladyhood was not applied to slave women. They were treated like slave men as a lower species of animals.

Brutality was administered not only by masters and foremen but also by mistresses, reflecting the fact that White women were just as much participants in this system of slavery as were White men. For every Angelina and Sarah Grimke there were numerous of those like their mother who not only condoned slavery but thought that abolitionists like Angelina and Sarah were agitators, if not in fact heretics.

b. *Black Women's Experience Compared to White Women's Experience After Slavery*

The abolition of slavery left intact the basic relationship between Black women and White women in particular and Black people and White people in general. For many Black people, emancipation meant slavery without chains.

The end of slavery as a formal, legal institution brought neither change in the image of, nor significant change in the condition of Black people in the United States. The image that Blacks were inferior and that they were intended to service white America remained intact. Consequently, when freed Blacks, sought work they were relegated in the labor market to the same service jobs and menial work which had been forced upon them during slavery. For Black men this meant plantation/ farm work, factory work, other menial jobs and often unemployment.[5] For many Black women this meant doing the same work as Black men as well as employment as domestic servants. Black women made up a significant percentage of domestic service workers.[6]

In David Katzman's description, domestic service in the South was a caste system, and domestic labor a part of the larger racial-caste structure which reproduced the social relations of slavery. Blacks were servants and Whites were masters and never were the two to be changed. The domination/subordination relationship within the house hold mirrored the White/Black relationship in general and especially in the South.[7]

In this privatized world of the family the continuation of many of the oppressive practices of slavery can be detected. Though legal slavery was abolished, the relations of Blacks and Whites characteristic of slavery, remained for decades thereafter. Three dimensions of this situation are important for our topic: 1) Physical brutality toward Blacks was continued, and even extended to violence outside of the work context. 2) The immediate relationship between White women and Black women did not change; White women were still oppressors and Black women were still the oppressed. 3) As a part of this continued relationship, Black women were still treated as property. These dynamics between White and Black women represent some of the negative dimensions of Black women's experience.

What is apparent in this historical context is how Black women's experience involves a convergence of racism, sexism, and classism. Within the limited arena of domestic labor, the sexist assumption that women's place is (only) in the home is reconfirmed, as well as the classist practice of paying those who do "menial" jobs little or nothing, and the assumption that such work is more appropriately done by those of the servant class. These patterns are compounded by the racist assumption that White women need protection from actual work and therefore should function in a supervisory capacity.[8] Consequently, as Hooks observes,

> many Black women experienced white women as the white supremacist group who most directly exercised power over them, often in a manner far more brutal and dehumanizing than that of racist White men. (Even) today, despite predominant rule by White supremacist patriarchs, Black women often work in a situation where the immediate supervisor, boss, or authority figure is a White woman.[9]

Thus when theologians speak about women's experience as the source for doing feminist theology, it is necessary to specify which women's experience is being referred to, for the above discussion demonstrates that the experiences of White women and Black women have been far from the same.

2. *Feminist Theology as Racist*

It would be inaccurate to assert that because feminist theology is White, it is also racist. To be White does not necessarily mean to be racist, though the behavior of Whites makes the distinction difficult. Nevertheless, my claim that feminist theology is racist is best supported by a definition of racism.

Racism, according to Joel Kovel ". . . is the tendency of a society to degrade and do violence to people on the basis of race, and by whatever mediations may exist for this purpose."[10] These mediations are manifested in different forms, and are carried on through various media: the psychology, sociology, history, economics and symbolism of the dominant (White) group. Racism is the domination of a people which is justified by the dominant group on the basis of racial distinctions. It is not only individual acts but a collective, institutionalized activity. As C. Eric Lincoln observed,

> [f]or racism to flourish with the vigor it enjoys in America, there must be an extensive climate of acceptance and participation by large numbers of people who constitute its power base. It is the consensus of private persons that gives racism its derivative power. . . . The power of racism is the power conceded by those respectable citizens who by their actions or inaction communicate the consensus which directs and empowers the overt bigot to act on their behalf.[11]

Even if some individual feminists are not racists, the movement has been so structured, and therefore takes on a racist character. In a racist society, the oppressor assumes the power of definition and control while the oppressed is objectified and perceived as a thing.[12] As such, White women have defined the movement and presumed to do so not only for themselves but also for non-White women. They have misnamed themselves by calling themselves feminists when in fact they are White feminists, and by appealing to women's experience when in fact they appeal almost exclusively to their own experience. To misname themselves as "feminists" who appeal to "women's experience" is to do what oppressors always do; it is to define the rules and then solicit others to play the game. It is to presume a commonality with oppressed women that oppressed women themselves do not share. If White women's analysis were adequate, they would be more precise in naming their own movement and would not presume to name or define the experiences of others. They have simply accepted and participated in the racism of the larger American society when they have done so. This partially accounts for the negative response which Black women have had with respect to feminism.

Brenda Eichelberger identifies five categories of reasons that lead to Black women's rejection of White feminism.

1) Class differences mean that while Black women are dealing with "survival" issues, White women are dealing with "fulfillment" issues. 2) Negative imagery of Black women derived from physical and cultural stereotypes has resulted in the debased treatment of Black women. 3) The naivete, or basic lack of knowledge of Black women about the women's movement results in their inability to see the relationship between feminist issues and the Black struggle. 4) Black women perceive White feminists to be racists who are interested in them only in order to accomplish the White women's agenda. 5) There is a concern that an alliance of Black women with White women in a feminist agenda may be "detrimental to black men" and therefore divisive of the Black community.[13]

The hostility towards the feminist movement elaborated by some critics focuses on its implications for family life.

Many view feminism as a direct threat to Black family life. Sociologist Iva Carruthers refers to feminism as "one of the most serious assaults on African familyhood.[14] This feminist movement, she maintains, is a "White-family affair" and is therefore totally irrelevant "to the real needs of Black women."[15] Deborah Hines distinguishes between Black women's reality and White women's reality.

> Black women find it extremely difficult to ally themselves with those who say, "We have all suffered the same," when we know it isn't so. . . . We are being told that apples and oranges are the same, when we can see that they are not. You cannot easily substitute one for the other in a recipe. Their odors are different. They appeal to people differently. Even a blind person can tell them apart. Yet, a steady stream of rhetoric is aimed at convincing Black women how much alike their lives, experiences, wishes and decisions are to those of our stepsisters.[16]

To say that many Black women are suspicious of the feminist movement, then, is to speak mildly about their responses to it. Put succinctly, women of the dominant culture are perceived as the enemy. Like their social, sexual and political White male partners, they have as their primary goal the suppression, if not oppression, of the Black race and the advancement of the dominant culture. Because of this perception, many believe that Black feminism is a contradiction in terms.

B. *Towards A New Black Women's Consciousness*

In spite of the negative responses of Black women to the White women's liberation movement described, there has been a growing feminist consciousness among them, coupled with the increased willingness to do an independent analysis of sexism. This is creating an emerging Black perspective on feminism. Black feminism grows out of Black women's tri-dimensional reality of race/sex/class. It holds that full human liberation cannot be achieved simply by the elimination of any one form of oppression. Consequently, real liberation must be "broad in the concrete;"[17] it must be based upon a multi-dimensional analysis. Recent writings by secular Black feminists have challenged White feminist analysis and Black race analysis, particularly by introducing data from Black women's experience that has been historically ignored by White feminists and Black male liberationists.

A review of a selected group of literature follows: The first of these publications, *The Black Woman* (1970), an anthology collected by Toni Cade[18] was representative of a variety of disciplines and perspectives. It broke the silence of Black women, declaring that they have a voice that must be heard apart from Black men and White women. Later Ntozake Shange published *For Colored Girls Only Who Have Considered Suicide When the Rainbow is Enuf* (1975)[19], following controversial responses to its production on Broadway. In this choreopoem, Shange exposes the pains and struggles of Black women in Black male/female relationships. Criticized for lacking a social and political context, her poem focussed exclusively upon the physical and especially psychological strains of Black women. The work's significance, however, is that it exposed some of the internal problems of the Black community as they relate to sexism.

Barbara Smith's essay "Toward a Black Feminist Criticism"[20] (1977), should be noted because it represented the beginnings of an emergent Black feminist theoretical perspective. She articulated an "approach to literature that embodies the realization that the politics of sex as well as the politics of race and class are crucially interlocking factors in the words of Black women writers. . . ."[21]

In 1978, Sharon Harley and Rosalyn Terborg-Penn edited *Afro-American Women*,[22] a book of historical and biographical essays which addressed some issues of race and sex in the labor force, the women's movement, and the White community and Black communities. They also provided some data on the contributions of Black women. In the same year Michelle Wallace, from a perspective similar to Shange's, published a controversial critique of the Black Liberation Movement. In her book, *Black Macho and the Myth of the Superwoman*,[23] she attributed the plight of Black women to Black men's exaggeration of White patriarchally prescribed roles for men, which results in Black male machoism.

By 1981 several other major publications appeared that developed a critique inclusive of the issues of racism, sexism and classism. Angela Davis' *Women, Race and Class*[24] explored the interrelationships between racism, sexism, and labor issues, and is aimed particularly at identifying the class bias that affects the analysis of women's histories. Bell Hooks' *Ain't I A Woman? Black Women and Feminism*[25] simultaneously challenged the White woman's liberation movement for its racism and the Black liberation movement for its sexism. The following year, this tri-dimensional analysis was extended in *All the Women are White, and all the Blacks are Men, But Some of Us are Brave*,[26] a volume edited by Gloria Hull, Patricia Scott and Barbara Smith. These essays seek to advance Black women's studies, by clarifying how analyses of racism, sexism and classism may genuinely illumine Black women's reality. More recently Alice Walker's novel, *The Color Purple*,[27] which received the Pulitzer Prize, portrays the troubles of a Black girl/ woman entangled in an oppressive web created by the racism of White America, but in doing so she focused clearly upon the brutal sexism of Black men. In her subsequent collections of prose, *In Search of Our Mother's Garden*, Walker proposes the term womanist, in contradistinction to feminist, to denote feminists of color.[28]

The publications of Black feminists continues to escalate. In 1984 a significant historical volume on Black women appeared by Paula Giddings, entitled *When and Where I Enter*.[29] This work is an historical account of the impact of Black women on race and sex in America. She chronicles these struggles through the nineteenth and twentieth centuries.

Another significant work of literary analysis is Gloria Wade-Gayles' *No Crystal Stair: Visions of Race and Sex in Black Women's Fiction*[30] Wade-Gayles examines the conditions, contradictions and challenges of Black women from 1946 to 1976, through literature. Most recently, Bell Hooks published her second volume, *Feminist Theory: From Margin to Center,*[31] that continues to identify the limitations of bourgeois White feminism and explores the broader implications of a feminism based upon multi-dimensional analysis of oppression.

In few of the above mentioned writings do Black women employ only a gender analysis to treat Black women's reality. Whereas Shange focuses chiefly upon sexism, Wallace, like Walker, presumes that White racism has had an adverse affect upon the Black community in a way that confuses and reinforces the already existing sexism. Harley, Terborg Penn, Giddings and Wade-Gayles all recognize the inclusiveness of the oppressive reality of Black women as they endure racism and sexism and economic oppression. Smith, Hull (et al.), Hooks and Davis particularly explore the implications of this tri-dimensional oppression of Black women. It is clear that through these and other works, Black women have either articulated Black feminist perspectives or develop grounds for doing so. These perspectives, however, have not led to the resolution of tensions between Black women and White women.

On the contrary, the possibly irreparable nature of these tensions is implied in Walker's suggestion that the experience of being a Black woman or a White woman is so different that another word is required to describe the liberative efforts of Black women. Her suggestion that the word "womanist" is more appropriate for Black women is derived from the sense of the word as it is used in Black communities:

> Womanist from womanish. (Opp. of "girlish,"
> i.e., frivolous, irresponsible, not serious.) A Black
> feminist or feminist of color. From the Black folk

expression of mothers to female children, "You
acting womanish," i.e., like a woman. Usually
referring to outrageous, audacious, courageous or
willful behavior. Wanting to know more and in
greater depth than is considered "good" for one.
Interest in grown-up doings. Acting grown up.
Being grown up. Interchangeable with another
black folk expression: "You trying to be grown."
Responsible. In charge. Serious.[32]

Womanists were Sojourner Truth, Jarena Lee, Amanda Berry
Smith, Ida B. Wells, Mary Church Terrell, Mary McLeod
Bethune, Fannie Lou Hamer and countless others not
remembered in any historical study. A womanist then is a
strong Black woman who has sometimes been mislabeled as a
domineering castrating matriarch. A womanist is one who
has developed survival strategies in spite of the oppression
of her race and sex in order to save her family and her
people. Walker's womanist notion suggests not "the
feminist," but the active struggle of Black women that makes
them who they are. For some Black women that may involve
being feminine as traditionally defined, and for others it
involves being masculine as stereotypically defined. In
either case, womanist just means *being* and *acting* out who you
are. It is to the womanist tradition that Black women must
appeal for the doing of theology.

C. *Conclusion: The Beginnings of a Womanist Theology with Special Reference to Christology*

Womanist theology begins with the experiences of Black
women as its point of departure. This experience includes not
only Black women's activities in the larger society but also in
the churches and reveals that Black women have often
rejected the oppressive structure in the church as well. A
brief review of the literature demonstrates this fact.

1. *Emerging Black Women's Literature in the Church*

Several works have recently appeared which lay the groundwork for the development of a Black woman's perspective in theology, although at this early stage, they have appeared primarily in collections of essays in Black and feminist theological works.

In "Black Women and the Churches: Triple Jeopardy," Theressa Hoover analyzed the position of Black women in predominantly White denominations, though she also mentions some of the problems in Black denominations.[33] She locates the source of Black woman's survival in a faith which has always strengthened them to struggle against the odds. Pauli Murray, in "Black Theology and Feminist Theology: A Comparative View," employs the "inclusionary" principle of White feminist theology to challenge proponents of Black theology to adopt a spirit of cooperation towards liberation and reconciliation and to take women's role more seriously.[34] In "Black Theology and the Black Woman," I challenge Black theology and the Black church to realize its own proclamation of liberation as the central message of the gospel by extending this principle to Black women.[35] In "Tasks of a Prophetic Church" I define the task of Black feminist liberation theology to be that of exposing the various forms of oppression: racism, classism, sexism and imperialism.[36] I contend that they are all interconnected and none of these forms of oppression can be eliminated by challenging them separately. At the request of a group of Black seminarian women, James Cone has published an essay entitled "New Roles of Women in the Ministry: A Theological Appraisal," which challenges the Black church to divest itself of traditional oppressive attitudes towards women.[37] Later Cone treats the theme of feminism in the Black Church in two of his books in Black theology. In *My Soul Looks Back*, he includes a discussion of "Black Theology, Feminism and Marxism" and in *For My People*, he devotes a chapter to "Black theology, Black Churches and Black Women."[38] He traces Black feminism in the 19th and 20th centuries and elaborates some of the forms of sexism in the Black Church. Cone moves to challenge Black male ministers and theologians to advance Black women's liberation in the church and society. James Evans has written an essay entitled "Black Theology and Black Feminism."[39] Like Cone, he challenged Black theologians to address sexism.

Other articles helped to fill the historical vacuum of Black women's contribution to Black religion particularly in Pentecostal traditions. Pearl Williams-Jones in "Pentecostal Women: A Minority Report," identifies Black women leaders of the 19th and 20th centuries who have held positions and power beyond the spheres usual for women.[40] James S. Tinney in "The Feminist Impulse in Black Pentecostalism"[41] has provided an "historical theological overview of women in Black Pentecostalism." Cheryl Gilkes' "Together and in Harness: Women's Tradition in the Sanctified Church," specifies the activities and strengths of women in Black holiness traditions and identifies how their contributions are irreplaceable, especially in light of how patriarchy and racism impinge upon their participation.[42]

A number of graduate theses have also appeared to contribute to the development of Black women's theological perspective. Delores Williams' *The Black Woman Portrayed in Selected Black Imaginative Literature and some Questions for Black Theology*,[43] explores Black women's image (as mother) through the antebellum slave narrative literature and post-bellum literary material such as blues and spirituals. Williams suggests that given the peculiar reality of Black Women, perhaps the dominant Jewish and Christian biblical story of woman which focuses on Sarah, wife of Abraham, is an inadequate model for Black women. She proposes Hagar, the slave woman, as the correlative of Black women's experience. She challenges Black theologians to re-examine the biblical sources of Christian traditions for a Black liberation Theology that could be inclusive of the liberation of Black women.

Acknowledging grounding in both Black and Feminist analyses, LaTaunya Maria Bynum, in *Black Feminist Theology: A New Word About God*,[44] compares the theology of James Cone and Rosemary Ruether and concludes that neither is sufficient to illumine the reality of Black women. Black women must develop a perspective which is both Black and feminist, and which affirms the revolutionary message of Jesus as freedom.

In her dissertation, *Resources for a Constructive Ethic for Black Women with Special Attention to the Life and Work of Zora Neal Hurston*,[45] Katie Cannon explores the possibility of the literary tradition of Black women as the most adequate source for a constructive Black women's ethic. Having engaged some dimensions of Hurston's work with Black theologians Howard Thurman and Martin Luther King, Jr., Cannon concludes that even though Black theologians generally ignore the "victimization of gender discrimination," these two theologians have identified three themes (*imago dei*, love and justice, and community) which Black women need in order to ensure their dignity as persons. These themes, she concludes, were operative in Hurston's work and in the literature of many Black women writers.

Jualynne Dodson has contributed research tracing the history and development of the African Methodist Episcopal Church that gives central attention to the limited data about women's activities in the 19th century. *Women's Collective Power in the African Methodist Episcopal Church*,[46] focuses upon "preaching women" and "missionary women." She offers a historical synopsis of their contribution to the church, particularly as these initiated structural changes in church life.

In a similar vein, Evelyn Brooks in *The Women's Movements in the Baptist Church, 1880-1920*,[47] traces the development of Black Baptist women's activities, exploring the intersection and interaction of race, class and gender consciousness of those women who created the Women's Convention Auxiliary of the National Baptist Convention, and who thereby provided an arena for the leadership of Black Baptist women.

Though diverse and somewhat more descriptive than normative, these works lay the historical foundation that is needed for the development of a constructive black woman's theological perspective. This perspective in theology which I am calling womanist theology draws upon the life and experiences of some Black women who have created meaningful interpretations of the Christian faith.

2. The Starting Point for Womanist Theology

Because it is important to distinguish Black and White women's experiences, it is also important to note these differences in theological and Christological reflection. To accent the difference between Black and White women's perspective in theology, I maintain that Black women scholars should follow Alice Walker by describing our theological activity as "womanist theology." The term "womanist" refers to Black women's experiences. It accents, as Walker says, our being responsible, in charge, outrageous, courageous and audacious enough to demand the right to think theologically and to do it independently of both White and Black men and White women.

Black women must do theology out of their tri-dimensional experience of racism/sexism/classism. To ignore any aspect of this experience is to deny the holistic and integrated reality of Black womanhood. When Black women, say that God is on the side of the oppressed, we mean that God is in solidarity with the struggles of those on the under side of humanity.

In a chapter entitled "Black Women: Shaping Feminist Theory," Hooks elaborates the interrelationship of the threefold oppressive reality of Black women and shows some of the weaknesses of White feminist theory. Challenging the racist and classist assumption of White feminism, Hooks writes:

> Racism abounds in the writings of white
> feminists, reinforcing white supremacy and
> negating the possibility that women will bond
> politically across ethnic and racial boundaries.
> Past feminist refusal to draw attention to and
> attack racial hierarchy suppressed the link
> between race and class. Yet class structure in
> American society has been shaped by the racial
> politics of white supremacy.[48]

This means that Black women, because of oppression
determined by race and their subjugation as women, make up
a disproportionately high percentage of the poor and
working classes. However, the fact that Black women are a
subjugated group even within the Black community and the
White women's community does not mean that they are alone
in their oppression within those communities. In the women's
community poor White women are marginalized, and in the
Black community, poor Black men are also discriminated
against. This suggests that classism, as well as racism and
sexism, has a life of its own. Consequently, simply addressing
racism and sexism is inadequate to bring about total
liberation.[49] Even though there are dimensions of class
which are not directly related to race or sex, classism impacts
Black women in a peculiar way which results in the fact that
they are most often on the bottom of the social and economic
ladder. For Black women doing theology, to ignore classism
would mean that their theology is no different from any
other bourgeois theology. It would be meaningless to the
majority of Black women, who are themselves poor. This
means that addressing only issues relevant to middle class
women or Blacks will simply not do: the daily struggles of
poor Black women must serve as the gauge for the
verification of the claims of womanist theology.

3. *The Use of the Bible in the Womanist Tradition*

Theological investigation into the experiences of Christian Black women reveals that Black women considered the Bible to be a major source for religious validation in their lives. Though Black women's relationship with God preceded their introduction to the Bible, this Bible gave some content to their God-consciousness.[50] The source for Black women's understanding of God has been twofold: first, God's revelation directly to them, and secondly, God's revelation as witnessed in the Bible and as read and heard in the context of their experience. The understanding of God as creator, sustainer, comforter, and liberator took on life as they agonized over their pain, and celebrated the hope that as God delivered the Israelites, they would be delivered as well. The God of the Old and New Testament became real in the consciousness of oppressed Black women. Though they were politically impotent, they were able to appropriate certain themes of the Bible which spoke to their reality. For example, Jarena Lee, a nineteenth century Black woman preacher in the African Methodist Episcopal Church constantly emphasized the theme "Life and Liberty" in her sermons which were always biblically based. This interplay of scripture and experience was exercised by many other Black women. An ex-slave woman revealed that when her experience negated certain oppressive interpretations of the Bible given by White preachers, she, through engaging the biblical message for herself rejected them. Consequently, she also dismissed White preachers who distorted the message in order to maintain slavery. Her grandson, Howard Thurman, speaks of her use of the Bible in this way:

> "During the days of slavery," she said, "the master's minister would occasionally hold services for the slaves. Always the white minister used as his text something from Paul. 'Slaves be obedient to them that are your masters . . ., as unto Christ.' Then he would go on to show

> how, if we were good and happy slaves, God
> would bless us. I promised my Maker that if I
> ever learned to read and if freedom ever came, I
> would not read that part of the Bible."[51]

What we see here is perhaps more than a mere rejection of a White preacher's interpretation of the Bible, but an exercise in internal critique of the Bible. The Bible must be read and interpreted in the light of Black women's own experience of oppression and God's revelation within that context. Womanists must, like Sojourner, "compare the teachings of the Bible with the witness" in them.[52]

To do Womanist Theology, then, we must read and hear the Bible and engage it within the context of our own experience. This is the only way that it can make sense to people who are oppressed. Black women of the past did not hesitate in doing this and we must do no less.

4. *The Role of Jesus in the Womanist Tradition*

In the experiences of Black people, Jesus was "all things."[53] Chief among these however, was the belief in Jesus as the divine co-sufferer, who empowers them in situations of oppression. For Christian Black women in the past, Jesus was their central frame of reference. They identified with Jesus because they believed that Jesus identified with them. As Jesus was persecuted and made to suffer undeservedly, so were they. His suffering culminated in the crucifixion. Their crucifixion included rape, and babies being sold. But Jesus' suffering was not the suffering of a mere human, for Jesus was understood to be God incarnate. As Harold Carter observed of Black prayers in general, there was no difference made between the persons of the trinity, Jesus, God, or the Holy Spirit. "All of these proper names for God were used interchangeably in prayer language. Thus, Jesus was the one who speaks the world into creation. He was the power behind the Church. . . .[54]

Black women's affirmation of Jesus as God meant that White people were not God. One old slave woman clearly demonstrated this as she prayed:

"Dear Massa Jesus, we all uns beg Ooner [you] come make us a call dis yere day. We is nutting but poor Etiopian women and people ain't tink much 'bout we. We ain't trust any of dem great high people for come to we church, but do' you is de one great Massa, great too much dan Massa Linkum, you ain't shame to care for we African people."[55]

This slave woman did not hesitate to identify her struggles and pain with those of Jesus. In fact, the common struggle made her know that Jesus would respond to her beck and call.

"Come to we, dear Massa Jesus. De sun, he hot too much, de road am dat long and boggy (sandy) and we ain't got no buggy for send and fetch Ooner. But Massa, you 'member how you walked dat hard walk up Calvary and ain't weary but tink about we all dat way. We know you ain't weary for to come to we. We pick out de torns, de prickles, de brier, de backslidin' and de quarrel and de sin out of you path so dey shan't hurt Ooner pierce feet no more."[56]

As she is truly among the people at the bottom of humanity, she can make things comfortable for Jesus even though she may have nothing to give him—no water, no food—but she can give tears and love. She continues:

"Come to we, dear Massa Jesus. We all uns ain't got no good cool water for give you when you thirsty. You know, Massa, de drought so long, and the well so low, ain't nutting but mud to drink.

> But we gwine to take de 'munion cup and fill it
> wid de tear of repentance, and love clean out of
> we heart. Dat all we hab to gib you, good
> Massa."[57]

For Black women, the role of Jesus unraveled as they
encountered him in their experience as one who empowers the
weak. In this vein, Jesus was such a central part of Sojourner
Truth's life that all of her sermons made him the starting
point. When asked by a preacher if the source of her
preaching was the Bible, she responded "No honey, can't
preach from de Bible–can't read a letter."[58] Then she
explained; "When I preaches, I has jest one text to preach
from, an' I always preaches from this one. My text is, 'When I
found Jesus!'"[59] In this sermon Sojourner Truth recounts the
events and struggles of her life from the time her parents
were brought from Africa and sold "up an' down, an' hither
an' yon ..."[60] to the time that she met Jesus within the context
of her struggles for dignity of Black people and women. Her
encounter with Jesus brought such joy that she became
overwhelmed with love and praise:

> Praise, praise, praise to the Lord! An' I begun to
> feel such a love in my soul as I never felt before–
> love to all creatures. An' then, all of a sudden, it
> stopped, an' I said, Dar's de white folks that
> have abused you, an' beat you, an' abused your
> people–think o' them! But then there came
> another rush of love through my soul, an' I cried
> out loud–'Lord, I can love *even de white folks!*[61]

This love was not a sentimental, passive love. It was a tough,
active love that empowered her to fight more fiercely for the
freedom of her people. For the rest of her life she continued
speaking at abolition and women's rights gatherings,
condemning the horrors of oppression.

5. *The Significance of Jesus in the Womanist Tradition*

More than anyone, Black theologians have captured the essence of the significance of Jesus in the lives of Black people which to an extent includes Black women. They all hold that the Jesus of history is important for understanding who he was and his significance for us today. By and large they have affirmed that this Jesus is the Christ, that is, God incarnate. They have argued that in the light of our experience, Jesus meant freedom.[62] They have maintained that Jesus means freedom from the sociopsychological, psychocultural, economic and political oppression of Black people. In other words, Jesus is a political messiah.[63] "To free (humans) from bondage was Jesus' own definition of his ministry."[64] This meant that as Jesus identified with the lowly of his day, he now identifies with the lowly of this day, who in the American context are Black people. The identification is so real that Jesus Christ in fact becomes Black. It is important to note that Jesus' blackness is not a result of ideological distortion of a few Black thinkers, but a result of careful Christological investigation. Cone examines the sources of Christology and concludes that Jesus is Black because "Jesus was a Jew." He explains:

> It is on the basis of the soteriological meaning of the particularity of his Jewishness that theology must affirm the christological significance of Jesus' present blackness. He *is* black because he was a Jew. The affirmation of the Black Christ can be understood when the significance of his past Jewishness is related dialectically to the significance of his present blackness. On the one hand, the Jewishness of Jesus located him in the context of the Exodus, thereby connecting his appearance in Palestine with God's liberation of oppressed Israelites from Egypt. Unless Jesus were truly from Jewish ancestry, it would make little theological sense to say that he is the

> fulfillment of God's covenant with Israel. But on
> the other hand, the blackness of Jesus brings out
> the soteriological meaning of his Jewishness for
> our contemporary situation when Jesus' person is
> understood in the context of the cross and res-
> urrection are Yahweh's fulfillment of his
> original intention for Israel....[65]

The condition of Black people today reflects the cross of Jesus.
Yet the resurrection brings the hope that liberation from
oppression is immanent. The resurrected Black Christ
signifies this hope.

Cone further argues that this christological title, "The
Black Christ" is not validated by its universality, but, in
fact, by its particularity. Its significance lies in whether or
not the christological title "points to God's universal will to
liberate particular oppressed people from inhumanity."[66]
These particular oppressed peoples to which Cone refers are
characterized in Jesus' parable on the Last Judgment as "the
least." "The least in America are literally and symbolically
present in Black people."[67] This notion of "the least" is
attractive because it descriptively locates the condition of
Black women. "The least" are those people who have no
water to give, but offer what they have, as the old slave
woman cited above says in her prayer. Black women's
experience in general is such a reality. Their tri-dimensional
reality renders their particular situation a complex one. One
could say that not only are they the oppressed of the
oppressed, but their situation represents "the particular
within the particular."

But is this just another situation that takes us deeper into
the abyss of theological relativity? I would argue that it is
not, because it is in the context of Black women's experience
where the particular connects up with the universal. By this
I mean that in each of the three dynamics of oppression,
Black women share in the reality of a broader community.
They share race suffering with Black men; with White
women and other Third World women, they are victims of

sexism; and with poor Blacks and Whites, and other Third World peoples, especially women, they are disproportionately poor. To speak of Black women's tri-dimensional reality, therefore, is not to speak of Black women exclusively, for there is an implied universality which connects them with others.

Likewise, with Jesus Christ, there was an implied universality which made him identify with others–the poor, the woman, the stranger. To affirm Jesus' solidarity with the "least of the people" is not an exercise in romanticized contentment with one's oppressed status in life. For as the Resurrection signified that there is more to life than the cross for Jesus Christ, for Black women it signifies that their tri-dimensional oppressive existence is not the end, but it merely represents the context in which a particular people struggle to experience hope and liberation. Jesus Christ thus represents a three-fold significance: first he identifies with the "little people," Black women, where they are; secondly, he affirms the basic humanity of these, "the least"; and thirdly, he inspires active hope in the struggle for resurrected, liberated existence.

To locate the Christ in Black people is a radical and necessary step, but an understanding of Black women's reality challenges us to go further. Christ among the least must also mean Christ in the community of Black women. William Eichelberger was able to recognize this as he further particularized the significance of the Blackness of Jesus by locating Christ in Black women's community. He was able to see Christ not only as Black male but also Black female.

> God, in revealing Himself and His attributes from time to time in His creaturely existence, has exercised His freedom to formalize His appearance in a variety of ways. . . . God revealed Himself at a point in the past as Jesus the Christ a Black male. My reasons for affirming the Blackness of Jesus of Nazareth are much different from that of the white apologist.

... God wanted to identify with that segment of
mankind which had suffered most, and is still
suffering.... I am constrained to believe that God
in our times has updated His form of revelation
to western society. It is my feeling that God is
now manifesting Himself, and has been for over
450 years, in the form of the Black American
Woman as mother, as wife, as nourisher, sustainer and preserver of life, the Suffering
Servant who is despised and rejected by men, a
personality of sorrow who is acquainted with
grief. The Black Woman has borne our griefs and
carried our sorrows. She has been wounded
because of American white society's
transgressions and bruised by white iniquities. It
appears that she may be the instrumentality
through whom God will make us whole.[68]

Granted, Eichelberger's categories for God and woman are
very traditional. Nevertheless, the significance of his
thought is that he was able to conceive of the Divine reality
as other than a Black male messianic figure.

6. Challenges for Womanist Christology

Although I have argued that the White feminist
analysis of theology and Christology is inadequate for
salvific efficacy with respect to Black women, I do contend
that it is not totally irrelevant to Black women's needs. I
believe that Black women should take seriously the feminist
analysis, but they should not allow themselves to be coopted
on behalf of the agendas of White women, for as I have
argued, they are often racist unintentionally or by intention.
The first challenge therefore, is to Black women.
Feminists have identified some problems associated with
language and symbolism of the church, theology, and
Christology. They have been able to show that exclusive

masculine language and imagery are contributing factors undergirding the oppression of women.

In addressing the present day, womanists must investigate the relationship between the oppression of women and theological symbolism. Even though Black women have been able to transcend some of the oppressive tendencies of White male (and Black male) articulated theologies, careful study reveals that some traditional symbols are inadequate for us today. The Christ understood as the stranger, the outcast, the hungry, the weak, the poor, makes the traditional male Christ (Black and White) less significant. Even our sisters, the womanist of the past though they exemplified no problems with the symbols themselves, they had some suspicions about the effects of a male image of the divine, for they did challenge the oppressive and distorted use of it in the church's theology. In so doing, they were able to move from a traditional oppressive Christology, with respect to women, to an egalitarian Christology. This kind of equalitarian Christology was operative in Jarena Lee's argument for the right of women to preach. She argued ". . . the Saviour died for the woman as well as for the man."[69] The crucifixion was for universal salvation, not just for male salvation or, as we may extend the argument to include, not just for White salvation. Because of this Christ came and died, no less for the woman as for the man, no less for Blacks as for Whites.

> If the man may preach, because the Saviour died for him, why not the woman? Seeing he died for her also. Is he not a whole Saviour, instead of half one? as those who hold it wrong for a woman to preach, would seem to make it appear.[70]

Lee correctly perceives that there is an ontological issue at stake. If Jesus Christ were a Savior of men then it is true the maleness of Christ would be paramount.[71] But if Christ is a Saviour of all, then it is the humanity–the wholeness–of Christ which is significant. Sojourner was aware of the same tendency of some scholars and church leaders to link the maleness of Jesus and the sin of Eve with the status of women and she challenged this notion in her famed speech "Ain't I A Woman?"

> Then that little man in black there, he says women can't have as much rights as men, 'cause Christ wasn't a woman! Where did your Christ come from? Where did your Christ come from? From God and a woman. Man had nothing to do with Him.
> If the first woman God ever made was strong enough to turn the world upside down all alone, these women together ought to be able to turn it back, and get it right side up again! And now they is asking to do it, the men better let them.[72]

I would argue, as suggested by both Lee and Sojourner, that the significance of Christ is not his maleness, but his humanity. The most significant events of Jesus Christ were the life and ministry, the crucifixion, and the resurrection. The significance of these events, in one sense, is that in them the absolute becomes concrete. God becomes concrete not only in the man Jesus, for he was crucified, but in the lives of those who will accept the challenges of the risen Saviour the Christ.

For Lee, this meant that women could preach; for Sojourner, it meant that women could possibly save the world; for me, it means today, this Christ, found in the experiences of Black women, is a Black woman. The commitment that to struggle not only with symptoms (church structures, structures of society), as Black women have done, but with causes (those beliefs which produce and re-inforce structures) yield deeper theological and christological questions having to do with images and symbolism. Christ challenges us to ask new questions demanded by the context in which we find ourselves.

The second challenge for Black women is that we must explore more deeply the question of what Christ means in a society in which class distinctions are increasing. If Christ is among "the least" then who are they? Because our foreparents were essentially poor by virtue of their race, there was no real need for them to address classism as a separate reality. Today, in light of the emerging Black middle class we must ask what is the impact of class upon our lives and the lives of other poor Black and Third World women and men.

Another way of addressing the class issue in the church is to recognize the fact that although our race/sex analyses may force us to realize that Blacks and women should share in the leadership of the church, the style of leadership and basic structures of the church virtually insure the continuation of a privileged class.

Contemporary Black women in taking seriously the Christ mandate to be among the least must insist that we address all three aspects of Black women's reality in our analyses. The challenge here for contemporary Black women is to begin to construct a serious analysis which addresses the structural nature of poverty. Black women must recognize that racism, sexism and classism each have lives of their own, and that no one form of oppression is eliminated with the destruction of any other. Though they are interrelated, they must all be addressed.

The third and final challenge for Black women is to do constructive Christology. This Christology must be a liberating one, for both the Black women's community and the larger Black community. A Christology which negates Black male humanity is still destructive to the Black community. We must, therefore, take seriously only the usable aspects of the past.

To be sure, as Black women receive these challenges, their very embodiment represents a challenge to White women. This embodiment (of racism, sexism and classism) says to White women that a wholistic analysis is a minimal requirement for wholistic theology. The task of Black women then, is constructive.

As we organize in this constructive task, we are also challenged to adopt the critical stance of Sojourner with respect to the feminist analysis as reflected in her comment:

> I know that it feel a kind o' hissin' and ticklin' like to see a colored woman get up and tell you about things, and woman's rights. We have all been thrown down so low that nobody thought we' ever get up again, but we have been long enough trodden now; we will come up again, and now I am here. . . .
>
> . . . I wanted to tell you a mite about Woman's Rights, and so I came out and said so. I am sittin' among you to watch; and every once in a while I will come out and tell you what time of night it is.[73]

NOTES

[1] Herbert Aptheker, ed., *A Documentary History of the Negro People in the United States: From Colonial Times thru the Civil War I* (New York: The Citidel Press, 1971); Herbert Aptheker, ed., *A Documentary History of the Negro People in the United States: From Reconstruction Years to the Founding of the NAACP in 1910 II* (Secaucus, N.J.: The Citadel Press, 1972); Herbert Aptheker, ed., *A Documentary History of the Negro People in the United States: From the Emergence of the NAACP to the Beginning of the New Deal, 1910-1932* (Secaucus, N.J.: The Citadel Press, 1973). For a combination of Historical and sociological studies see August Meier and Elliott Rudwick, eds., *The Making of Black America: The Origins of Black Americans, I* (New York: Atheneum, 1969); and Meier and Rudwick, *The Making of Black America: The Black Community in Modern America. II* (New York: Atheneum, 1973).

[2] For a comparative study of American Slavery and slavery in other places, see Stanley M. Elkins, "Slavery in Capitalist and Non-Capitalist Cultures" in *The Black Family: Essays and Studies*

(Belmont, California: Wadworth Publishing Company, Inc., 1971), pp. 23-16. Elkins says:

> Neither in Brazil nor in Spanish America did slavery carry with it such precise and irrevocable categories of perpetual servitude, "durante vita" and "for all generations," as in the United States. The presumptions in these countries, should the status of a colored person be in doubt, was that he was free rather than a slave," quoted from William Lau Mathieson, *British Slavery and its Abolition* (London: Longmans Green, 1926), pp. 37-38. A slave could be free by a number of ways: (1) he could buy his own freedom. (2) In Cuba and Mexico, the Negro could demand a price declaration which he/she could pay by installments. (3) In Brazil the parent of 10 children might demand his/her freedom. (Johnston, *Negro in the New World*, p. 89) (4) The medieval Spanish code provided for termination of the slave's service if he denounced cases of treason, murder, counterfeiting, or the rape of a virgin or if other meritorious acts are performed (p. 15).

3 Several biographies of Black women slaves have appeared. Among them are: John Collins, *The Slave-Mother* (Philadelphia: #31 North Fifth Street, 1855). This is a brief account of a runaway slave mother who strategically gave up her infant to gain freedom for them both. Victoria Earle, *Aunt Lindy: A Story Founded on Real Life* (New York: J. J. Little and Co., 1893). This is the story (fictionalized) of an ex-slave Black woman (and Black man) who discovered that a burn victim placed in her care was her ex-master. After a religious meeting she decided to nurse him rather than let him die, consequently in appreciation he helped them to locate their son whom he had sold years earlier. Sarah R. Levering, *Memoirs of Margaret Jane Black of Baltimore Md.*, (Philadelphia: Innes and Son, 1879). Levering gives *her* a brief account of the life of Blake. Blake's mother is said to prefer slavery to freedom for herself and her daughter, Margaret. Leverling's paternalistic/maternalistic and racist perspective made it impossible to see that perhaps Margaret's mother was not rejecting freedom, but the un-bearable difficulties her weakling and sickly daughter would have to experience as a freedperson right after the war. Jim Bearden and Linda Jean Butler, *The Life and Times of Mary Shadd Cary*

(Toronto, Ontario: New Canada Publication, a division of NC Press Ltd., 1977). This is a biography of a free Negro woman, who was dedicated to education of Blacks, abolition and women's rights. Also see Conrad Earl, *Harriet Tubman* (Washington, D.C.: The Associated Publishers, Inc., 1943); Sarah Bradford's *Scenes in the life of Harriet Tubman* (1869). *Aunt Sally: A Narrative of the Slave Life and Purchase of the Mother of Rev. Isaac Williams of Detroit, Michigan* (Wheaton, Illinois: Syndale House Publishers, Inc., 1979). First published in 1858 by the American Reform Tract Book Society of Cincinnati, Ohio.

The interplay of racism and sexism is more dramatic in autobiographies and slave narratives. Among the published ones are: Linda Brent, *Incidents in the Life of a Slave Girl* (New York: A Harvest Book, Harcourt, Brace, Jovanovich, Inc.,, ed. L. Marie Child (originally published in 1861). New introduction and notes by Walter Teller, 1973. Brent speaks of the physical and mental violence of slavery and other injustices. She appeals to northerners to stop sending fugitive slaves back to the South. Elizabeth Keckley, *Behind the Scenes: Thirty Years a Slave, and Four Years in the White House* (New York: G. W. Carleton and Co., Publishers, 1868). Though attempting to be kind and restrained in her accounts, nonetheless Keckley likewise reveals many of the atrocities of slave existence. Susie King Taylor *Reminiscences of my Life in Camp* (Boston: The Author, 1902). This is an account of Taylor's work among the 33 U.S. Colored Troops.

[4] From the point of view of White men, Black women existed not only to serve White women's domestic needs but also to bear the brunt of their sexual exploitation. See discussion in Mary Berry and John Blassingame, *The Black Experience in America* (New York: Oxford University Press, 1982), chapter 4. Also see Calvin Hernton, *Sex and Racism in America* (New York: Grove Press, Inc. 1965).

[5] See statistics as summarized in the U. S. Department of Commerce, Bureau of the Census, *The Social and Economic Status of the Black Population in the U. S.: American Historical View, 1790-1978* (Current Population Reports Special Studies Series #80). To see the consistent high unemployment rates of Blacks relative to whites (and Black men relative to White men), see reports from the U. S. Department of Labor, Bureau of Labor Statistics.

[6] Major studies on Domestic servants are: David Katzman, *Seven Days a Week: Women and Domestic Service in Industrializing America* (New York: Oxford University Press, 1978);

Daniel Sutherland, *Americans and Their Servants: Domestic Service in the United States From 1800-1920* (Baton Rouge, La.: Louisiana State University Press, 1981). Faye E. Dudden, *Serving Women: Household Service in Nineteenth-Century America* (Middletown, Connecticut: Wesleyan University Press, 1983). For particular Black emphasis see: Elizabeth Ross Haynes, *Negroes in Domestic Service in the United States* (Washington, D.C.: The Association for the Study of Negro Life and History, Inc., 1923), Reprinted from *The Journal of Negro History*, Vol. VIII, #4 (October 1923). W. E. B. DuBois included in *The Philadelphia Negro* a study of Domestic Servants conducted by Isabel Eaten, "Special Report on Negro Domestic Service in the Seventh Ward" (Millwood, New York: Kraus-Thomas Organization Ltd., 1973). Literary studies include Alice Childress, *Like One of the Family . . . Conversations From a Domestic Life* (Brooklyn, New York: Independence Publishers, 1956) and Trudier Harris, *From Mammy to Militant: Domestics in Black American Literature* (Philadelphia: Temple University Press, 1982).

White females (especially immigrants) used domestic service as a stepping stone to other more decent women's occupations–office clerks, stenographers, typists, bookkeepers, cashiers, accountants, store clerks and saleswomen, and telephone operators. For Black women, domestic service was permanent. In 1890 and 1920 while White female servants declined significantly, Black women in this field increased to 40%. In 1920 they were 73% of all laundresses. In 1910 and 1920 Black women were 0.5% and 1.4% in non-agricultural occupations while (native born) White women were 32.1 and 37.1 in such occupations. By 1920 only 7% native born and 20% immigrant women were servants. Katzman, *Seven Days A Week*, pp. 72-73.

Two reasons can be deduced, from the studies, for the high percentage of Blacks in domestic service. (1) Recognizing that race relations and domestic service were intertwined, Katzman quotes Orra Langhorne's report in 1890 that "among the white people of the South, difficulties about servants are generally spoken of as "trouble with Negroes; –Negroes and servants being synonymous terms in the average White Southerner's vocabulary." (Katzman, *Seven Days A Week*, p. 185). See also Orra Langhorne, "Southern Workman" (October 1890) in Charles E. Wynes (ed.) *Southern Sketches from Virginia 1881-1901* (Charlottesville, Virginia, 1964), p. 100. (2) Sutherland suggests as another reason for the high percentage of Black domestic servants that negative attitudes towards "new immigration" resulting in their seldom employment as servants. Far worst than the heathen Irish were the culture and tradition differences of Poles, Bohemians, Hungarians, Italians, and Jews of all nations. They were seldom employed as servants partially because Americans disliked and distrusted them. [(Sutherland, *Americans, and Their Domestics*, p. 59); see also Mary Grove Smith, "Immigration as a Source of Supply for Domestic Workers," *Bulletin of Inter-Municipal Committee on Household Research*, II (May 1906); Rose Cohen, *Out of the Shadows* (New York; Jerome S. Ozer, 1971), 158-59, 171-72; Elizabeth H. Pleck, "A Mother's Wages: Income Earning Among Married Italian and Black women, 1896-1911," In Michael Gordon (ed.), *The American Family in Social-Historical Perspective* (New York: St. Martins Press, 1978), 495.] (3) A third factor in the high percentage of Blacks as domestics is that while native-White women had non-service occupations opened to them, Blacks were excluded from occupational mobility. Sutherland, Ibid., see also Mary White Ovington, "The Colored Woman in Domestic Service in New York City," *Bulletin of Inter-Municipal Committee on Household Research*, (May 1905), 10-12.

7 Comparing the South with the North and West, Katzman notes that servants were rarely found in lower middle or working class families. However, in the former slave states, Back servants were equally common in households headed by wage earners as in those headed by white collar workers. He further notes that the South has been called a "house-wife's utopia." Katzman, *Seven Days A Week*, p. 185. Of course this reflected the fact that Black labor was cheap.

8 Because of the strenuousness of housework and the delicateness of White women's physical make-up, White women were taught that they needed protection from the dangers of housework. Katzman recalls:

> During the late nineteenth century, medical authorities cautioned women against demanding and enduring physical labor. According to medical guidebooks, adolescent middle-class girls should be excused from such hard physical labor as strenuous domestic chores. More mature women were advised against physical activity during menstruation, and it was widely thought that regular work schedules were injurious to a woman's health. (Katzman, p. 149).

9 Hooks, *Feminist Theology*, p. 49.

[10] Joel Kovel, *White Racism: A Psychohistory* (New York: Columbia University Press, 1984), p. x.

[11] C. Eric Lincoln, *Race Religion and the Continuing American Dilemma* (New York: Hill and Wang, 1984), pp. 11-12.

[12] Kovel, *White Racism*, passim.

[13] Brenda Eichelberger, "Voices of Black Feminism," *Quest: A Feminist Quarterly* III (Spring):pp. 16-23.

[14] Iva Carruthers, "War in African Familyhood," in *Sturdy Black Bridges: Visions of Black Women in Literature*, eds. Roseann P. Bell, Bettye J. Parker and Beverly Guy-Sheftall (New York: Anchor Books, Doubleday, 1979), p. 9.

[15] *Ibid.*, p. 9.

[16] Deborah Hines, "Racism Breeds Stereotypes," *The Witness*, 65 (February 1982), p. 7.

[17] This phrase is used by Anna Cooper in *A Voice From the South By A Black Woman of the South* (Xenia, Ohio, 1892), quoted in Hooks *Ain't I A Woman*, p. 193-194. I use it here to characterize Black women's tri-dimensional experience. To be concerned about Black Woman's issues is to be *concrete*. Yet because of their interconnectedness with Black men (racism), White women (sexism) and the poor (classism), it is also to be, at the same time, concerned with broad issues.

[18] Cade (New York: Macmillan Publishing Co., Inc., 1970).

[19] Shange (New York: Macmillan Publishing Co., Inc. 1975).

[20] Smith (Trumanburg, New York: The Crossing Press, 1977), p. 3. Originally published in *Conditions: Two* (October 1977). Brenda Eichelberger's "Voices on Black Feminism" also appeared in 1977, in *Quest* III (Spring, 1977). In this essay she interviews eight Black women on Black women's response to the women's movement and their thoughts on the need for Black feminism.

[21] *Ibid.*, Smith, "Towards a Black. . .," p. 3.

[22] Harley and Terborg-Penn (New York: Kennikat Press, 1978).

[23] Wallace (New York: Dial Press, 1978).

[24] Davis (New York: Vintage Book, 1981).

[25] Hooks (Boston: South End Press, 1981).

[26] Hull, et al. (Old Westbury, New York: The Feminist Press, 1982).

[27] Walker (New York: Harcourt, Brace and Jovanovich, Publishers, 1982).

228   White Women's Christ and Black Women's Jesus

Walker (New York: Harcourt, Brace and Jovanovich, Publishers, 1983).

[29] Giddings (New York: William Morrow and Company, Inc., 1984). Other collections of historical documents include Gerda Lerner, *Black Woman in White America*, and Bert Lowenberg and Ruth Bogin, eds. of *Black Women in Nineteenth-Century American Life: Their Words, Their Thoughts, Their Feelings* (University Park, Pennsylvania: The Pennsylvania State University Press, 1976). In *We Are Your Sisters: Black Women in the Nineteenth Century*, Dorothy Sterling (ed.) brings together a primary source of Black women—letters, interviews, diaries, autobiographies organizational records and newspaper accounts. (New York: W. W. Norton and Company, 1984).

[30] Wade-Gayles (New York: Pilgrim Press, 1984).

[31] Hooks (Boston: South End Press, 1984).

[32] Walker, *In Search . . .*, p. xi.

[33] Theressa Hoover, "Black Women and the Churches: Triple Jeopardy" in *Black Theology: A Documentary History*, eds. Gayraud Wilmore and James Cone (New York: Orbis Books, 1979), pp. 377-388. This article was originally published in *Sexist Religion and Women in the Church: No More Silence*! ed. Alice Hageman (New York: Association Press 1974).

[34] Pauli Murray, "Black Theology and Feminist Theology: A Comparative View," in *Black Theology.*, eds. Wilmore and Cone, pp. 398-417.

[35] Jacquelyn Grant, "Black Theology and The Black Woman," in *Black Theology*, eds. Wilmore and Cone, pp. 418-433.

[36] Idem, "Tasks of a Prophetic Church," in *Theology in the Americas*, Cornell West (New York: Orbis Books, 1982), pp. 136-142.

[37] James Cone, "New Roles of Women in the Ministry: A Theological Appraisal," in *Black Theology*, eds. Wilmore and Cone, pp. 380-397.

[38] Idem, *My Soul Looks Back* (Nashville: Abingdon Press, 1983), and James Cone, *For My People: Black Theology and the Black Church* (New York: Orbis Books, 1984).

[39] James Evans, "Black Theology and Black Feminism," *Journal of Religious Thought* 38 (Spring/Summer, 1981), pp. 43-53.

[40] Pearl Williams Jones, "A Minority Report: Black Pentecostal Women," *Spirit: A Journal of Incident to Black Pentecostalism* I (No. 1, 1977), pp. 31-44.

[41] An unpublished paper.

[42] Cheryl Gilkes, "Togetherness and in Harness: Women's Traditions in the Sanctified Church" (publication forthcoming in *Signs* Quarterly).

[43] Delores Williams, *The Black Woman Portrayed in Selected Black Literature and Some Questions for Black Theology* (M.A. Thesis, Columbia University and Union Theological Seminary, 1975).

[44] LaTaunya Marie Bynum, *Black Feminist Theology: A New Word About God* (D. Min.thesis, School of Theology at Claremont, 1980).

[45] Katie G. Cannon, *Resources for a Constructive Ethic for Women with Special Attention to the Life and Work of Zora Neale Hurston* (Ph.D. dissertation, Union Theological Seminary, 1983).

[46] Jualynne Dodson, *Women's Collective Power in the African Methodist Episcopal Church* (Ph.D. dissertation, University of California at Berkerly, 1983).

[47] Evelyn Brooks, *The Women's Movement on the Black Baptist Church, 1880-1920* (Ph.D. dissertation, University of Rochester, 1984).

[48] Hooks, *Feminist Theology*, p. 3.

[49] This is reflected in the fact that the Black movement (Civil Rights/Black Power) has resulted in advancement of only some Blacks, primarily men, creating an emergent Black middle class. Likewise, the women's movement has meant progress for some women, primarily White, resulting in the increased class stratification in the women's community.

[50] Cecil Wayne Cone, *Identity Crisis in Black Theology* (Nashville, Tennessee: African Methodist Episcopal Church, 1975), passim, especially Chapter II.

[51] Howard Thurman, *Jesus and the Disinherited* (Nashville: Abingdon Press, 1949), pp. 30-31.

[52] Olive Gilbert, *Sojourner Truth: Narrative and Book of Life*, (1850 and 1875; reprint ed., Chicago: Johnson Publishing Co., Inc., 1970), p. 83.

[53] Harold A. Carter, *The Prayer Tradition of Black People* (Valley Forge: Judson Press, 1976). Carter, in referring to traditional Black prayer in general, states that Jesus was revealed as one who "was all one needs!" p. 50.

[54] *Ibid.*

[55] *Ibid.*, p. 49.

[56] *Ibid.*

[57] *Ibid.*

[58] Gilbert, *Book of Life*, p. 118.

[59] *Ibid.*, p. 119.

[60] *Ibid.*

[61] *Ibid.*, p. 122.

[62] J. D. Roberts, *A Black Political Theology* (Philadelphia: The Westminster Press, 1974), p. 138. See especially Chapter 5. See also Noel Erskine, *Decolonizing Theology: A Caribbean Perspective* (New York: Orbis Books, 1980), p. 125.

[63] Roberts, *A Black Political Theology*, p. 133.

[64] Albert Cleage, *The Black Messiah* (New York: Sheed and Ward, 1969), p. 92.

[65] Cone, *God of the Oppressed*, p. 134.

[66] *Ibid.*, p. 135.

[67] *Ibid.*, p. 136.

[68] William Eichelberger, "Reflections on the Person and Personality of the Black Messiah," *The Black Church*, p. 54.

[69] Jarena Lee, *Religious Experiences and Journal of Mrs. Jarena Lee* (Philadelphia, 1849), pp. 15-16.

[70] *Ibid.*, p. 16.

[71] There is no evidence to suggest that Black women debated the significance of the maleness of Jesus. The fact is that Jesus Christ was a real crucial figure in their lives. Recent feminist scholarship, as reflected in the discussion of Chapters III, IV and V, has been important in showing the relation between the maleness of Christ and the oppression of women.

[72] Truth, "Ain't I A Woman," in *Feminism*, ed. Schneir, p. 94.

[73] *Ibid.*, pp. 96-98.

BIBLIOGRAPHY

Articles

Alexander, John. "A Conversation with Virginia Mollenkott." *The Other Side Magazine* 12 (May-June 1976):21-30, 73-75.

Baker, Ella and Cooke, Marvel. "The Bronx Slave Market." *The Crisis* 42 (November 1935):330-331 and 340.

Barrabee, Susan Copenhover. "Education for Liberation: Women in the Seminary." In Women's Liberation and the Church, pp. 47-59. Edited by Sarah Bentley Doely. New York: Association Press, 1970.

Brock, Rita. "The Feminist Redemption of Christ." In *Christian Feminism: Visions of a New Humanity*, pp. 55-74. Edited by Judith Weidman. New York: Harper and Row, 1984.

Carruthers, Iva. "War in African Familyhood." In *Sturdy Black Bridges: Visions of Black Women in Literature*, pp. 8-17. Edited by Roseann P. Bell, Bettye Parker, and Beverly Guy-Sheftall. New York: Anchor Books, Doubleday, 1979.

Christ, Carol. "A Review of Feminist Literature." *Religious Studies Review* III (October, 1977):203-207.

Clifton, Lucille. "To Ms. Ann." *An Ordinary Woman.* New York: Random House, 1974, p. 24.

"The Communique of Council of Visioners of the Feminist Theological Institute Inc." October 1981. (Photocopy)

Cone, James. "New Roles in the Ministry: A Theological Appraisal." In *Black Theology: A Documentary History, 1966-1979*, pp. 389-417. Edited by Gayraud Wilmore and James Cone. Maryknoll, New York: Orbis Books, 1979.

Conversation with Gayraud Wilmore. New York Theological Seminary, August 1984.

Cook, Mary. "The Work for Baptist Women." In *The Negro Baptist Pulpit: A Collection of Sermons and Papers on Baptist Doctrine and Missionary and Educational Work.* Edited by E. M. Brawley. Philadelphia: American Baptist Publication Society, 1890.

COWAC. "The History Statement from the 1976 Resource Kit." *Statements of History of the Task Force on Women and the Council on Women and the Church.*

Daly, Mary. "The Courage to See: Religious Implications of the New Sisterhood." *The Christian Century* 88 (September 22, 1971):1108-1111.

Daly, Mary. "The Spiritual Revolution: Women's Liberation as Theological Re-education." *Andover Newton Quarterly* 12 (March 1972).

Daly, Mary. "The Women's Movement: An Exodus Community." *Religious Education* 67 (September-October 1972):327-333.

Danner, Margaret. "Women's Lib." In *Sturdy Black Bridges*, p. 356. Edited by Roseann Bell, Bettye Parker and Beverly Guy-Sheflall. New York: Anchor Books, 1979.

Dodson, Jualynne. "Nineteenth Century A.M.E. Preaching Women." In *Women in New Worlds*, pp. 276-289. Edited by Hilah F. Thomas and Rosemary Skinner. Nashville: Abingdon, 1981.

Eaton, Isabel. "Special Report on Negro Domestic Service in the Seventh Ward." In *The Philadelphia Negro*, pp. 427-509. Edited by W. E. B. DuBois. Millwood, New York: Organization Ltd., 1973.

Eichelberger, Brenda. "Voices of Black Feminism." *Quest: A Feminist Quarterly* III (Spring):16-28.

Eichelberger, William. "Reflections on the Person and Personality of the Black Messiah." *The Black Church* II (n.d.): 14-16.

Elkins, Stanley M. "Slavery in Capitalist and Non-Capitalist Cultures." In *The Black Family: Essays and Studies*, pp. 13-16. Belmont, California: Wadworth Publishing Company, Inc. 1971.

English, Jane. "Introduction." In *Feminism and Philosophy*, pp. 1-3. Edited by Mary Vetterling-Braggin, Frederick A. Elliston and Jane English. Totowa, New Jersey: Littlefield, Adams & Company, 1977.

Evans, James. "Black Theology and Black Feminism." *Journal of Religious Thought* 33 (Spring/Summer, 1981):43-53.

"Feminist Theological Institute, Inc., Statement," November 1980.

Fiorenza, Elizabeth. "Feminist Theology and New Testament Interpretation." *Journal for the Study of the Old Testament.* Issue 22 (February 1982):32-46.

Fiorenza, Elizabeth. "To Comfort or to Challenge: Theological Reflections on the Pre-Conference Process." In *New Woman, New Church, New Priestly Ministry*, pp. 43-60. Edited by Maureen Dwyer. Rochester, New York: Kirk-Wood Press, 1980.

"The General Association of Massachusetts (Orthodox) to the Churches Under Their Care, 1837." In *Feminist Papers: From Adams to de Beauvoir*. Edited by Alice Rossi. New York: Bantam Books, 1974.

Gere, Judy and Mills, Virginia. "95 Theses on Patriarchal Oppression of Women." In *Moving Toward Full Personhood: A Six-Session Seminar on the Changing Status of Women.* Edited by The Task Force on Women Presbyterian Church.

"The Gender Factor in Math." *Time Magazine,* 15 December 1980.

Gilkes, Cheryl. "Togetherness and in Harness: Women's Traditions in the Sanctified Church." (Publication forthcoming in *Signs* Quarterly).

Goldstein, Valerie Saiving. "The Human Situation in Feminine View." *The Journal of Religion* 40 (April 1960):100-112.

Govaart-Halkes, Tine. "Developments in the Roman Catholic Church Regarding the Question of the Ordination of Women." In *What is Ordination Coming To?* pp. 30-41. Edited by Brigalia Bam. Geneva: World Council of Churches, 1971.

Grant, Jacquelyn. "The African Methodist Episcopal Church and Women." *Working Paper II of the AME Church,* 1980.

Grant, Jacquelyn. "Black Theology and the Black Woman." In *Black Theology: A Documentary History, 1966-1979,* pp. 418-433. Edited by Gayraud Wilmore and James Cone. New York: Orbis Books, 1979.

Grant, Jacquelyn. "The Status of Women in the African Methodist Episcopal Church." *The Voice of Missions.* (October 1976).

Grant, Jacquelyn. "Tasks of a Prophetic Church." In *Theology in the Americas,* pp. 136-42. Edited by Cornell West. Maryknoll, New York: Orbis Books, 1982.

Green, Clifford. "Liberation Theology: Karl Barth on Women and Men." *Union Theological Seminary Quarterly* XXIX (Spring/Summer 1974): 221-231.

Grimke, Sarah. "Letter on the Equality of the Sexes." In *Feminist Papers: From Adams to de Beauvoir*, pp. 306-318. Edited by Alice Rossi. New York: Bantam, 1973.

Gross, Rita. "Androcentrism and Androgyny in the Methodology of History of Religion." In *Beyond Androcentrism: New Essays on Women and Religion*, pp. 7-21. Edited by Rita Gross. Missoula, Montana: Scholars Press, 1977.

Harding, Vincent. "Black Theology and the American Christ." In *Black Theology: A Documentary History*, pp. 35-42. Edited by Gayraud Wilmore and James Cone. New York: Orbis Books, 1979.

Hare, Nathan. "What Will It Take for the Black Man to Rise Again." *Black Male/Female Relationships.* (Winter 1982).

Hendry, George. "Christology." In *The Dictionary of Christian Theology*, pp. 51-64. Edited by Alan Richardson. London: SCM Press Ltd., 1976.

Heyward, Carter. "Jesus, Lord or Brother." A sermon delivered in James Memorial Chapel, Union Theological Seminary November 8, 1978. (Photocopy)

Hines, Deborah. "Racism Breeds Stereotypes." *The Witness,* 65 (February 1982):pp. 5-8.

Hoover, Theressa. "Black Women and the Churches: Triple Jeopardy." In *Black Theology: A Documentary History, 1966-1975*, pp. 377-388. Edited by Gayraud Wilmore and James Cone. Maryknoll, New York: Orbis Books, 1979.

Jaggar, Alison. "Political Philosophy of Women's Liberation." In *Feminism and Philosophy*, pp. 5-21. Edited by Vetterling-Braggin, Frederick A. Elliston and Jane English. Totowa, New Jersey: Littlefield, Adams and Company, 1977.

Johnson, J. A. "The Need for a Black Christian Theology." *Journal of the Interdenominational Theological Center* II (Fall 1974):19-29.

Kimbrall, Gayle. "From Motherhood to Sisterhood: The Search for Female Religious Imagery in Nineteenth and Twentieth Century Theology." In *Beyond Androcentrism: New Essays on Women and Religion*, pp. 259-265. Edited by Rita Gross. Missoula Montana: Scholars Press, 1977.

"Language About God: Opening the Door." *Advisory Council on Discipleship of Worship.* New York: The United Presbyterian Church in the U.S.A., 187th General Assembly, May 1975.

LaRue, Linda. "The Black Movement and Women's Liberation." *Contemporary Black Thought: The Best from the Black Scholar*, pp. 116-125. Edited by Robert Chrisman and Nathan Hare. New York: The Bobbs-Merrill Company, Inc., 1973.

Morrison, Toni. "What the Black Woman Thinks About Women's Liberation." *The New York Times Magazine*, 22 August 1971.

Murray, Pauli. "Black Theology and Feminist Theology: A Comparative View." In *Black Theology: A Documentary History, 1966-1979*, pp. 398-417. Edited by Gayraud Wilmore and James Cone. New York: Orbis Books, 1979.

Ovington, Mary White. "The Colored Woman in Domestic Service in New York City." *Bulletin of Inter-Municipal Committee on Household Research*, I, May 1905.

Plaskow, Judith. "Blaming the Jews for the Birth of Patrirachy." In *Nice Jewish Girls*, pp. 250-254. Edited by Evelyn Torton Beck. Watertown, Massachusetts: Persephone Press Inc., 1982.

Romero, Joan Arnold. "The Protestant Principle: A Woman's Eye View of Barth and Tillich." In *Religion and Sexism: Images of Women in the Jewish and Christian Traditions*, pp. 319-340. Edited by Rosemary Ruether. New York: Simon and Schuster, 1974.

Rossi, Alice. "Introduction: Social Roots of the Woman's Movement in America." In *The Feminist Papers: From Adams to de Beauvoir*, pp. 241-281. Edited by Alice Rossi. New York: Bantam, 1973.

Ruether, Rosemary. "A Religion for Women: Sources and Strategies." *Christianity and Crisis* 39 (December 10, 1979):307-311.

Ruether, Rosemary. "Christology and Feminism." *An Occasional Paper* of the Board of Higher Education and Ministry of the United Methodist Church I (December 25, 1976).

Ruether, Rosemary. "Crisis in Sex and Race: Black Theology vs. Feminist Theology." In *Mission Trends 4: Liberation Theologies*, pp. 175-187. Edited by Gerald Anderson and Thomas Stanksy. Grand Rapids: William B. Eerdman's Publishing Co., 1979.

Ruether, Rosemary. "Feminism and Patriarchal Religion: Principles of Ideological Critique of the Bible." *Journal for the Study of the Old Testament* Issue 22 (February 1982):54-66

Ruether, Rosemary. "Goddesses and Witches: Liberation and Countercultural Feminism." The *Christian Century* 97 (September 10-17, 1980):842-847.

"What Do the Synoptic Say? The Sexuality of Jesus." *Christianity and Crisis* II (May 29, 1978):134-137.

Sepher, Franjo Cardinal. "Vatican Declaration." *Origins, N.C. Documentary Service* VI (February 3, 1977).

Smith, Barbara. "Toward a Black Feminist Criticism." In *Conditions: Two*. Trumanburg, New York: The Crossing Press, October 1977; reprinted., Trumanburg, New York: Out and Out Books, The Crossing Press, 1977.

Smith, Mary Grove. "Immigration as a Source of Supply for Domestic Workers." *Bulletin of Inter-Municipal Committee on Household Research*, II, May 1906.

Sojourner Truth. "Ain't I A Woman?" In *Feminism: The Essential Historical Writings*, pp. 93-95. Edited by Mariam Schneir. New York: Vintage Books, 1977.

Storrie, Kathleen. "New Yeast in the Dough: Jesus Transforms Authority." *Daughters of Sarah* January/February 1984.

The Status and Role of Women in Program and Policy Making Channels. The United Methodist Church General Conference, 1972.

Stuart, The Rev. David R. (Pseud). "My Objections to Ordaining Women." In *The Ordination of Woman Pro and Con*, pp. 44-53. Edited by Michael P. Hamilton and Nancy S. Montgomery. New York: Morehouse-Barlow Company, 1975.

Swidler, Leonard. "Jesus Was a Feminist." *South East Asia Journal of Theology* 13 (1971):102-110.

Wilcox, Preston. "Is There Life for Black Leaders After ERA?" *Black Male/Female Relationships* II (No. 1):53-56.

Wilmore, Gayraud. "The Black Messiah: Revising the Color Symbolism of Western Christianity." *Journal of Interdenominational Theological Center* II (Fall 1974):8-18.

Williams-Jones, Pearl. "A Minority Report: Black Pentecostal Women." *Spirit: A Journal Incident to Black Pentecostalism* I (No. 1, 1977):31-44.

Wright, Nathan. "Black Power: A Religious Opportunity." In *Black Theology : A Documentary History*, 1966-1979, pp. 48-61. Edited by Gayraud Wilmore and James Cone. Maryknoll, New York: Orbis Books, 1979.

Books

Appiah-Kubi, Kofi and Torres, Sergio, eds. *African Theology Enroute*. Maryknoll, New York: Orbis Books, 1979.

Aptheker, Bettina. *Women's Legacy: Essays in Race, Sex, and Classes in American History*. Amherst, Massachusetts: The University of Massachusetts Press, 1982.

Aptheker, Bettina. *A Documentary History of the Negro People in the United States: From Reconstruction Years to the Founding of the NAACP in 1910*. II. Secaucus, New Jersey: The Citadel Press, 1972.

Aptheker, Bettina. *A Documentary History of the Negro People in the United States: From the Emergence of the NAACP to the Beginning of the New Deal*, 1910-1932. III. Secaucus, New Jersey: The Citadel Press, 1972.

Aptheker, Herbert, ed. *A Documentary History of the Negro People in the United States: From Colonial Times thru the Civil War (I)*. New York: The Citadel Press, 1971.

Aunt Sally. *A Narrative of the Slave Life and Purchase of the Mother of Rev. Isaac Williams of Detroit Michigan.* Wheaton, Illinois: Tyndale House Publishers, Inc., 1979.

Barth, Karl. *Church Dogmatics.* Vol. III, Part 4. Edinburgh: T & T Clark, 1974.

Bearden, Jim and Butler, Linda Jean. *The Life and Times of Mary Shadd Cary.* Toronto, Ontario: New Canada Publication, a division of NC Press, Ltd., 1977.

Berry, Mary and Blassingame, John. *The Black Experience in America.* New York: Oxford University Press, 1982.

Bliss, Kathleen. *The Service and Status of Women in the Churches.* London: SCM Press Ltd., 1952.

Bonhoeffer, Dietrich. *Christ The Center.* New York: Harper & Row, Publisher, 1960.

Bonino, Jose Miquez. *Doing Theology in a Revolutionary Situation.* Philadelphia: Fortress Press, 1975.

Botkin, B. A., ed. *Lay My Burden Down: A Folk History of Slavery.* Chicago: University of Chicago Press, 1945.

Bradford, Sarah. *Scenes in the Life of Harriet Tubman.* 1869.

Brent, Linda. *Incidents in the Life of a Slave Girl.* New York: A Harvest Book, Harcourt, Brace and Jovanovich, Inc. L. Marie Child, ed. 1861.

Brooks, Evelyn. *The Women's Movement on the Black Baptist Church, 1880-1920.* Ph.D. dissertation, University of Rochester, 1984.

Bruce, Michael and Duffield, E. G., eds. *Why Not? Priesthood and the Ministry of Women: A Theological Study.* Sutton Courtenay: Marcham Manor Press, 1972.

Bullough, Vern L. *The Subordinate Sex: A History of Attitudes Toward Women.* Baltimore, Maryland: Penguin Books, Inc., 1973.

Bynum, LaTaunya Marie. *Black Feminist Theology: A New Word About God.* D. Min. thesis, School of Theology at Claremont, 1980.

Cannon, Katie G. *Resources for a Constructive Ethic for Women With Special Attention to the Life and Work of Zora Neal Hurston.* Ph.D dissertation, Union Theological Seminary, 1983.

Carter, Harold A. *The Prayer Tradition of Black People.* Valley Forge: Judson Press, 1976.

Childress, Alice. *Like One of the Family . . . Conversations From a Domestic Life.* Brooklyn, New York: Independence Publishers, 1956.

Christ, Carol, ed. *Diving Deep and Surfacing: Women Writers on Spiritual Quest.* Boston: Beacon Press, 1980.

Christ, Carol, ed. *Womanspirit Rising.* New York: Harper and Row, 1979.

Clark, Stephen. *Man and Woman in Christ, An Explanation of the Roles of Men and Women in Light of Scripture and Social Science.* Ann Arbor, Michigan: Servant Books, 1980.

Cleage, Albert. *The Black Messiah.* New York: Sheed and Ward, 1968.

Clifton, Lucille. *An Ordinary Woman*. New York: Random House, 1974.

Clinton, Catherine. *The Plantation Mistress: Woman's World in the Old South*. New York: Pantheon Books, 1982.

Coan, Josephus R. *Daniel Alexander Payne: Christian Educator* Philadelphia: The A.M.E. Book Concern, 1935.

Cohen, Rose. *Out of the Shadows*. New York: Jerome S. Ozer, 1971.

Collins, John. *The Slave Mother*. Philadelphia: #31 North Fifth Street, 1855.

Collins, Sheila. *A Different Heaven and Earth*. Valley Forge, Pennsylvania: Judson Press, 1974.

Cone, Cecil. *Identity Crisis in Black Theology*. Nashville, Tennessee: African Methodist Episcopal Church, 1975.

Cone, James. *A Black Theology of Liberation*. New York: Lippincott, 1970.

Cone, James. *Black Theology and Black Power*. New York: The Seabury Press, 1969.

Cone, James. *For My People: Black Theology and the Black Church*. Maryknoll, New York: Orbis Books, 1984.

Cone, James. *God of the Oppressed*. New York: Seabury Press, 1975.

Cone, James. *My Soul Looks Back*. Nashville: Abingdon Press, 1983.

Cooper, Anna. *A Voice From the South by a Black Woman of the South*. Xenia, Ohio: Aldine Printing House, 1892.

The Cornwall Collection. *Your Daughters Shall Prophesy.* New York: The Pilgrim Press, 1980.

Cott, Nancy. *The Bonds of Womanhood: Woman's Sphere in New England.* New York: Yale University Press, 1972.

Daly, Mary. *Beyond God the Father.* Boston: Beacon Press, 1973.

Daly, Mary. *The Church and the Second Sex.* New York: Harper and Row Publishers, 1975.

Daly, Mary. *Gynecology: The Metaethics of Radical Feminism.* Boston: Beacon Press, 1978.

Daly, Mary. *Pure Lust: Elemental Feminist Philosophy.* Boston: Beacon Press, 1984.

Davis, Angela. *Women, Race and Class.* New York: Random House, 1983.

Davis, John Jefferson. *Foundations of Evangelical Theology.* Grand Rapids, Michigan: Baker Book House, 1984.

Dayton, Donald. *Discovering an Evangelical Heritage.* New York: Harper and Row Publishers, 1976.

de Beauvoir, Simone. *The Second Sex.* New York: Vintage Books, 1952.

Dodson, Jualynne. *Women's Collective Power in the African Methodist Episcopal Church.* Ph.D. dissertation, University of California at Berkeley, 1983.

Driver, Tom. *Christ in a Changing World.* New York: Crossroad, 1981.

Dudden, Faye E. *Serving Women: Household Service in Nineteenth Century America.* Middletown, Connecticut: Wesleyan University Press, 1983.

Duster, Alfreda M. ed. *Crusade for Justice: The Autobiography of Ida B. Wells.* Chicago: The University of Chicago Press, 1970.

Dwyer, Maureen. Editor. *New Woman, New Church, New Priestly Ministry.* Rochester, New York: Kirkwood Press, 1980.

Earl, Conrad. *Harriet Tubman.* Washington, D.C.: Associated Publishers, Inc., 1943.

Earle, Victoria. *Aunt Lindy: A Story Founded on Real Life.* New York: J. J. Little and Co., 1893.

Eisenstein, Zillah. *The Radical Future of Liberal Feminism.* New York: Longman, 1981.

Elshtain, Jean. *Public Man Private Woman.* New Jersey: Princeton University Press, 1981.

Engels, Friedrick. *The Origin of the Family, Private Property and the State.* New York: International Publishers, 1970.

Ermarth, Margaret Sittler. *Adam's Fractured Rib.* Philadelphia: Fortress Press, 1970.

Erskine, Noel. *Decolonizing Theology: A Caribbean Perspective.* Maryknoll, New York: Orbis Books, 1980.

Evans, Sarah. *Personal Politics: The Roots of Women's Liberation in the Civil Rights Movement and the New Left.* New York: Vintage Books, 1979.

Fabella, Virginia, ed. *Asia's Struggle for Full Humanity.* Maryknoll, New York: Orbis Books, 1980.

Fabella, Virginia, and Torres, Sergio, eds. *Irruption of the Third World: Challenge to Theology.* Maryknoll, New York: Orbis Books, 1983.

Feuerbach, Ludwig. *The Essence of Christianity.* New York: Harper and Row, 1975.

Firestone, Shulamith. *Dialectic of Sex.* New York: Bantam Books, 1972.

Fiorenza, Elizabeth. *In Memory of Her: A Feminist Theological Reconstruction of Christian Origins.* New York: Crossroad, 1983.

Flexner, Eleanor. *Century of Struggle: The Women's Rights Movement in the United States.* Cambridge, Massachusetts: The Belknap Press of Harvard University Press, 1975.

Foh, Susan. *Woman and the Word of God.* Grand Rapids, Michigan: Baker Book House, 1979.

Friedan, Betty. *The Feminine Mystique.* New York: Dell Publishing Co., 1963.

Friedan, Betty. *The Second Stage.* New York: Summit Books, 1981.

Fuller, Reginald. *The Foundations of New Testament Christology.* New York: Charles Scribner's & Sons, 1965.

Giddings, Paula. *When and Where I Enter . . . The Impact of Black Women on Race and Sex in America.* New York: William Morrow and Company, Inc., 1984.

Gilbert, Olive. *Sojourner Truth: Narrative and Book of Life.* 1850 and 1875; reprinted., Chicago: Johnson Publishing Company, Inc., 1970.

Goldberg, Steven. *The Inevitability of Patriarchy.* New York: William Morrow Company, Inc., 1973.

Goldenberg, Naomi. *The Changing of the Gods: Feminism and the End of Traditional Religions.* Boston: Beacon Press, 1979.

Gordon, Michael, ed. *The American Family in Social-Historical Perspective.* New York: St. Martins Press, 1978.

Gray, Elizabeth Dodson. *Green Paradise Lost.* Wellesley, Massachusetts: Roundtable Press, 1979.

Gray, Elizabeth Dodson. *Patriarchy as a Conceptual Trap.* Wellesley Massachusetts: Roundtable Press, 1982.

Gray, Glenn J. *The Warriors: Reflections on Men in Battle.* New York: Random House, 1969.

Griffin, David. *A Process Christology.* Philadelphia: The Westminster Press, 1973.

Grillmeier, Aloys. *Christ in Christian Tradition.* New York: Sheed and Ward, 1964.

Grimke, Angelina E. *An Appeal to the Christian Women of the South.* New York: American Antislavery Society, 1836.

Guttierrez, Gustavo. *A Theology of Liberation.* New York: Orbis, 1973.

Hahn, Ferdnand; Lohff, Wenzel, and Boenkamm, Gunter. *What Can we Know About Jesus?* Philadelphia: Fortress Press, 1969.

Harnack, Adolf. *History of Dogma*. Vol. IV. New York: Dover Publishers, 1974.

Harris, Trudier. *From Mammy to Militant: Domestic in Black American Literature*. Philadelphia: Temple University Press, 1982.

Harvey, Van A. *The Historian and the Believer*. New York: Macmillan Publishing Co., Inc., 1966.

Haynes, Elizabeth Ross. *Negroes in Domestic Service in the United States*. Washington, D.C.: The Association for the Study of Negro Life and History, Inc., 1923.

Heilbrun, Carolyn. *Toward A Recognition of Androgyny*. New York: Harper Colophon Books, 1973.

Henry, Carl. *God Revelation and Authority*. 6 vols. Waco, Texas: Word Books, 1976.

Hernton, Calvin. *Sex and Racism in America*. New York: Grove Press, Inc., 1965.

Hewitt, Emily C. and Hiatt, Suzanne R. *Women Priests: Yes or No?* New York: The Seabury Press, 1973.

Heyward, Carter. *A Priest Forever: The Formation of a Woman and a Priest*. New York: Harper and Row Publishers, 1976.

Heyward, Carter. *The Redemption of God: A Theology of Mutual Relation*. Washington, D.C.: University Press of America, 1982.

Hooks, Bell. *Ain't I A Woman? Black Women and Feminism*. Boston: South End Press, 1981.

Hooks, Bell. *Feminist Theory: From Margin to Center*. Boston: South End Press, 1984.

Hull, Gloria; Scott, Patricia; and Smith, Barbara. *All the Women Are White, and All the Blacks Are Men, But Some of Us Are Brave.* Old Westbury, New York: The Feminist Press, 1982.

Jaggar, Alison and Rothenberg, P. *Feminist Frameworks: Alternative Theoretical Accounts of the Relations Between Women and Men.* New York: McGraw-Hill Book Company, 1978.

Jewett, Paul. *The Ordination of Women.* Grand Rapids, Michigan: William B. Eerdmans Publishers, 1980.

Jewett, Paul. *Man as Male and Female.* Grand Rapids, Michigan: William B. Eerdmans Publishing Company, 1975.

Jones, William. *Is God a White Racist?* New York: Anchor/Doubleday, 1973.

Kantzer, Kenneth S. and Gundry, Stanley N., etc. *Perspectives on Evangelical Theory.* Grand Rapids, Michigan: Baker Book House, 1984.

Karenga, Maulana. *Introduction to Black Studies.* Los Angeles: Kawaida Publications, 1982.

Kaseman, Ernest. *Jesus Means Freedom.* Philadelphia: Fortress Press, 1972.

Katzman, David. *Seven Days a Week: Women and Domestic Service in Industrializing America.* New York: Oxford University Press, 1978.

Kaufman, Gordon. *An Essay in Theological Method.* Missoula, Montana: Scholar Press, 1975.

Keckley, Elizabeth. *Behind the Scenes: Thirty Years a Slave, and Four Years in the White House.* New York: G. W. Carleton and Company Publishers, 1868.

Keller, Rosemary Skinner; Queen, Louise L.; and Thomas, Hilah, eds. *Women in New Worlds: Historical Perspective in the Wesleyan Tradition.* II. Nashville: Abingdon, 1982.

Kelly, Jr. N. D. *Early Christian Doctrine.* New York: Harper and Row, 1960.

Kelsey, George. *Racism and the Christian Understanding of Man.* New York: Charles Scribner's Sons, n.d.

Klooster, Fred. *Quests for the Historical Jesus.* Grand Rapids, Michigan: Baker Book House, 1977.

Knox, John. *Jesus Lord and Christ.* New York: Harper and Brothers Publishers, 1958.

Kovel, Joel. *White Racism: A Psychohistory.* New York: Columbia University Press, 1984.

Kraditor, Aileen S. *The Ideas of the Women Suffrage Movement.* New York: Columbia University Press, 1965.

Kraditor, Aileen S. *Up From the Pedestal: Selected Writings in the History of American Feminism.* Chicago: Quadrangle Books, 1968.

Kramer, Heinrich, and Sprenger, James. *The Malleus Maleficarum.* Translated by Rev. Montague Summers. New York: Dover, 1971.

Lee, Jarena. *Religious Experiences and Journals of Mrs. Jarena Lee.* Philadelphia: 1849.

Leith, John, ed. *Creeds of the Churches.* New York: Anchor Books, 1963.

Lerner, Gerda. *Black Women in White America: A Documentary History.* New York: Vintage Books, 1973.

Lerner, Gerda. *Liberation Theology: Human Hope Confronts Christian History and American Power.* New York: Paulist Press, 1972.

Lerner, Gerda. *The Women in American History.* Reading Massachusetts: Addison Wesley Publishing Company, 1971.

Leverling, Sarah R. *Memoirs of Margaret June Black of Baltimore Md.*, Philadelphia: Mines and Son, 1879.

Lincoln, C. Eric. *Race, Religion and the Continuing American Dilemma.* New York: Hill and Wang, 1984.

Lohse, Bernhard. *A Short History of Christian Doctrine: From the First Century to the Present.* Philadelphia: Fortress Press, 1966.

Lorde, Audre. *Sister Outsider: Essays and Speeches.* New York: The Crossing Press, 1984.

Lowenberg, Bert, and Bogin, Ruth, eds. *Black Women in Nineteenth-Century American Life: Their Words, Their Thoughts Their Feelings.* University Park, Pennsylvania: The Pennsylvania State University Press, 1976.

Lutz, Alma. *Created Equal, A Biography of Elizabeth Cady Stanton.* New York: John Day, 1940.

Lutz, Alma. *Crusade for Freedom: Women of the Antislavery Movement.* Boston: Beacon Press, 1968.

Mathieson, William Law. *British Slavery and its Abolition.* London: Longmans Green, 1926.

Matthaei, Julie A. *An Economic History of Women in America.* New York: Schocker Books, 1982.

Meier, August, and Rudwick, Elliot, eds. *The Making of Black America: The Origins of Black Americans I.* New York: Atheneum, 1969.

Meier, August, and Rudwick, Elliot, eds. *The Making of Black America: The Black Community in Modern America II.* New York: Atheneum, 1973.

Millett, Kate. *Sexual Politics.* New York: Equinox Books published by Avon, 1970.

Mollenkott, Virginia Ramey. *The Divine Feminine: The Biblical Imagery of God as Female.* New York: Crossroad, 1984.

Mollenkott, Virginia Ramey. *Speech, Silence, Action! The Cycle of Faith.* Nashville: Abingdon, 1980.

Mollenkott, Virginia Ramey. *Women, Men and the Bible.* Nashville: Abingdon, 1977.

Moltmann, Jurgen. *The Crucified God.* New York: Harper and Row Publishers, 1974.

Monteval, Marion. *The Klan Inside Out.* Westport, Connecticut: Negro Universities Press, 1970.

Montaqu, Ashley. *The Natural Superiority of Woman.* New York: Collier Books, Macmillan Publishing Company, Inc., 1978.

Morgan, Marabel. *The Total Woman.* Old Tappen, New Jersey: Fleming H. Revell Company, 1973.

Morgan, Robin. *Sisterhood is Powerful.* New York: Vintage Books, 1970.

Mudhubuti, Haki. *Enemies: The Clash of Races.* Chicago: Third World Press, 1978.

The National Council of Christian Churches. *Inclusive Language Lectionary: Readings for Year A.* Philadelphia: The Westminster Press 1983.

Niebuhr, H. Richard. *Christ and Culture.* New York: Harper & Brothers Publishers, 1951.

Norris, Richard A. Jr. *The Christological Controversy.* Philadelphia: Fortress Press, 1980.

Ochshorn, Judith. *The Female Experience and the Nature of the Divine.* Bloomington, Indiana: Indiana University Press, 1981.

O'Collins, Gerald. *What Are They Saying About Jesus?* New York: Paulist Press, 1977.

O'Neil, William. *Everyone Was Brave: The Rise and Fall of Feminism in America.* Chicago: Quadrangle Books, 1969.

O'Neil, William. *The Woman Movement: Feminism in the United States and England.* New York: Barnes and Noble, Inc., 1969.

Pannenberg, Wolfhart. *Jesus-God and Man.* Philadelphia: The Westminster Press, 1974.

Patterson, Bob E. *Carl F. H. Henry.* Waco, Texas: Word Book, 1983.

Perdue, Charles L. Jr.; Barden, Thomas E., and Phillips, Robert K. Compilers and editors. *Weevils in the Wheat: Interviewers with Virginia Ex-Slaves.* Bloomington: Indiana University Press, 1980.

Perrin, Norman. *The Kingdom of God in the Teaching of Jesus.* London: SCM Press Ltd., 1963.

Plaskow, Judith. *Sex, Sin, and Grace: Women's Experience and the Theologies of Reinhold Niebuhr and Paul Tillich.* Washington, D.C.: University Press of America, Inc., 1980.

Porteus, S. C. and Babcock, Marjorie E. *Temperament and Race.* Boston: Richard G. Badger Publishers, The Gorham Press, 1926.

Proctor, Priscilla, and Proctor, William. *Women in the Pulpit: Is God an Equal Opportunity Employer?* Garden City, New York: Doubleday and Company, Inc., 1976.

Richardson, Alan. *Creeds in the Making: A Short Introduction to the History of Christian Doctrine.* London: Student Christian Movement Press, 1951.

Roberts, J. Deotis. *A Black Political Theology.* Philadelphia: The Westminster Press, 1974.

Roberts, J. Deotis. *Black Theology Today: Liberation and Contextualization.* New York: The Edwin Mellen Press, 1983.

Roberts, J. Deotis. *Liberation and Reconciliation.* Philadelphia: The Westminister Press, 1971.

Roberts, J. Deotis. *Roots of a Black Future.* Philadelphia: The Westminister Press, 1982.

Robinson, James. *The New Quest of Historical Jesus.* New York: Macmillan Publishing Company, Inc. 1968.

Rosaldo, Michelle Zimbalist, and Lamphere, Louise, eds. *Women, Culture, and Society.* Stanford: Stanford University Press, 1974.

Rossi, Alice. *Feminist Papers From Adam to de Beauvoir.* New York: Bantam Books, 1974.

Rothman, Sheila M. *Woman's Proper Place: Practices, 1870 to the Present.* New York: Basic Books, Inc., Harper Colophon Books, 1978.

Ruether, Rosemary. *Disputed Questions: On Being a Christian.* Nashville: Abingdon, 1982.

Ruether, Rosemary. *Faith and Fratricide: The Theological Roots of Anti-Semitism.* New York: The Seabury Press, 1974.

Ruether, Rosemary. *Liberation Theology.* New York: Paulist Press, 1972.

Ruether, Rosemary. *Mary: the Feminine Face of the Church.* Philadelphia: The Westminster Press, 1977.

Ruether, Rosemary. *New Woman, New Earth: Sexist Ideologies and Human Liberation.* New York: The Seabury Press, 1975.

Ruether, Rosemary, ed. *Religion and Sexism: Images of Woman in the Jewish and Christian Traditions.* New York: Simon and Schuster, 1974.

Ruether, Rosemary. *Sexism and God-Talk: Toward a Feminist Theology.* Boston: Beacon Press, 1983.

Ruether, Rosemary. *To Change the World: Christology and Cultural Criticism.* New York: Crossroads Publishing Company, 1981.

Ruether, Rosemary, and Mclaughlin, Eleanor, eds. *Women of Spirit: Female Leadership in the Jewish Christian Traditions.* New York: Simon and Schuster, 1979.

Rupp, George. *Christologies and Cultures.* Paris: Mouton, 1974.

Russell, Letty. *Becoming Human.* Philadelphia: The Westminster Press, 1982.

Russell, Letty. *The Future of Partnership.* Philadelphia: the Westminster Press, 1979.

Russell, Letty. *Human Liberation in a Feminist Perspective: A Theology.* Philadelphia: The Westminster Press, 1974.

Russell, Letty. *The Liberating Word: A Guide to Non-Sexist Interpretation of the Bible.* Philadelphia: The Westminster Press, 1976.

Scanzoni, Letha, and Hardesty, Nancy. *All We're Meant to Be: A Biblical Approach to Women's Liberation with Study Guide.* Texas: Word Books, 1977.

Schaef, Anne Wilson. *Women's Reality: An Emerging Female System in the White Male Society.* Minneapolis, Minnesota: Winston Press, Inc., 1981.

Schillebeeckx, Edward, and Iersel, Basvan. Editors. *Jesus Christ and Human Freedom.* New York: Herder and Herder, 1974.

Schneir, Miriam. *Feminism: The Essential Historical Writings.* New York: Vintage Books, 1972.

Sellers, R. V. *The Council of Chalcedon: A Historical and Doctrinal Survey.* London: S.P.C.K., 1953.

Seminary Quarter at Grailville. *Women United in Theologizing and Action.* Summer 1978.

Shange, Ntozake. *For Colored Girls Who Have Considered Suicide When the Rainbow is Enuf.* New York: Macmillan Publishing Co., Inc., 1975.

Sillen, Samuel. *Women Against Slavery.* New York: Massen and Mainstream, 1955.

Simmons, William J. *The Klan Unmasked.* Atlanta, Georgia: William E. Thompson Publishing Co., 1923.

Smith, Charles Spencer. *A History of the African Methodist Episcopal Church.* Philadelphia: The A.M.E. Book Concern, 1922.

Sobrino, Jon. *Christology at the Crossroads.* Maryknoll, New York: Orbis Books, 1978.

Soelle, Dorothy. *Beyond Mere Obedience.* Minneapolis: Augsburg Publishing House, 1970.

Soelle, Dorothy. *Christ the Representative: An Essay in Theology After the Death of God.* Philadelphia: Fortress Press, 1967.

Spretnak, Charlene, ed. *The Politics of Women's Spirituality: Essays on the Rise of Spiritual Power Within the Feminist Movement.* Garden City, New York: Anchor Books, 1982.

Stampp, Kenneth. *The Peculiar Institution: Slavery in the Antebellum South.* New York: Alfred A. Knopf, 1969.

Stanton, Elizabeth C. *Eighty Years and More (1815-1897): Reminiscence of Elizabeth Cady Stanton.* New York: European Publishing Co., 1898.

Sterling, Dorothy, ed. *We Are Your Sisters: Black Women in the Nineteenth Century.* New York: W. W. Norton and Company, 1984.

Sutherland, Daniel. *Americans and Their Servants: Domestic Service in the U.S. from 1800-1920.* Baton Rouge, La.: Louisiana State University Press, 1981.

Swidler, Leonard. *Biblical Affirmations of Woman.* Philadelphia: The Westminster Press, 1979.

Taylor, Susie King. *Reminiscences of My Life in Camp.* Boston: The Author, 1902.

Thistlethwaite, Susan Brooks. *Metaphors for the Contemporary Church*. New York: The Pilgrim Press, 1983.

Thomas, Hilah F. and Keller, Rosemary Skinner, eds. *Women in New Worlds: Historical Perspective in the Wesleyan Tradition*. I. Nashville: Abingdon, 1981.

Tillich, Paul J. *Systematic Theology*. I. Chicago: The University of Chicago Press, 1951.

Torres, Sergio, and Eagleson, John, eds. *The Challenge of Basic Christian Communities*. Maryknoll, New York: Orbis Books, 1981.

Thurman, Howard. *Jesus and the Disinherited*. Nashville: Abingdon Press, 1949.

Tyler, Charles. *The K.K.K.* New York: The Abbey Press, 1902.

Ulanov, Ann Belford. *Receiving Woman: Studies in the Psychology and Theology of the Feminine*. Philadelphia: The Westminster Press, 1981.

The United Methodist Church Study Commission. *The Status and Role of Women in Program and Policy Making Channels of the United Methodist Church*. The 1972 General Conference and Actions of the General Conference on the participation of Women in Programs and Policy Making Channels of the United Methodist Church.

U.S. Department of Commerce, Bureau of the Census. *The Social and Economic Status of the Black Population in the U.S.: American Historical Views*, 1790-1978.

Van deGeer, Haye. *Women Priests in the Catholic Church?* Philadelphia: Temple University Press, 1973.

Verdesi, Elizabeth Howell. *In But Still Out: Women in the Church.* Philadelphia: The Westminster Press, 1973.

Vetterling-Braggin, Mary; Ellison, Frederick A.; and English, Jane, eds. *Feminism and Philosophy.* Totowa, New Jersey: Littlefield, Adams and Company, 1977.

Wade-Gayles, Gloria. *No Crystal Stair: Visions of Race and Sex in Black Women's Fiction.* New York: The Pilgrim Press, 1984.

Wahlberg, Rachel. *Jesus According to a Woman.* New York: Paulist Press, 1975.

Walker, Alice. *The Color Purple.* New York: Harcourt, Brace and Jovanovich Publishers, 1982.

Walker, Alice. *In Search of My Mother's Garden.* New York: Harcourt, Brace and Jovanovich, 1983.

Washbourn, Penelope. *Becoming Woman: The Quest for Wholeness in Female Experience.* New York: Harper and Row Publishers, 1977.

Wells, Ida B. *A Red Record: Tabulated Statistics in the United States 1892-1893-1894.* Chicago: Donohue and Henneberry.

West, Cornell. *Prophesy Deliverance: An Afro-American Revolutionary Christianity.* Philadelphia: The Westminster Press, 1982.

Williams, Delores. *The Black Women Portrayed in Selected Black Literature and Some Questions for Black Theology.* M.A. thesis, Columbia University and Union Theological Seminary, 1975.

Wilmore, Gayraud and Cone, James. *Black Theology: A Documentary History, 1966-1979.* Maryknoll, New York: Orbis Books, 1979.

Wright, Bishop R. R. *The Bishops of the A.M.E. Church.*
Nashville: The A.M.E. Church Sunday School Union, 1963.

Wynes, Charles, ed. *Southern Sketches from Virginia, 1881-1901.*
Charlottesville, Virginia: 1964.

Zahrnt, Heinz. *The Historical Jesus.* Translated by J. S. Bowden.
New York: Harper and Row Publishing Co., 1963.

PRECIS

In this work, I explore the development and limitations of feminist Christology. Utilizing the method of contextualization, I argue that the christologies of feminists are best understood within the larger feminist theological discussion of women which emerges from the experiences of White women.

The problematic of Christology for feminists is two-fold: (1) the Jesus of history is proclaimed as the Christ–the unique God-bearer; and (2) this maleness of the Christ figure was often used as an oppressive weapon against women. Feminist theologians, employing women's experience as the primary source, and sexism as the starting point for theology, have reinterpreted Jesus Christ in the light of their experiences. I have shown that women's experience in feminist theology means White women's experience. Therefore, feminist theology lacks the universal import which is claimed by some of its proponents. Although it is true that sexism is cross-cultural, it is not true that the analysis of White women is adequate to address the concerns of non-White and non-Western women. In this work I argue that feminist theology suffers from the same problem as the nineteenth-century feminist movement–that is, it is a single issue movement; its issue is sexism. As such, it could not possibly address adequately the reality of non-White women in general, and Black women in particular. Racism/sexism/classism as a corporate point of departure for doing theology and Christology is embraced as an appropriate and corrective approach in theology. This tri-dimensional analysis is more consistent with the way Jesus identified the Christ. Because he locates the Christ among the most oppressed peoples, he minimizes the possibility of a single issue and elitist analysis, which changes the oppressive condition of only a few, yet leaves intact the oppression of the masses of people. The basic contention here, then, is that the Christ is more likely to be found in the community of Black women.

Curriculum Vitae

Jacquelyn Grant is a native of Georgetown, South Carolina where she received her early education. She received the B.A. in French from Bennett College, Greensboro, North Carolina; the M.Div. in Systematic Theology from Turner Theological Seminary at the Interdenominational Theological Center, Atlanta, Georgia; and the M.Phil. and Ph.D. from Union Theological Seminary, New York.

Ms. Grant's academic experience includes working as a tutor in systematic theology at Union Theological Seminary and a Research/Resource Associate in Women's Studies at Harvard Divinity School. She has been visiting lecturer at Candler School of Theology, Atlanta, Georgia, and Princeton Theological Seminary, Princeton, New Jersey. Presently, she is teaching systematic theology at the Interdenominational Theological Center, where she is also founder and director of Black Women in Church and Society, a program geared toward the leadership development of Black women, and the enhancement of participation of Black women in the church.

Among her awards and honors are: the ITC Scholarship; Union Theological Seminary Scholarship; the Rockefeller Doctoral Fellowship; Annual Theological Scholarship of the African Methodist Episcopal Church; the AMEC Women's Missionary Society Scholarship; the Dissertation Year Fellowship of the Fund for Theological Education; the DuBois Fellowship of the DuBois Institute for Afro-American Research, Harvard University; and the United Methodist Women's Theological Scholarship.

Her publications include the following: "Black Theology and the Black Woman" in *Black Theology: A Documentary History, 1966-1979* 257 (Maryknoll, New York: Orbis Books, 1979); "Tasks of a Prophetic Church" in *Theology in the Americas*, edited by Cornell West (Maryknoll, New York: Orbis Books, 1982); and "A Black Response to Feminist Theology" in *Women's Spirit Bonding*, edited by Janet Kalven and Mary Buckley (New York: The Pilgram Press, 1984).

Ms. Grant is an ordained elder in the African Methodist Episcopal Church and serves as Associate Minister at Flipper Temple AME Church in Atlanta, Georgia.